KV-429-274

POLISH NATIONAL INCOME AND PRODUCT
IN 1954, 1955, AND 1956

 EAST CENTRAL EUROPEAN STUDIES
OF COLUMBIA UNIVERSITY

POLISH
NATIONAL INCOME
AND PRODUCT
IN 1954, 1955, AND 1956

By THAD PAUL ALTON
AND
ANDRZEJ KORBONSKI
BOGDAN MIECZKOWSKI
LEON SMOLINSKI

COLUMBIA UNIVERSITY PRESS 1965

NEW YORK AND LONDON

Copyright © 1965 Columbia University Press

Library of Congress Catalog Card Number: 65-13617

Printed in the United States of America

EAST CENTRAL EUROPEAN STUDIES
OF COLUMBIA UNIVERSITY

The East Central European Studies comprise scholarly books prepared under the auspices of the Institute on East Central Europe of Columbia University or through other divisions of the University. The publications of these studies is designed to enlarge our understanding of an important region of the world, which, because of its relative inaccessibility in the recent past as well as because of the linguistic problems it presents, has been somewhat neglected in serious academic study. The faculty of the Institute on East Central Europe, without necessarily endorsing the conclusions reached by the authors, believe that these studies contribute substantially to knowledge of the area and should serve to stimulate further inquiry and research.

EAST CENTRAL EUROPEAN STUDIES

THE COMMUNIST PARTY OF BULGARIA: ORIGINS AND

DEVELOPMENT, 1883–1936   JOSEPH ROTHSCHILD

YUGOSLAVIA IN CRISIS, 1934–1941   J. B. HOPTNER

THE FIRST PARTITION OF POLAND   HERBERT H. KAPLAN

CZECHOSLOVAK NATIONAL INCOME AND PRODUCT,

1947–1948 AND 1955–1956

THAD PAUL ALTON AND ASSOCIATES

POLISH-SOVIET RELATIONS, 1932–1939

BOHDAN B. BUDUROWYCZ

HUNGARIAN NATIONAL INCOME AND PRODUCT IN 1955

THAD PAUL ALTON AND ASSOCIATES

POLITICS OF SOCIALIST AGRICULTURE IN POLAND:

1945–1960   ANDRZEJ KORBONSKI

POLISH NATIONAL INCOME AND PRODUCT IN 1954,

1955, AND 1956   THAD PAUL ALTON AND ASSOCIATES

PREFACE

This volume is the third in a series on the national income of countries in East Central Europe. Like its companion volumes on Czechoslovakia and Hungary, it is part of a larger study of the structure, growth, and performance of the Soviet-type economies carried on by the Research Project on National Income in East Central Europe.

Much attention has been drawn recently to the evolving nationalistic trends in economic policy and planning in the Soviet-type economies. Though many of the expectations raised by the Polish revolt of October, 1956, have been poorly realized, nonetheless Poland, the most populous country in East Central Europe, has gained the distinction of decollectivizing its agriculture, following the lead given earlier by Yugoslavia. Poland has also been exceptional in the volume and quality of its statistical publications and has been unique in publishing a detailed planned state budget. This is not to say that the Polish statistical information can be used uncritically, for here, as in other Soviet-type economies, there are differences in concepts, peculiarities of prices, and varying reliability of reporting by economic sectors that require discriminating attention on the part of the student.

Our concern in this study is to present a cross-section view of economic activity as it is summarized in the gross national product. We are not concerned with the rate of growth or with the size of the Polish economy in comparison with other economies; instead we seek to show the relative contributions of sectors of production—industry, agriculture, and so forth—to the GNP and the relative shares of final uses—personal consumption, government consumption, gross investment, and defense—in the GNP. We do this, first, in current transaction prices, in order to show the actual articulation of the various sectors, and, second, in adjusted factor cost, in order to exhibit the allocation of resources in more meaningful terms than market prices alone permit.

We have made a special effort to provide extensive documentation of our sources and full description of the procedures supporting our estimates in order to permit readers to follow the work in detail. Although at some points we have found it necessary to make rough estimates, we have tried in such instances to stay within reasonable limits, imposed in part by the comprehensive national accounting approach that we followed.

The study was carried out as a team effort, all of the authors participating in many phases of the work in either direct or advisory roles. Special note should be taken of the work on the state budget and the agricultural sector by Dr. Korbonski. Dr. Mieczkowski prepared the initial drafts of the wage and salary estimates and of various household sector expenditures. Dr. Smolinski worked on the enterprise sector accounts and coordinated many of the estimates. I am primarily responsible for the foreign sector accounts, the eventual factor cost adjustments, detailed review of all estimates, and the final drafting of the study.

The authors are happy to acknowledge their debt to Professors Abram Bergson and Harold Barger for reading and commenting on portions of an early version of the study and to Professor John Michael Montias for reading a later draft and offering a number of helpful criticisms. We are likewise indebted to Dr. Maurice Ernst and Professor Boris P. Pesek for similar help and for a number of consultations on research problems. Our colleagues, Drs. Alexej Wynnyczuk, Gregor Lazarcik, and Laszlo Czirjak helped us in frequent discussions based on their knowledge of other Soviet-type economies. We are also appreciative of the thorough editing by Mrs. Kathryn W. Sewny. Finally, to all those who have helped us in typing, in library service, in statistical computations, and in other ways, we express our thanks and appreciation. Any errors or limitations of the study are of course the sole responsibility of the authors.

THAD PAUL ALTON

New York, N.Y.
February, 1965

CONTENTS

Abbreviations Used for Polish Documents   xv

I   Introduction   1

II   Sectoral and Consolidated Accounts   13

III   Gross National Product by Sector of Origin and by End Use at Market Prices   55

IV   Gross National Product at Factor Cost   67

V   Economic Implications   86

Appendixes

A   Notes to Household Sector Accounts (Tables 1A, 1B, and 1C)   101

B   Notes to Economic Enterprise Sector Accounts (Tables 2A, 2B, and 2C)   119

C   Notes to Government Sector Accounts (Tables 3A, 3B, and 3C)   125

D   Notes to Foreign Sector Accounts (Tables 4A, 4B, and 4C)   128

E   National Wage Bill   137

F   Selected Estimates in Agriculture   161

G   The State Budget   171

H   Notes to Tables 6 and 7   203

I   Notes to Tables 8 and 9   212

Sources Cited   235

Key to Table Items   243

Index   245

TABLES

1A	Household Sector Production Account	13
1B	Household Sector Appropriation Account	14
1C	Household Sector Capital Account	15
2A	Enterprise Sector Production Account	15
2B	Enterprise Sector Appropriation Account	16
2C	Enterprise Sector Capital Account	17
3A	Government Sector Production Account	17
3B	Government Sector Appropriation Account	18
3C	Government Sector Capital Account	18
4A	Foreign Sector Production Account	19
4B	Foreign Sector Appropriation Account	19
4C	Foreign Sector Capital Account	19
5A	Consolidated Production Account	20
5B	Consolidated Appropriation Account	20
5C	Consolidated Capital Account	21
6	Gross National Product by Sector of Origin in Current Market Prices	56
7	Gross National Product by End Use in Current Market Prices	62
8	GNP by Sector of Origin at Factor Cost	77
9	GNP by End Use at Market Prices and at Factor Cost	82
10	GNP by Sector of Origin at Market Prices and at Factor Cost	87
11	GNP by Sector of Origin at Factor Cost in 1955: Czechoslovakia, Hungary, and Poland	89
12	Resource Allocation in Czechoslovakia, Hungary, Poland, and the USSR in 1955	92
13	Sources of Polish Finance	93
14	Polish Official National Income Statistics, 1956	95
15	Polish National Income at 1956 "Conventional Prices"	98

APPENDIX TABLES

A1 Income of Self-Employed Outside Agriculture   102
A2 Retail Trade Sales for Consumption   105
A3 Purchases of Services by Households   109
A4 Gross Rent, Cash and Imputed   114
D1 Polish Foreign Trade Estimates   134
E1 Total Wage Bill   138
E2 Wage-like Payments in Enterprise Sector   159
F1 Farm Income   162
F2 Derivation of the Index of Realized Farm Prices
    for 1956   167
F3 Farm Consumption in Kind   169
G1 State Budget Revenues   172
G2 State Budget Expenditures   177
G3 Budget Expenditures on Health, Education,
    and Welfare   186
G4 Budgetary Expenditure on Administration, Justice,
    and Internal Security   198
G5 Budgets of Quasi-Governmental Organizations   200
H1 Indirect Tax Receipts by Sector   205
H2 Subsidy Payments by the Receiving Sector   207
H3 Depreciation Allowances by Sector   209
I1 Gross National Product by Sector of Origin
    at Factor Cost   214
I2 Current Values of Fixed and Working Capital   216
I3 Fixed Capital in the Polish Economy   218
I4 Fixed Capital Stock in the Polish Economy,
    by Sector of Ownership   220
I5 Adjusted Depreciation Allowances   225
I6 GNP by End Use   227
I7 Government Sector Services at Factor Cost   233

ABBREVIATIONS USED
FOR POLISH DOCUMENTS

BBM	*Biuletyn budownictwa mieszkaniowego*
BS	Poland. Główny urząd statystyczny. *Biuletyn statystyczny*
DN	Poland. Główny urząd statystyczny. *Dochód narodowy Polski*
DU	Poland. Rada Ministrów. *Dziennik ustaw*
GP	*Gospodarka planowa*
MRS	Poland. Główny urząd statystyczny. *Mały rocznik statystyczny*
NR	*Nowe rolnictwo*
RPG	*Rocznik polityczny i gospodarczy*
RS	Poland. Główny urząd statystyczny. *Rocznik statystyczny*
SC	Poland. Główny urząd statystyczny. *Statystyka cen*
SIB	Poland. Główny urząd statystyczny. *Statystyka inwestycji i budownictwa*
SK	Poland. Główny urząd statystyczny. *Statystyka kultury*
WNBP	*Wiadomości narodowego banku polskiego*
ZER	*Zagadnienia ekonomiki rolnej*
ZG	*Życie gospodarcze*

POLISH NATIONAL INCOME AND PRODUCT
IN 1954, 1955, AND 1956

I. INTRODUCTION

The purpose of the present study is to show the structure of the Polish economy in the years 1954, 1955, and 1956, first, in current market prices and, second, at factor cost. We are concerned with the relative shares contributed to the gross national product by the various sectors of production—industry, agriculture, construction, forestry, transportation, and various other services—and with the allocation of the product to final uses—personal consumption, government consumption, defense, and gross investment. Both bases of valuation are of interest: in market prices we are able to follow actual transactions; at factor cost we gain an insight into the dimensions of the economic activity in terms of the services of labor and other factors of production that were used up in production.

The factor cost structure is the principal goal of our research; the market price valuations, besides being of interest for their possible use in eventual international comparisons and for a knowledge of the articulation of economic activities, are an essential intermediate step toward the factor cost structure. The latter is particularly important in Soviet-type economies, where relative prices are seriously distorted by turnover taxes, the irregular incidence of the formal profit category, and various subsidies. For most other national economies the structure of the national product at market prices affords a reasonably close approximation to the structure at factor cost; in the Soviet-type economies, however, the structure at market prices available for a truncated concept of national income, excluding services not directly related to material production, is seriously misleading as to the resource cost involved. In particular, the distortions introduced by Polish prices greatly exaggerate the contribution of industry in relation to that of agriculture and very seriously overstate personal consumption in relation to investment. Our estimates should therefore serve to add meaning and perspective to the Polish national income statistics.

This study was carried out as part of a larger project on the structure and growth of the economies of East Central Europe. Besides Poland, the countries covered include Czechoslovakia, Hungary, and Bulgaria.[1] Although the results of the present work will be used in a companion study of the growth of the Polish economy, we are not concerned here with showing any changes in the size of the gross national product or its components in the period covered. Our results are expressed in current prices and costs. No attempt was made to show the results in constant prices, and we would caution against superficial inferences as to changes in magnitude based on changes in relative structure.

ACCOUNTING FRAMEWORK

In order to facilitate the derivation of a consistent set of national income aggregates we employed a double-entry system of national accounting based on four decision-making sectors and their transactions in regard to production, the disposal of current income, and saving and investment. We divided the domestic economy into three sectors—households, government, and business enterprise; the foreign, or "rest-of-the-world," sector serves to close the system. Three accounts were set up for each sector: (A) a production account, showing the transactions related to productive activity; (B) an appropriation account, showing the disposal of current income gained from productive activity or by transfers from other sectors; and (C) a capital account, showing transactions related to savings and investment.[2]

---

[1] Studies of the structure of the Czechoslovak and Hungarian economies have already been published. See Alton and associates, *Czechoslovak National Income and Product, 1947–1948 and 1955–1956,* and their *Hungarian National Income and Product in 1955.*

[2] A detailed description of this type of accounting is given in United Nations, *A System of National Accounts.* See also an earlier discussion in Stone, "Functions and Criteria of a System of Social Accounting," pp. 1–74, and the more

For many purposes in our study we found it necessary to provide a more detailed classification, particularly in the enterprise sector. Thus, in many instances agriculture receives a distinct treatment, although it is not formally designated as a fifth basic sector. Further detail reflecting the nature and articulation of economic activity is given in the various kinds of transactions that are recorded. These include subcategories of goods and services as well as several types of financial transfers.

The household sector is defined to include all individuals who are normal residents and all private nonprofit organizations that are supported mainly by members' contributions and are not primarily serving business organizations or acting as agencies of the government. Although we show in the household production account the activity of domestic servants and religious organizations, this perhaps arbitrary distinction from enterprise activity is not particularly significant since in any event it disappears upon consolidation of the sectoral production accounts. The enterprise sector comprises all establishments producing goods for sale at a price intended to cover roughly the costs of production. Thus it includes farms, professional services, all business enterprises regardless of ownership (state, cooperative, and private), transportation and communication services, financial services, housing, and such units formally included in the government as in fact are engaged in production for sale as defined above. The government sector includes all the agencies of general government that supply services to the community but normally not for sale, regardless of whether these agencies are supported by government budgets or operate on extrabudgetary funds. Thus we included in the government sector the Communist party, subsidiary political organizations, labor unions, and other organizations where it was clear that they operated as government agencies even though much of their direct support came from special assessments on their members. The foreign, or rest-of-the-world, sector accounts for the external transactions of the economy and thus closes the system.

---

recent recommendations by the Organization for European Economic Cooperation, *A Standardized System of National Accounts,* 1958 ed. (Paris, 1959).

The contents of the three accounts for each sector that we mentioned above will be evident from the entries shown in the tables. In general, the receivables on the production account refer to current account sales to other sectors, actual or imputed sales to capital formation (including changes in stocks), and subsidies; payables in the account reflect charges against the product, namely, purchases from other sectors, indirect taxes, provisions for capital consumption, and actual or imputed payments to labor and other factors of production. Although we proceed in a formal way by treating turnover taxes as indirect taxes, it is worth while noting at the outset that in fact these taxes are regarded by spokesmen for the Soviet-type economies as embodying a return to state ownership and control of the economy, and definitely not as similar in function to indirect taxes in a capitalist economy. It is clear that most of the return to nonlabor factors of production has been caught up in the turnover taxes. At a later stage we take cognizance of this in our adjustments of the gross national product to factor cost.

The appropriation account provides details of the transactions showing the disposition of each sector's current income. As such, it includes various transfers to and from the government and between one sector and another.

The capital account shows the sources of capital funds (saving, capital consumption allowances, and various tranfers between sectors) and their allocation to gross investment.

Upon consolidation of the sectoral accounts we derive the familiar national income and product aggregates: the gross national product from the production accounts, national income and net national product from the appropriation accounts, and gross investment from the capital accounts. Because of the poorly defined character of the turnover tax, the figures derived for national income upon consolidation (GNP minus capital consumption allowances and minus indirect taxes plus subsidies) must be regarded simply as a formal consequence of the classification of this tax. As we remarked above, the turnover tax in fact includes returns to nonlabor factors of production, and we therefore find it necessary to adjust the formal results to what we believe is a reasonable approximation to factor cost.

We provide separate capital accounts for the individual sectors, but because of incomplete information some of the transactions reflecting flows between capital accounts rest on more or less reliable assumptions; upon consolidation, however, any imprecision here vanishes in the summary statement.

SETTING OF THE STUDY [3]

Poland emerged from the Second World War with her area reduced by about 20 percent and with her boundaries displaced toward the west, having ceded a large but poorly industrialized and low-yield agricultural area in the east to the USSR and having taken over a smaller but relatively well-industrialized and higher yield agricultural area from Germany. As a result of war losses, Hitler's policy of extermination of Jews and other groups, and transfers at the end of the war, Poland's population had declined from about 35 million in 1939 within its prewar boundaries to about 24 million in 1948 within its postwar boundaries. The actual loss would, of course, have been greater if account were taken of what would have been the normal increase in population in the absence of war. Despite economic potential gained by the acquisition of the western territories, the economy suffered from immense destruction of fixed capital assets, livestock, and inventories.

With the help of the United Nations Relief and Rehabilitation Administration, substantial reconstruction was achieved by the end of 1946, and a Three-Year Plan aiming at more comprehensive reconstruction was undertaken for the years 1947–49. Although this plan was initiated under some expectation that it would represent a harmonious joint effort by the private, cooperative, and state-owned sectors, it soon became evident that the

[3] For an extensive discussion of Poland's economic system, policies, and development see Alton, *Polish Postwar Economy;* Montias, *Central Planning in Poland;* Taylor, *The Economic Development of Poland, 1919–1950;* and the sources cited by these authors.

economic system, its institutions, and scheme of planning and control would be patterned after the Soviet economy. This evolution, paralleled in other countries falling within the Soviet sphere in East Central Europe, was the consequence of Soviet policy carried out by subservient national Communist parties under the shadow of Soviet military force. Government by coalition quickly gave way to forthright domination by the Communist Party, which either engorged its rivals or transformed them into impotent shells obediently seconding the Communist policies. Organized opposition was not allowed.

The issue of nationalism versus Soviet dominance was settled in 1948 in connection with the Soviet-Yugoslav dispute. Yugoslavia shared boundaries with Italy and Greece, thus making possible easy access to support from the west, and the country was not liberated by Soviet forces. Tito's failure to bow to Stalin's will led to the Yugoslavs being purged from the Cominform, the Soviet-dominated organization of representatives of the Communist parties in Czechoslovakia, Bulgaria, Hungary, Poland, Rumania, Yugoslavia, France, and Italy. The other parties acknowledged Soviet authority and proceeded to purge themselves of nationalist elements. In Poland, Wladyslaw Gomułka, the Secretary-General of the Polish Workers' Party, was removed from office and later imprisoned for his nationalist tendencies, including his reluctance to force the collectivization of agriculture. Thereafter, until 1956, Marxist-Leninist-Stalinist ideology as elaborated in Soviet experience became the guide to Polish economic organization. In at least one major respect, however, the Polish economy proved recalcitrant: the peasants stubbornly resisted collectivization, and its slow pace and eventual successful reversal in 1956 were unique within the Soviet sphere.

State control over the economy was rapidly extended by the Soviet-sponsored government as Poland was liberated. In 1946 large- and medium-sized enterprises in transportation, communication, and industry were nationalized. Subsequently, private enterprise, wherever it occurred, was subject to discriminatory measures of taxation, supply of raw materials, and licensing. By the period of our study, 1954–56, private enterprise had become relatively insignificant in every branch of production except agriculture. In this sector the state and collective farms progressively increased their shares of the total agricultural land until in 1956 they accounted for 13.8 and 9.6 percent, respectively, the remainder being in private farms.[4] In the last quarter of 1956, however, the collective farm sector almost disappeared.[5] At the same time Gomułka returned to the leadership of the United Workers' Party, and the Polish government began to show a small measure of independence from Moscow in matters of economic policy. Shortly thereafter there was a small revival of handicrafts and other private small-scale enterprise.

The Polish economic system in 1954–56 closely resembled its Soviet model. Economic planning and control were highly centralized. Production goals were relatively highly detailed, and major emphasis was placed on quantitative fulfillment of goals, cost considerations being of secondary importance. The notion that the planned economy should represent collaboration among the private, cooperative, and state-owned sectors had perished during the Three-Year Plan. By the outset of the Six-Year Plan in 1950, the state was predominant in all sectors, except agriculture; private enterprise was rapidly shrinking or being converted into cooperatives operating under rigorous state control. Although private agriculture was being subjected progressively to increasing discriminatory pressures vis-à-vis the collective farms in such matters as the land tax in kind, compulsory deliveries at low state-set prices to the state monopoly for agricultural procurements, and the supply of fertilizers, most of the farmers successfully resisted these pressures as well as attempts at outright compulsion.

Poland's Six-Year Plan (1950–55) set ambitious goals for the growth of the economy, especially in mining, metallurgy, and machine building, and some of these targets were raised in the subsequent annual plans. In an endeavor to reach the targets, direct controls were applied to assignment of specialized personnel and graduates of vocational schools and higher institutions, and

[4] *RS 1957,* p. 124.
[5] By 1958 it represented only 1 percent of the agricultural land (*RS 1959,* p. 171).

the educational system was geared to the requirements of the planned economy.

By the latter part of 1953, however, following the lead of the USSR, Poland revised her economic plans for 1954–55 to give more attention to the lagging agricultural sector, to increase the output of consumer goods so as to realize at least in part some of the goal of raising the level of consumption, and to alleviate some of the disproportions between sectors of production that resulted from the poorly coordinated development of the earlier years. In particular, planned investment in 1954–55 was to stay at the absolute level reached in 1953, which would mean a decline in its share of the rising national product. In the subsequent Five-Year Plan the drive for a higher rate of investment and more rapid growth were to be resumed, but the events of 1956 leading to some lessening of Soviet domination delayed the drive.

In general, the years 1950–56 were characterized by over-ambitious, poorly executed investment plans, waste in the use of labor and capital, and a policy of coercion and inadequate rewards to producers that led to a serious decline in morale throughout the economy. Although the economy grew under this regimen, the gains were realized at a higher cost than was necessary.

The Six-Year Plan set the goal for growth of national income for 1955 at 212 (1949 = 100), but the official realized index, in 1956 prices, was only 174.[6]

We shall not go into any detail here concerning our independent measures of Polish economic growth, except to indicate that our preliminary results, based on Polish production statistics in general combined within individual branches by 1956 prices and aggregated by sectors using estimated gross value added at factor cost as weights, showed the 1955 index for GNP at 139 (1949 = 100).[7] The difference between the official measure and ours, of course, reflects in part the broader coverage of GNP as compared to the Polish concept of national income (essentially

[6] *RS 1959*, p. 58. The planned figure is shown in Alton, *Polish Postwar Economy*, p. 117, citing Hilary Minc.

[7] Our results will be published separately in a study of Polish economic growth.

net material production, although it includes purchases from nonmaterial service sectors), and in part the different weights and methodology. It is not always clear what procedures were followed in the derivation of the Polish indexes.

In any event, the average rate of growth, though high, should not be regarded as particularly exceptional, given the reserves of labor and production capacity within the postwar boundaries. The disaffection of the population was made clear in riots and demonstrations in Poznan and elsewhere, and it eventually led to a confrontation with the Soviet leadership in 1956 at which some of Poland's economic grievances against the USSR were recognized.

NOTES ON SOURCES

After the Second World War Poland resumed publication of some statistical information, but in comparison with the prewar period the coverage was far less comprehensive. As the Communists consolidated their hegemony, even this small flow of information greatly diminished, and by 1951 it almost completely disappeared. Annual statistical yearbooks were published for the years 1946–50; a national income study was completed for 1947; and a statistical monthly was published by the Central Statistical Office until it finally shrunk out of sight in 1951. In 1956, however, the flow of statistical publication was resumed, most prominently with the publication of the statistical yearbook for 1955, the first since 1950. Succeeding issues of the yearbook became more comprehensive, and discussions in economic periodicals gained in seriousness and perception in contrast to their sterility before the thaw.

We found the publications of the Polish Central Statistical Office particularly useful in our study. Besides its statistical yearbooks and monthly statistical news, it published, among others, special volumes on industry, agriculture, investment and construction, prices, and national income. Two volumes of the latter series, *Dochód narodowy Polski* (National Income of Poland), one for 1954 and 1955 and the other for 1956, were of evident relevance to our work. Although their coverage is incomplete because of the restricted definition of national income they apply and although we could not accept the aggregate measures that they provide on other grounds, including the defective prices in which they are expressed as well as some double counting allowed under their concept of national income but inadmissible under ours, we nonetheless made use of selected components that we could identify as being directly applicable or could adjust to our definitions. The state budgets for 1957 and 1958 similarly provided information useful in estimating items in the government accounts. Both contained a fairly detailed breakdown of expenditures in most government departments that was helpful conceptually and provided some basis for quantitative estimates for earlier years. Other sources that we consulted were economic periodicals and monographs, technical journals, economic textbooks, and newspapers.

The reliability of data gleaned from these sources varies according to the source, the year, and the economic sector to which they apply. On the whole, the information for 1955 and, especially, 1956 is more detailed and reliable than that for 1954. With the passage of time and the concomitant gradual relaxation of restrictions on the flow of economic statistics, the coverage of many series has been expanded, definitions of concepts more explicitly stated, and the desire and ability to inform more pronounced. In general, statistics of the private sector, particularly private farming, tend to be less reliable than for the socialized sector. This may be owing in part to the inevitable difficulties connected with collecting data from millions of small production units and in part to the widespread evasion practiced by reporting units to escape levies and restrictions imposed on them by the government.

The main issue concerning Polish statistics in recent years is their trustworthiness. If the published information reflects merely fabrication, research on the Polish economy would become almost impossible. Fortunately, our detailed examination of Polish statistical materials yields no evidence of deliberate falsification of primary data. Although statistics still serve propaganda purposes in Poland, this goal is achieved primarily by manipulation of data or withholding of information rather than by free invention. This view is supported by the mutual consistency of data derived from various sources, by the evident use of the published data for operational purposes within Poland, and by checks with statistics of other countries.

It does not follow that Polish statistics can be used uncritically. Correction, adjustment, and qualification are called for in numerous instances. Following the consolidation of Communist rule in 1949 until 1956, many previously available statistical series became state secrets. In the absence of primary data, the student had to contend with poorly defined, often contradictory summary measures, indexes, and percentages with unspecified bases. Although the situation has improved a great deal since 1956, there are still areas where the basic information is lacking and where, as always, great care must be exercised in the use of the more aggregated measures.

Among the areas of Polish statistics that are still poorly illuminated were foreign trade, business profits and losses, state subsidies to enterprises, military expenditures, and some aspects of agricultural incomes and outlays. In these fields, however, as well as in other economic areas, it is nonetheless true that there is generally more information available than for most other Soviet-type economies, and particularly for the USSR. For this reason, some of our findings may throw light on these problem areas in the other economies. In particular, the reader's attention is drawn to Appendix G on the state budget. This is probably the most comprehensive and detailed presentation available for any Soviet-type economy.

Because of the limitations of Polish statistics, we have stressed thorough documentation of our findings, outlining in considerable detail the methodology we followed and indicating the reliability of our estimates. Our aim has been to provide all the necessary information to enable a serious student to check our sources and results. In some instances we have had to settle for very rough estimates, which may not significantly affect the relative structure of the national product but which might prove of questionable value in a more limited, precise inquiry. Readers who are familiar with the problems of national income accounting in almost any country will recognize the necessities we faced and no doubt will have been faced with similar problems in their own areas of inquiry.

OUTLINE OF THE STUDY

In Chapter II we provide the basic sectoral and consolidated national accounts. The contents, and in some cases the derivation, of each entry are commented upon in the accompanying text. Detailed sources and methodology are set forth in Appendixes A through D for the sectoral accounts proper, and for convenience of documentation cross references are made to Appendixes E, F, and G, which give in detail the estimates of wages and salaries, agricultural incomes, and government revenues and expenditures, respectively.

Chapter III presents the gross national product by sectors of origin of product and by final uses in current market prices. Appendix H provides detailed supporting documentation and amplification of some of the summary items drawn from the sectoral and consolidated accounts given in Chapter II.

Chapter IV provides an adjustment of the GNP aggregates at market prices to convert them into factor cost. The purpose of the adjustment, its rationale, its methodology, and its limitations are discussed in the text; detailed estimative procedures and sources are given in Appendix I.

In Chapter V we present some of the economic implications of our study, particularly a discussion of resource allocation, sources of finance for government outlays and gross investment, and the relation of our findings to Polish official national income studies.

Finally, we should like to invite the reader's attention to the list of abbreviations (p. xiii) and to the key to items in Tables 1–4 (p. 243), which gives page references to both the text and appendix comments and documentation.

II. SECTORAL AND CONSOLIDATED ACCOUNTS

In Tables 1 through 4 we present the sectoral accounts for the Polish economy for the years 1954, 1955, and 1956. Table 5 consolidates these accounts to arrive at the conventional national income aggregates. The remarks that follow are intended to outline the content of the entries in the sectoral accounts and, in some instances, to discuss problems of methodology and reliability encountered in the derivation of particular estimates. Detailed derivation of entries is presented in appendix notes to the tables.

TABLE 1A

HOUSEHOLD SECTOR PRODUCTION ACCOUNT

(*Million zlotys*)

	1954	1955	1956
RECEIVABLE			
1. Sales to household appropriation account	842	840	774
A. Domestic services	266	280	269
B. Religious services	576	560	505
Total payable	842	840	774
PAYABLE			
2. Value added by sector	842	840	774
A. Money wages	601	614	618
B. Wages in kind	121	130	132
C. Social security	120	96	24
Total receivable	842	840	774

TABLE 1B
HOUSEHOLD SECTOR APPROPRIATION ACCOUNT
(*Million zlotys*)

	1954	1955	1956
RECEIVABLE			
1. Value added by household sector	842	840	774
2. Income from other sectors	154,516	166,425	197,760
A. Enterprise sector	124,446	135,178	163,386
(1) Cash income	100,462	109,519	130,259
a. Wages and salaries	73,651	79,607	92,686
b. Income of self-employed	6,410	6,784	7,970
c. Farm income	20,401	23,128	29,603
(2) Income in kind	23,663	25,323	31,970
a. Wages in kind	689	747	862
b. Farm consumption in kind	22,974	24,576	31,108
(3) Profits distributed to members of nonagricultural cooperatives	300	300	1,085
(4) Interest received from enterprise sector	21	36	72
B. Government sector	30,070	31,247	34,374
(1) Cash wages and salaries	14,993	15,541	17,551
a. Health, education and welfare	5,983	6,698	7,950
b. Administration and justice	3,448	3,753	4,332
c. Internal security	2,100	1,975	2,050
d. Armed forces	3,000	2,650	2,750
e. Quasi-governmental organizations	462	465	469
(2) Income in kind	3,792	3,377	3,019
a. Military subsistence	3,500	3,100	2,750
b. Other wages in kind	292	277	269
(3) Transfer payments	11,285	12,329	13,804
a. From government (cash and imputed)	11,134	12,174	13,622
b. From quasi-governmental organizations	151	155	182
Total receivable	155,358	167,265	198,534
PAYABLE			
3. Purchases of goods and services	155,238	166,588	189,704
A. From households	842	840	774
B. From enterprises	147,294	157,766	180,101
(1) Retail purchases for consumption	101,309	109,027	123,624
(2) Farm market purchases	5,803	6,431	7,100
(3) Services (excluding domestic)	7,944	8,563	9,117
(4) Purchases from handicraft	2,329	2,568	2,768
(5) Farm consumption in kind	22,974	24,576	31,108
(6) Wages in kind	981	1,024	1,131
(7) Military subsistence	3,500	3,100	2,750
(8) Housing: cash and imputed gross rent	2,454	2,477	2,503

TABLE 1B (Continued)

	1954	1955	1956
C. Payments to government	7,102	7,982	8,829
(1) Dues paid to quasi-governmental organizations	693	703	727
(2) Direct taxes	5,573	6,435	7,256
(3) Transfers	716	748	822
(4) Social security contributions	120	96	24
4. Saving	120	677	8,830
Total payable	155,358	167,265	198,534

TABLE 1C

HOUSEHOLD SECTOR CAPITAL ACCOUNT

(*Million zlotys*)

	1954	1955	1956
RECEIVABLE			
1. Saving	120	677	8,830
2. Transfers from foreign sector	550	925	1,500
Total receivable	670	1,602	10,330
PAYABLE			
3. Lending to enterprise sector	566	839	1,238
4. Transfers to enterprise sector	104	763	9,092
Total payable	670	1,602	10,330

TABLE 2A

ECONOMIC ENTERPRISE SECTOR PRODUCTION ACCOUNT

(*Million zlotys*)

	1954	1955	1956
RECEIVABLE			
1. Sales to other accounts	230,673	248,634	292,514
A. Sales to household appropriation account	147,294	157,766	180,101
B. Sales to government production account	14,212	17,916	19,175
C. Sales to government capital account	4,829	5,193	6,733
D. Sales to enterprise capital account	38,420	41,252	55,603
E. Sales to foreign sector	25,918	26,507	30,902
2. Inventory changes	14,700	16,000	14,160
3. Subsidy receipts, excluding foreign trade	12,559	17,089	14,689
A. State farms	2,403	3,624	3,865
B. MTS	711	784	1,123
C. Other enterprises	9,445	12,681	9,701
Total receivable	257,932	281,723	321,363

TABLE 2A (Continued)

PAYABLE

4. Purchases from foreign sector	16,200	19,500	29,800
5. Indirect taxes	73,058	74,871	63,231
A. Turnover tax and positive budget differences, excluding foreign trade	71,160	72,128	60,830
B. Other indirect taxes	1,898	2,743	2,401
6. Capital consumption allowances	10,846	12,498	20,632
7. Value added by sector	157,828	174,854	207,700
A. Compensation of employees	85,179	92,078	106,989
(1) Cash wages and salaries	73,651	79,607	92,686
(2) Social security contributions	10,839	11,724	13,441
(3) Wages in kind	689	747	862
B. Interest payments to households	21	36	72
C. Profits and incomes of self-employed	72,628	82,740	100,639
Total payable	257,932	281,723	321,363

TABLE 2B

ECONOMIC ENTERPRISE SECTOR APPROPRIATION ACCOUNT

(*Million zlotys*)

	1954	1955	1956
RECEIVABLE			
1. Value added by sector	157,828	174,854	207,700
2. Transfer receipts from government	390	435	510
A. Interest payments	40	35	60
B. Prizes	350	400	450
Total receivable	158,218	175,289	208,210
PAYABLE			
3. Compensation of employees (cash and in kind)	74,340	80,354	93,548
4. Social security contributions	10,839	11,724	13,441
5. Interest payments to households	21	36	72
6. Direct taxes	14,339	17,295	20,566
7. Transfers to government	3,455	2,437	2,139
8. Incomes of nonagricultural self-employed	6,410	6,784	7,970
9. Farm consumption in kind	22,974	24,576	31,108
10. Farm income	20,401	23,128	29,603
11. Profits distributed to members of nonagricultural cooperatives	300	300	1,085
12. Retained earnings	5,139	8,655	8,678
Total payable	158,218	175,289	208,210

TABLE 2C

ECONOMIC ENTERPRISE SECTOR CAPITAL ACCOUNT

(*Million zlotys*)

	1954	1955	1956
RECEIVABLE			
1. Retained earnings	5,139	8,655	8,678
2. Capital consumption allowances	10,846	12,498	20,632
3. Capital transfers from government	40,708	37,376	38,616
A. Fixed capital	25,229	26,871	29,417
B. Capital repairs	1,117	1,468	1,873
C. Working capital	14,312	8,960	7,263
D. Repayment of internal debt	50	77	63
4. Borrowing from households	566	839	1,238
5. Capital transfers from households	104	763	9,092
Total receivable	57,363	60,131	78,256
PAYABLE			
6. Gross enterprise investment	53,120	57,252	69,763
A. Additions to fixed capital	33,153	34,978	46,527
B. Capital repairs	5,267	6,274	9,076
C. Increase in inventories	14,700	16,000	14,160
7. Capital transfers to government	3,796	2,280	7,353
8. Lending to government	447	599	1,140
Total payable	57,363	60,131	78,256

TABLE 3A

GOVERNMENT SECTOR PRODUCTION ACCOUNT

(*Million zlotys*)

	1954	1955	1956
RECEIVABLE			
1. Value of government services	34,606	38,570	41,791
PAYABLE			
2. Compensation of employees	18,785	18,918	20,570
A. Cash wages	14,993	15,541	17,551
B. In kind	3,792	3,377	3,019
3. Social security contributions	1,609	1,736	2,046
4. Current purchases	14,212	17,916	19,175
5. Net purchases from abroad	0	0	0
Total payable	34,606	38,570	41,791

TABLE 3B
GOVERNMENT SECTOR APPROPRIATION ACCOUNT
(*Million zlotys*)

	1954	1955	1956
RECEIVABLE			
1. Income from other sectors	110,402	116,045	110,252
A. Indirect tax receipts	73,058	74,871	63,231
B. Direct tax receipts	19,912	23,730	27,822
(1) From households	5,573	6,435	7,256
(2) From enterprises	14,339	17,295	20,566
C. Social security contributions	12,568	13,556	15,511
D. Dues paid to quasi-governmental organizations	693	703	727
E. Transfers	4,171	3,185	2,961
(1) From households	716	748	822
(2) From enterprises	3,455	2,437	2,139
Total receivable	110,402	116,045	110,252
PAYABLE			
2. Purchases from government production account	34,606	38,570	41,791
3. Transfers	11,675	12,764	14,314
A. To households	11,285	12,329	13,804
B. To enterprises	390	435	510
4. Subsidies to enterprise sector, excluding foreign trade	12,559	17,089	14,689
5. Saving	51,562	47,622	39,458
Total payable	110,402	116,045	110,252

TABLE 3C
GOVERNMENT SECTOR CAPITAL ACCOUNT
(*Million zlotys*)

	1954	1955	1956
RECEIVABLE			
1. Saving	51,562	47,622	39,458
2. Capital transfers from enterprise sector	3,796	2,280	7,353
3. Borrowing from enterprise sector	447	599	1,140
Total receivable	55,805	50,501	47,951
PAYABLE			
4. Government investment	4,829	5,193	6,733
5. Capital transfer	50,008	43,376	37,316
A. To enterprise sector	40,708	37,376	38,616
B. To foreign sector (net)	9,300	6,000	− 1,300
6. Net lending to foreign sector	968	1,932	3,902
Total payable	55,805	50,501	47,951

TABLE 4A
FOREIGN SECTOR PRODUCTION ACCOUNT
(*Million zlotys*)

	1954	1955	1956
RECEIVABLE			
1. Imports	16,200	19,500	29,800
2. Balance on production account	9,718	7,007	1,102
Total receivable	25,918	26,507	30,902
PAYABLE			
3. Export of goods and services	25,918	26,507	30,902
A. Commercial exports	25,000	25,100	28,400
B. Transit services (net)	360	424	664
C. Maritime services	558	983	1,838
Total payable	25,918	26,507	30,902

TABLE 4B
FOREIGN SECTOR APPROPRIATION ACCOUNT
(*Million zlotys*)

	1954	1955	1956
RECEIVABLE			
1. Surplus of nation on current account	9,718	7,007	1,102
PAYABLE			
2. Balance on production account	9,718	7,007	1,102

TABLE 4C
FOREIGN SECTOR CAPITAL ACCOUNT
(*Million zlotys*)

	1954	1955	1956
RECEIVABLE			
1. Net transfers from government	9,300	6,000	− 1,300
2. Net lending to rest of world by government	968	1,932	3,902
Total receivable	10,268	7,932	2,602
PAYABLE			
3. Surplus of nation on current account	9,718	7,007	1,102
4. Transfers to household sector	550	925	1,500
Total payable	10,268	7,932	2,602

TABLE 5A
CONSOLIDATED PRODUCTION ACCOUNT
(*Million zlotys*)

	1954	1955	1956
RECEIVABLE			
1. Sales by enterprise sector	190,543	204,211	242,437
A. Household appropriation account	147,294	157,766	180,101
B. Government capital account	4,829	5,193	6,733
C. Enterprise capital account	38,420	41,252	55,603
2. Inventory changes in enterprise sector	14,700	16,000	14,160
3. Value of domestic and religious services sold to household appropriation account	842	840	774
4. Value of government services on production account	34,606	38,570	41,791
5. Foreign sector balance on production account	9,718	7,007	1,102
Gross national product	250,409	266,628	300,264
PAYABLE			
6. Indirect taxes less subsidies	60,499	57,782	48,542
7. Capital consumption allowances	10,846	12,498	20,632
8. National income	179,064	196,348	231,090
A. Value added by enterprise sector	157,828	174,854	207,700
B. Compensation of employees outside enterprise sector	21,236	21,494	23,390
(1) Household sector	842	840	774
(2) Government sector	20,394	20,654	22,616
Gross national product	250,409	266,628	300,264

TABLE 5B
CONSOLIDATED APPROPRIATION ACCOUNT
(*Million zlotys*)

	1954	1955	1956
RECEIVABLE			
1. National income	179,064	196,348	231,090
A. Value added by household sector	842	840	774
B. Value added by enterprise sector	157,828	174,854	207,700
C. Value added by government sector	20,394	20,654	22,616
2. Indirect taxes less subsidies	60,499	57,782	48,542
Net national product	239,563	254,130	279,632
PAYABLE			
3. Household consumption	148,136	158,606	180,875
A. Purchases from household	842	840	774
B. Purchases from enterprises	147,294	157,766	180,101
4. Value of government services	34,606	38,570	41,791
5. Saving	56,821	56,954	56,966
A. Households	120	677	8,830
B. Enterprises	5,139	8,655	8,678
C. Government	51,562	47,622	39,458
Net national product	239,563	254,130	279,632

Table 5C

CONSOLIDATED CAPITAL ACCOUNT

(*Million zlotys*)

	1954	1955	1956
RECEIVABLE			
1. Saving	56,821	56,954	56,966
2. Capital consumption allowances	10,846	12,498	20,632
3. Net capital transfers to households from rest of the world	550	925	1,500
Total receivable	68,217	70,377	79,098
PAYABLE			
4. Gross domestic investment	57,949	62,445	76,496
A. Gross enterprise investment	53,120	57,252	69,763
B. Government investment	4,829	5,193	6,733
5. Net lending to rest of the world	968	1,932	3,902
6. Net capital transfers from government to rest of the world	9,300	6,000	− 1,300
Total payable	68,217	70,377	79,098

HOUSEHOLD SECTOR PRODUCTION ACCOUNT (TABLE 1A)

Production activity in the household sector is defined to consist of domestic services on a wage basis and religious services by ecclesiastical personnel. Expenditure on domestic services is estimated from available information on the numbers of full-time domestic servants and their average cash wage and from assumptions as to the numbers of part-time domestic help. Total earnings of domestic servants are assumed to be equally divided between cash wages and wages in kind. Expenditure on religious services is estimated on the basis of numbers of ecclesiastical personnel and their assumed average wages.

HOUSEHOLD SECTOR APPROPRIATION ACCOUNT (TABLE 1B)

Value added by sector (item 1). This item represents the value of domestic and religious services purchased by households including social security contributions paid for full-time domestic help.

Cash wages and salaries received from the enterprise sector (item 2A1a). These consist of earnings of employees of socialized and private enterprise. Earnings of employees of state farms and MTS are included, as well as wage payments to hired help in agricultural producer cooperatives.[1] On the other hand, cash income received by members of producer cooperatives on the labor-day basis is treated under farm income (item 2A1c) and that received by members of labor cooperatives under distributed profits (see below, item 2A3).

Our estimating procedure is described, step by step, in Appendix E. One methodological issue, however, deserves a brief mention at this stage. While our main sources were the official data on the "wage bill in the national economy," they were found to suffer from a downward bias on a number of counts. They are based on a restrictive definition of wages that excludes various types of payments made to employees, such as prizes and payments out of the director's fund,[2] as well as some categories of wage and salary payments. We adjusted our estimates upward to take account of the omissions.

Income of self-employed (item 2A1b). This item covers the net income of owners of private nonfarming enterprise including professional services. The official Polish statistics of "income of private enterprise" in 1954 and 1955 are net income figures derived as residuals of net output after subtracting the amounts paid as wages to hired labor, social security contributions, and taxes.[3] Net income thus computed encompasses an element of entrepreneurial "wage" (the amount that he could earn by working as an employee elsewhere) as well as an element of pure profit or loss. Following the practice of the Western national income accounting, these two elements are not presented separately, although such a refinement might be of interest from the viewpoint of the theory of distribution.

Farm income (item 2A1c). This has been calculated as the

---

[1] The term MTS, an acronym for "machine-tractor stations," is drawn from discussions of the Soviet economy. It is used here to represent the Polish state and village machinery centers (*państwowe ośrodki maszynowe* [POM] and *gminne ośrodki maszynowe* [GOM], respectively).

[2] We use the term "director's fund," which has become familiar from discussions of the Soviet economy, to represent the corresponding Polish "plant fund" (*fundusz zakładowy*).

[3] *DN 1954/55,* p. 4.

sum of farmers' receipts from centralized and decentralized state procurements and proceeds from sales in the free market. From the sum of these receipts, purchases of nonfarm inputs into production and payments of land tax were deducted, leaving as a residual net cash income of farmers.

We assumed that all of this residual was distributed to farmers, but this is an oversimplification where the collective farms are concerned. Collective farms pay out most of their income as members' shares based on their work; a part of the income, however, would normally be retained for collective purposes. The collective work of these farms accounted for only about 5 to 6 percent of the combined gross production of individual and collective farms in 1954 and 1955,[4] and in the last quarter of 1956 about 90 percent of them were dissolved. Moreover, the collective farms in many instances failed to observe their charter provisions about retention of income for collective purposes because their earnings were disappointing. Thus, any overestimate of farm income paid to households under our assumption very probably is insignificant.

Wages in kind (*item 2A2a*). This item includes such commodities as coal and sugar distributed to employees (*deputaty*), free uniforms, housing, and food. Our estimates are based on official figures relative to the wage totals plus an upward adjustment for incomplete coverage.

Farm consumption in kind (*item 2A2b*). We show here the value of products produced and directly consumed by farmers. Our figures for 1954 and 1955 are based on official Polish estimates in average realized prices for marketed output. In 1956, however, the corresponding official estimate was expressed in prices paid to farmers for above-quota deliveries to the state procurement agencies. We deflated this figure to average realized prices by means of a specially constructed price index based on twelve products weighted by quantities consumed by the rural population.

Details of our estimates are shown in Appendix F. We dis-

[4] Poland, Główny urząd statystyczny, *Produkcja globalna i brutto rolnictwa przed wojną i w latach 1946–1958*, p. 3.

cuss there also the reasons for applying average realized prices. In brief, we believe that these prices come closer than other alternatives to corresponding to farmers' marginal rates of substitution between money income and income in kind.

Profits distributed to members of nonagricultural cooperatives (*item 2A3*). The statutes of labor cooperatives authorized them to distribute not more than 20 percent of net profits to members in 1954 and 1955 and 50 percent in 1956. Our estimates are based on information on profits and on the assumption that the actual distribution was the permissible maximum.

Interest received from the enterprise sector (*item 2A4*). The figures we show are interest on savings deposits by the population in the General Savings Bank.

Cash wages and salaries in government sector (*item 2B1*). The reliability of our estimates of cash wages in the government sector varies a great deal according to the branch. Firm figures were available for total wage bills in health, education, and welfare as well as in public administration. Their breakdown into cash and in-kind elements is also fairly reliable.

On the other hand, our figures for wage bills in internal security agencies, the armed forces, and, to a smaller extent, the quasi-governmental organizations are at best rough estimates. The margin of arbitrariness introduced by these elements is nevertheless preferred to distortions that would be caused by their complete omission. It may be noted that the assumptions on which our estimates of these magnitudes are based tend to be conservative in all cases. Actual wage payments to police, for example, may be underestimated, but they are not likely to be overestimated in our calculations.

A detailed step-by-step description of our estimating procedure is given in Appendix E. Cash wages in health, education, and welfare and in public administration were obtained by subtracting wages-in-kind from the sum of the personal and nonpersonal wage funds in each of these branches. Cash wage payments to internal security personnel were estimated from fragmentary information on the numbers in various classes of such personnel and on their average earnings. Our rough estimate of military pay was based on the total strength of the Polish armed forces and on some assumptions as to the average remuneration received by officers and by enlisted men. In particular, the average basic pay received by officers and specialists was assumed to be equal to the average salaries received by engineering and technical personnel in socialized industry.

Health, education, and welfare (item 2B1a). This item covers "social and cultural institutions," primarily government agencies providing health and educational services and institutions for child care. The wage bill in theaters, motion picture theaters, and other entertainment institutions and in state publishing houses is treated as belonging to the enterprise sector. Details of the computation are given in Appendix E.

Administration and justice (item 2B1b). Here belong wages and salaries received by employees of administrative agencies of central and local government and of judicial institutions. Contrary to the Polish statistical practice we do not include under this category the employees of financial institutions; they are treated, rather, as part of the enterprise sector. It could, of course, be argued that the same treatment should be accorded to at least part of the personnel employed by the industrial ministries and by central boards. Such personnel perform economic functions of planning and coordination that in a nonplanned economy are traditionally carried out by entrepreneurs. It would be very difficult, however, to draw any hard and fast line that would separate such employees from others who perform purely administrative functions. Polish statisticians have followed a vacillating course on this score. Thus, in national accounts for 1947 employees of central boards are considered as being engaged in the production of material goods (which very roughly corresponds to the Marxian counterpart of an "enterprise sector") whereas in later years their labor is treated as "unproductive." We follow the more recent practice, placing all employees of central boards and ministries in the government sector.

Internal security (item 2B1c). Here belong the money earnings of employees of the police, the full- and part-time employees of the voluntary police reserve, frontier guards, and personnel employed by the Ministry of the Interior.

Armed forces (item 2B1d). This item covers the cash earnings of officers, noncommissioned officers, and enlisted men in the Polish armed forces. Our figures are based on estimates of the strength of the military forces and average pay and allowances.

Quasi-governmental organizations (item 2B1e). We include here cash wages received by officials of the Communist Party, trade unions, youth organizations, and other organizations that were considered to be extensions of the formal government apparatus.

Military subsistence (item 2B2a). The value of military subsistence was estimated on the basis of information on the total strength of the Polish armed forces. Subsistence per capita was estimated by approximating the cost of clothing, food, and other supplies. Only major items were included in our estimate.

Other wages in kind (item 2B2b). Nonmilitary wages in kind in the government sector were calculated on the assumption that wages in kind amounted to the same percentage of the personal wage fund in the government sector as they did in the socialized enterprise sector.

Cash and imputed transfer payments from government (item 2B3a). Cash transfers include pensions and allowances paid by the social security administration and by the Ministry of Railroads as well as educational stipends. The latter include for the most part grants to students of technical and vocational schools and to university students and faculty and to a much lesser extent to high school students, artists, and others. Assistance both in money and in kind is included. Imputed transfers were taken equal to the wages and social security contributions for the clergy. We considered the latter as paid by the household sector, but in fact the remuneration was paid directly from government funds. The imputation is shown here to complete the rerouting of the transaction.

Transfer payments from quasi-governmental organizations

(*item 2B3b*). Included here are statutory benefits paid by trade unions.

Purchases from households (*item 3A*). The entry represents the value added by the household sector as transferred from the sector's production account. It consists of wages (both in cash and in kind) and social security contributions covering services rendered to households.

Retail purchases for consumption (*item 3B1*). Polish official statistics on retail trade embrace all sales by both socialized and private trade but exclude sales on the farmers' market (*targowisko*).[5] In the socialized sector they cover (*a*) all retail sales by trade outlets, restaurants, and cafeterias; (*b*) direct sales to households by distributors, wholesalers, and by the producing enterprises; and (*c*) wages paid in kind. Sales by all retail outlets are included, whether they belong to the retail trade enterprises or to the Workers' Supply Branches (Oddziały Zaopatrzenia Robotniczego). Retail sales embrace also the so-called "nonmarket" sales (*obrót pozarynkowy*), that is, sales to offices, enterprises, and institutions and to other nonhousehold buyers, as well as commission sales (*komis*) of used goods. The sales in restaurants and cafeterias include sales of both the public (open) establishments and the workers' cafeterias, which are open as a rule only to the employees of a given establishment. Retail sales are also assumed to include the value of goods delivered to the population through the so-called "internal exports" (PKO). (For explanation of internal exports, see note under Table IC, item 2.) Purchases of supplies by private retail stores from socialized retail establishments are omitted in the derivation of total retail sales in order to avoid double counting.[6]

In order to arrive at net retail purchases of consumer goods by households, the above total was diminished by retail purchases of producer goods on current and on capital account by the government and enterprise sectors, as well as by commission sales (less retail margin). A very similar procedure is followed by the Polish Central Statistical Office in its estimates of consumption

[5] *RS 1957*, p. 219.
[6] Cf. *DN 1954/55*, p. 20.

expenditure by households,[7] and by the United Nations in their estimates of Soviet consumption in 1955.[8]

Farm market purchases (*item 3B2*). These purchases are made in bazaars to which farmers bring their surplus produce after meeting state delivery quotas. Bazaar prices are set freely by supply and demand. They tend to be considerably above retail prices, the extent of difference being an index of the shortages of foodstuffs in socialized retail trade. Purchases from farmers by households are estimated as total free market sales by farmers less purchases from farmers by private retail trade (to avoid double counting with item 3B1).

Services (*excluding domestic*) (*item 3B3*). Purchases of services by households from the enterprise sector were estimated as the sum of household expenditures on utilities, transportation, communications, entertainment, professional services, and miscellaneous other services.

The reliability of our estimates varies according to the type of service, reflecting the uneven statistical coverage in Polish sources. Expenditures by households on gas, electricity, and water and urban transport could be estimated with a fair degree of reliability from the available information on the physical amounts purchased and on the prevailing rates. But household expenditures on transportation other than local and on communications and other services were more difficult to estimate. According to Marxian definitions, such services are not "productive," and statistical data referring to them have many gaps. Value figures for the most part are unavailable. In the case of transportation, the number of passenger-kilometers is given, but their distribution by classes according to the rates charged is missing. The rate charged per kilometer varied considerably depending on the type of train, class of service, type of ticket (one-trip, monthly, and so forth), and category of passengers (workers and school children, for example, were entitled to dis-

---

[7] *DN 1956*, p. 56.

[8] United Nations, *Economic Bulletin for Europe*, IX, No. 1 (May, 1957), 101.

counts ranging from 33 to 80 percent).[9] In the absence of such information, no meaningful estimates could be arrived at by using physical data alone, except in the case of urban transportation for which a separate estimate was made.

In the case of communications, the total number of parcels and letters handled by the postal authorities and of telephone calls and telegrams is known. No information is provided, however, on the amounts actually spent on those items by households as distinguished from enterprises and government. The amounts spent by the population on public entertainment are also somewhat conjectural.

Lacking actual value figures, our estimates for 1954 and 1955 were derived for the most part by extrapolating 1956 figures obtained from an official Polish source giving the percentage composition of household purchases and our estimate of the absolute value of one component, namely, cash rent. A subsequent comparison of the values of purchases of selected items thus obtained with figures taken directly from official statistics showed substantial agreement. Our extrapolations to 1954 and 1955 were based on indexes of the volume of services and related indicators. Thus, for example, for various transportation services we used passenger-kilometers or number of passengers. We did not attempt to deflate for price changes since the price level of services remained more or less constant during this period.

Purchases from handicraft (item 3B4). Purchases by households from handicraft establishments are treated here as a separate item, mainly in view of the fact that they consisted of purchases both of goods (such as shoes, clothes, and household utensils) and services (such as repairs). Our estimates were calculated from the official statistics of gross output and sales by handicraft to various categories of customers. We assumed that handicraft in this context refers to private handicraft only, since socialized handicraft had no special legal status of its own and was defined as any productive enterprise employing up to

9 *RS 1957,* p. 210.

five workers, regardless of the character of output, and as any service enterprise, regardless of the number of employees, if the work resembled that of a private handicraft enterprise.[10] Consequently, the Polish statistics do not usually show socialized handicraft as a separate sector but include it with socialized industry. We assumed then that the sales of socialized handicraft were included in the socialized retail trade figures and that no separate direct sales to households took place.

Farm consumption in kind (item 3B5). This item has been commented upon under item 2A2b, above.

Wages in kind (item 3B6). See comments under items 2A2a and 2B2b, above.

Military subsistence (item 3B7). See under item 2B2a, above.

Housing: cash and imputed gross rentals (item 3B8). Rents on dwellings in Poland were paid on the basis of the housing area occupied by the tenant. This covers, according to the official definition, the area of all usable space, including kitchens, bathrooms, halls, etc.[11] In the absence of official data on the total amount of rent paid by the population, our estimates were based on the total housing area in the socialized and private sectors and on rent rates. The most nearly complete information was available for 1956. Estimates for other years were obtained by working backward on the basis of information on new construction and retirement. Our estimates of the housing area in the socialized and private sectors were based on data of the Institute for Housing Construction (Instytut Budownictwa Mieszkaniowego [IBM]). These data were used for official planning purposes and were based on rather extensive surveys.

Dues paid to quasi-governmental organizations (item 3C1). We include here the Communist Party, trade unions, Association of Polish Youth, the Polish-Soviet Friendship Society, sports and tourist clubs, and secondary political parties. This procedure appears justified in view of the close affinity, bordering on identity, between these bodies and the government, which often uses such bodies rather than the official administrative machinery.

[10] *RS 1957,* p. 59.
[11] *DU 1953,* No. 35, Item 152; *RS 1957,* p. 264, Table 17 (290), footnote a.

The amount of dues paid was estimated on the basis of announced membership, assumptions concerning the varying proportions of dues-paying members (delinquency of dues being widespread, especially in 1956), and unofficial information on membership rates.

Direct taxes (*item 3C2*). This item represents primarily the tax on wages and salaries. Small sums representing other levies were also included here although there are some questions concerning their classification.

Transfers (*item 3C3*). Included here are fees for social, cultural, and health services, fines, and other miscellaneous payments.

Social security contributions (*item 3C4*). These cover payments on behalf of domestic servants.

Saving (*item 4*). This is the balancing item between receivables and payables. The large increase in saving between 1955 and 1956 may be partly explained by wage gains unaccompanied by a proportional increase in the supply of consumer goods and by the general uncertainty of the period during which the motivation for liquidity was likely to have been stronger than in the preceding period.

Household Sector Capital Account (Table 1C)

Saving (*item 1*). See the comments under the household sector appropriation account (Table 1B, item 4).

Transfers from foreign sector (*item 2*). This item includes the so-called "internal exports" (PKO) and various cash payments from abroad. The internal exports consist of sums received from abroad in foreign exchange which are paid to Polish households either as Polish currency or in the form of scarce consumer goods. The value of the latter is assumed to be included in retail sales to households.

Lending to enterprise sector (*item 3*). This item represents the increment in savings deposits held by the population in the savings banks.

Transfers to enterprise sector (*item 4*). This balancing item between payables and receivables represents an imputed transfer to finance investment.

Economic Enterprise Sector Production Account (Table 2A)

Sales to household appropriation account (item 1A). This was obtained from Table 1B as the sum of: retail trade purchases for consumption, farm market purchases, services (excluding domestic), purchases from handicraft, income in kind consumed on farms, wages in kind, military subsistence, and cash and imputed gross rentals.

Sales to government production account (item 1B). This item embraces sales to government administration and services, armed forces, and quasi-governmental organizations. More detailed discussion is found in connection with the government sector production account (see under Table 3A, item 4).

Sales to government capital account (item 1C). This item was calculated as the sum of purchases of fixed capital assets and capital repairs in health and educational facilities, in national defense, and in administration, minus nonbudget financed investment and minus investments in those business enterprises that in Polish official statistics are treated as part of government. Our estimates based on budget data are presented in detail in Appendix Table G2.

Sales to enterprise capital account (item 1D). These embrace net additions to fixed capital and capital repairs in the enterprise sector.

Sales to foreign sector (item 1E). This item represents the export of goods and services to foreign countries. See the comments under the foreign sector production account (Table 4A).

Inventory changes (item 2). The value of changes in inventories were taken from Polish official sources. The figures cover changes in inventories proper (*zapasy*) and in state reserves (*rezerwy*).

Subsidy receipts, excluding foreign trade (item 3). Total subsidy receipts by enterprises were based on official sources (see

Appendix Table G2). Subsidies to MTS and other enterprises included in the state budget were estimated independently and were added to the other enterprise subsidies. Subsidies to foreign trade enterprises, or so-called "negative budget differences" in foreign trade, were estimated separately in connection with the foreign sector production account (see note under Table 4A, items 1 and 3A). For an explanation of the positive and negative budget differences, see the note below under item 5A, paragraph 2.

Purchases from foreign sector (item 4). We show here the value of imports. For discussion of this entry, see the comments under the foreign sector production account (Table 4A, item 1).

Turnover tax and positive budget differences, excluding foreign trade (item 5A). Four categories are distinguished here:

1. Turnover taxes on goods. Turnover taxes are imposed on goods at certain stages in their production, usually at the factory level. Trade establishments are not subject to turnover tax "in principle" [12] but in fact do pay relatively minor amounts. (In 1956, 1.9 billion was paid on this account on agricultural goods alone.) [13] The Polish tax system differs in this respect from the Soviet pattern in which the turnover tax is collected primarily by trade rather than by production units.[14]

2. Positive budget differences. The line of division between so-called "positive budget differences" outside foreign trade and turnover taxes is a rather arbitrary one, drawn on administrative rather than on economic grounds. Like the turnover tax, positive budget differences are transferred by the enterprise to the budget. Their main purpose is to siphon off high profits realized by low-cost producers (see pp. 60–61).

We exclude budget differences in foreign trade at this stage because they already enter the prices of imports and exports.

3. Tax on services. This is essentially a sales tax on services corresponding to the turnover tax on goods.

4. Turnover taxes paid on exports. Enterprises selling their

[12] Weralski, *Finanse i kredyt,* Part I, p. 146.
[13] *RS 1957,* p. 57.
[14] Reniger, *Dochody państwowe,* p. 131.

goods to foreign trade organizations for export pay turnover tax, but the amounts in question are refunded to them by the state budget. We enter here the amounts paid by the enterprises since the sales to the foreign sector are shown in domestic prices including turnover tax.

Other indirect taxes (item 5B). We put here all those taxes imposed upon the enterprise sector, apart from turnover tax and positive budget differences, that are regarded by enterprises as business expense. The itemized amounts are tabulated in Appendix Table G1.

Capital consumption allowances (item 6). Our estimates for the most part were taken from official Polish sources. Even though our figures probably cover all sectors of the economy, they purport to measure depreciation allowances set aside by the enterprise sector but not the amounts of capital actually consumed in producing national income. It has been repeatedly stated by Polish economists that the rates of depreciation allowances, especially in the years prior to 1956, were set at a level that was too low and that substantially understated the actual consumption of capital.[15] The extent to which they were biased downward can be gathered from the fact that on January 1, 1956, depreciation rates were raised by an average of 50 percent in order to make them more realistic. In arriving at our estimates, we excluded from the official figures estimated depreciation on private and collective farms because it appears to be an imputation not corresponding to actual transactions.

In accordance with our theoretical framework, we assumed that capital consumption allowances refer to the enterprise sector alone. No depreciation is calculated for the government sector. Whereas the official figure we used for 1956 includes 82.6 million zlotys set aside as capital consumption allowances in the government sector, we assumed that this item refers to such fields of enterprise as publishing, entertainment, and some other business enterprises that in official data are considered part of the government sector.

---

[15] Fiszel, *Prawo wartości a problematyka cen w przemyśle socjalistycznym*, *passim*.

Compensation of employees (item 7A). This item is explained in Appendix E and in the household sector appropriation account (see under Table 1B, items 2A1a and 2A2a).

Interest payments to households (item 7B). This item represents interest on savings deposits.

Profits and incomes of self-employed (item 7C). Profits and incomes of self-employed is a residual item which covers farm investment in kind, farm income consumed in kind, profits distributed in labor cooperatives, net income from the sale of farm products by farmers, and undistributed profits of private enterprise.

Economic Enterprise Sector Appropriation Account (Table 2B)

Some of the entries in this account have already been discussed in connection with other accounts. Detailed derivation of the entries is given in Appendix B.

Value added by sector (item 1). This item was transferred from the enterprise sector production account.

Transfer receipts from government (item 2). The interest payment shown here refers to the internal debt. The amounts shown as prizes represent funds transferred to enterprises for special awards and bonuses.

Compensation of employees (item 3) and *Social security contributions (item 4)*. These entries represent wages and salaries in cash and in kind and payments on behalf of employees for social security insurance. See Appendix E, Table E1 for details.

Interest payments to households (item 5). This entry covers interest on personal savings deposits. Because the amounts are relatively insignificant and services rendered by banks to depositors are negligible, we did not attempt an imputation showing higher interest receipts diminished by service charges.

Direct taxes (item 6). These entries include the following components: (A) income tax paid by cooperatives; (B) transfers of profits from socialized enterprise to the state budget; (C) income tax on private enterprise, imposed according to differentiated progressive scales, the rates depending on the kind of activity from which income was derived; [16] and (D) land tax, paid by individual farmers and collective farms according to income derived from the land.

Transfer payments to government (*item 7*). These include administrative fees, fines, confiscations, and other miscellaneous payments.

Incomes of nonagricultural self-employed (*item 8*). This includes incomes of professions from private practice, entrepreneurial incomes from private enterprise other than farming, and "other cash incomes of the population." The figures for the latter were taken from Polish official sources and comprise such items as earnings of haulers, income derived from the sale of used bottles, crates, and other scrap, and income from other activities.

Farm consumption in kind (*item 9*). This represents the imputed value of that part of gross agricultural output that was consumed in kind by members of farm households. It was valued at average realized farm prices.

Farm income (*item 10*). This represents the net income from sale of farm products by farmers. We estimated this by subtracting total purchases of nonfarm inputs, payments of land tax, and wages from gross receipts from sale of farm products by individual farmers and owners of plots in producer cooperatives, and by adding income distributed to members of producer cooperatives on a labor-day basis. No deduction was made for estimated depreciation of fixed assets since it is improbable that significant depreciation reserves were established in this sector, and we are here concerned with actual money flows.

Profits distributed to members of nonagricultural cooperatives (*item 11*). This item represents that part of net cash income of labor cooperatives that was distributed to members.

Retained earnings (*item 12*). This is the balancing item between receivables and payables on the enterprise sector appropriation account.

[16] See Reniger, *Dochody państwowe*, pp. 204–13.

ECONOMIC ENTERPRISE SECTOR CAPITAL ACCOUNT (TABLE 2C)

Retained earnings (*item 1*). These figures were obtained in the enterprise sector appropriation account as the balancing entries (see under Table 2B, item 12).

Capital consumption allowances (*item 2*). These entries are explained in the enterprise sector production account (see under Table 2A, item 6).

Capital transfers from government (*item 3*). Government grants for fixed and working capital and capital repairs and amounts paid out to enterprises in repayment of internal debt were estimated from data on the state budget.

Borrowing from households (*item 4*). See note under the household sector capital account (Table 1C, item 3).

Capital transfers from households (*item 5*). See note under the household sector capital account (Table 1C, item 4).

Gross enterprise investment (*item 6*). Gross investment is defined as the sum of additions to fixed capital, capital repairs, and the value of change in inventories. We started with the value of each of these components for the enterprise and government sectors combined, taken directly or derived from official sources. Then we subtracted from these totals our independent estimates of the share of the government sector, thus deriving the figures for the enterprise sector as residuals.

In our estimating procedure we made occasional use of the formula adopted in Polish official statistics in which additions to fixed capital equal net investment plus capital consumption allowances less capital repairs. It enabled us to set up equations and estimate missing components from the available ones.

The breakdown of total investment between the enterprise and government sectors involved an adjustment of the official figures on investment in health and education (or "social and cultural institutions") since they include investment in publishing and entertainment establishments as well as in some *khozraschet* (that is, business) enterprises that we treat as part of the enterprise sector. Our estimates of investment in the government sector are therefore lower than implied by the official figures.

Inventories are regarded in Polish statistics as a part af "accumulation." They are usually lumped together with government reserve stocks of materials, but some indication of the composition is given in the detailed notes in Appendix B. Although there are some significant differences in the Polish official sources as to the 1955 absolute value of the increment to inventories as well as the value of fixed capital investment,[17] the use of the alternative figures would have relatively unimportant effect on the percentage composition of GNP by end use.

Capital transfers to government (item 7). This is the balancing item in the account. It includes surplus working capital[18] and surplus depreciation funds as well as an imputed transfer.

Lending to government (item 8). In earlier years the enterprise sector was lending funds to government by subscribing to state loans. The National Reconstruction Loan of 1946 was primarily subscribed by enterprises.[19] During the period 1954–56, however, lending to government took the form of compulsory investment of resources by savings banks and state insurance institutions. These operations could, in fact, be looked upon as transfers of capital to the state budget. Although these "investments" are regarded as returnable, no fixed term is set for repayment, which takes place "only in cases where it is justified by a given institution's concrete needs."[20] We followed the Polish practice of treating these transactions as loans to government.

GOVERNMENT SECTOR PRODUCTION ACCOUNT (TABLE 3A)

Value of government services (item 1). The value of government services is equal to amounts paid out as compensation of employees, social security contributions, purchases from enter-

---

[17] Cf. *DN 1954–55,* p. 3, and *DN 1956,* pp. 14, 51.
[18] See Weralski, *Finanse i kredyt,* Part I, pp. 124–25.
[19] See Reniger, *Dochody państwowe,* pp. 266–68.
[20] *Ibid.,* pp. 259–60.

prises on current account, and purchases of goods and services from the foreign sector. Government services corresponding to these inputs are valued at cost and are considered to be sold to the government appropriation account.

A small part of the cost of government services directly covered to some extent by charges to households is treated here as a transfer on the appropriation accounts. These payments (consisting mostly of fees for social and cultural services) were estimated in notes to the household sector appropriation account (see under Table 1B, item 3C3).

Compensation of employees (*item 2*). The following items are included:

i. Cash wages and salaries and wages in kind paid to the employees of public administration and of justice, health, education, and other social and cultural services. Entertainment and publishing, treated as part of educational services in Polish statistics, are excluded since we treat them as part of the enterprise sector.

ii. Wage bill of quasi-governmental organizations (trade unions, political parties, sports clubs).

iii. Wage bill of internal security forces, including civilian employees of the Ministry of the Interior.

iv. Armed forces pay and military subsistence.

Only item i and part of item iii (civilian employees) are included in the Polish official definition of the "wage fund in the national economy," and as such are covered in the official statistics. The remaining items were estimated on the basis of scattered information on the numbers involved and on average pay per head.

Social security contributions (*item 3*). Government sector employees are covered by social insurance, and contributions are made on behalf of employees for this purpose.

Current purchases from enterprises (*item 4*). Purchases by government on current account were derived as a residual in total budgetary expenditure in each year. The detailed estimate is shown in Appendix Table G2. Purchases by the military were estimated as a residual in the budgetary expenditure on national defense after subtraction of wages, military subsistence, and investment expenditure. In conformity with our concept of the government sector, we add to these figures estimated current purchases by quasi-governmental organizations.

Net purchases from abroad (item 5). The estimates, shown in detail in Appendix Table G2, are in the nature of an informed guess. They include the nonwage cost of diplomatic representation abroad and of economic and cultural cooperation with foreign countries. We assumed that the purchases of the foreign sector from the Polish government exactly offset the Polish government purchases from the foreign sector, so that the net purchases were zero.

GOVERNMENT SECTOR APPROPRIATION ACCOUNT (TABLE 3B)

The government appropriation account depends heavily on our analysis of the state budget presented in Appendix G. At various points in this analysis it was necessary to make simplifying assumptions in order to obtain at a later stage some of the important items in our accounts. At every point, however, we have tried to keep touch with reality by relating our assumptions to comparable known phenomena. Although some of our estimates on a more detailed level thus may suffer from varying degrees of arbitrariness, we have always observed the over-all constraints of known budget magnitudes. Hence, on an aggregated basis, we would expect our results to be more reliable than in the case of some of the detailed estimates.

Detailed derivation of entries in Table 3B is given in Appendix C. Our remarks below indicate in a general way the content of some of the entries and the character of the estimates.

Indirect tax receipts (item 1A). This item covers the turnover tax and various other taxes considered as costs from the point of view of the enterprise. In the case of the residential tax (*podatek od lokali*), which is known to be levied both on households and enterprises,[21] we assumed that 90 percent of it was paid by households and 10 percent by enterprises. Similarly, fees for

---

[21] Reniger, *Dochody państwowe,* pp. 175 ff.

transfer of property rights were assumed to be split evenly between households and the enterprise sector.

We made two important adjustments to the official budget revenue figures. First, we increased the turnover tax revenues by the estimated amount of turnover tax rebated to producers on exported goods. This item appears in the state budgets as a negative item among revenues.[22] Second, we diminished the revenue from positive budget differences, a kind of price equalization tax, by the amount realized from foreign trade. Both adjustments were made to insure consistency with our valuation of national product in domestic prices. In effect, we show the domestic enterprises paying and receiving domestic prices in transactions with the foreign sector.

Direct tax receipts (item 1B). We included in the direct tax receipts from households the tax on wages and salaries and miscellaneous other taxes. Direct tax receipts from enterprises include the income tax, land tax (based on income), and transfers of profits. The income tax in the socialized sector is imposed on cooperatives and amounts, as a rule, to one third of their profits as shown in the balance sheet. Private enterprises paying the income tax include handicrafts, professions, trade, services, and small industrial establishments.

Transfers of profits to the budget apply only to socialized enterprises. A part of total enterprise profits is allocated to the plant incentive fund (director's fund), a part to increases in working capital, and the balance, which may not be less than 10 percent of the total, to the state budget.[23]

Social security contributions (item 1C). We used the Polish official totals for payments by employers, including government.

Dues paid to quasi-governmental organizations (item 1D). These include membership dues of political parties, labor unions, and other organizations, all of which were considered as belonging to the government sector because of the governmental character of their activities and the unified government control over their operations.

Transfers from households (item 1E1). This item covers vari-

---

[22] See *DU 1957*, No. 25, p. 259.
[23] Reniger, *Dochody państwowe*, pp. 144, 152.

ous fines, fees, and stamp taxes. Although a part of these figures could be regarded as purchases from the government, for the sake of simplicity we decided to treat the entire amounts as transfers.

Transfers from enterprises (item 1E2). This item covers budget revenue from various administrative fees and fines and confiscations.

Purchase from the government production account (item 2). We show here an imputed sale of government services produced during the year, valued at cost (see note under Table 3A, item 1).

Transfers to households (item 3A). Included here are pensions, stipends, and allowances, provided to households by government proper and by labor unions, that we placed in the government sector.

Transfers to enterprises (item 3B). This item includes interest payments, which are explained in detail in connection with the enterprise sector appropriation account, and budget expenditure for prizes, which pass through the enterprise sector eventually to households (see note under Table 2B, item 2).

Subsidies to enterprise sector, excluding foreign trade (item 4). In the Polish terminology subsidies appear mainly in the form of "grants to cover planned losses" and "grants for special purposes." Both of these categories appear in the budget as part of current grants to business (*khozraschet*) enterprises and are distinct from the budget grants for investment and capital repairs. Losses are financed from the budget via the respective ministries and central boards. The main branches of the economy subsidized from the budget, whether in the form of grants or budget differences, were the foreign trade enterprises, coal mining, building materials industry, state farms, agricultural machinery stations, and residential housing.

Budget differences, as found in Polish statistics, are often separated into two categories: budget differences paid to, or received from, foreign trade enterprises, and budget differences that concern enterprises outside of foreign trade, namely, those in such sectors of the economy as industry, trade, and transportation. In some instances, negative budget differences are used to cover losses in enterprises for which a deficit has been planned. In other instances, they are used to equalize differences in profitability among enterprises belonging to a given branch of the economy. In a situation where some firms make huge profits and others make large losses, each firm establishes a so-called "internal accounting price" reflecting average cost, planned profits, and turnover tax. For efficient firms the internal accounting price is likely to lie below the selling price binding upon all firms. In such a case the difference between the selling price and the accounting price is positive, and it is transferred to the budget in the form of positive budget differences. On the other hand, when the accounting price is above the selling price, the difference is tranferred from the budget to the enterprise in the form of negative budget differences.

Negative budget differences result also from the sale of commodities at discriminatory prices varying according to the buyer and destination (for example, sales of industrial goods such as coal to farmers who signed delivery contracts with the socialized procurement organization). Finally, in some instances goods (such as coal) are sold at delivered prices, the selling price including the planned transportation costs. If the actual transportation costs differ from the planned, this gives rise to positive or negative budget differences.

In principle, the various enterprises pay the positive budget differences into and receive the negative budget differences from their central boards, which, in turn, settle their accounts with the state budget. According to Polish sources, these settlements are conducted separately for the positive and negative budget differences, which would seem to mean that the budget differences appear in the budget after having been netted out by the central boards and thus represent only a part of the total budget differences.[24] It may be added that some enterprises are accountable directly to the budget, without being required to pass through the intermediate central boards.

It appears from the foregoing discussion that our estimate of

[24] Weralski, *Finanse i kredyt,* Part I, pp. 156, 157–58.

total budget differences in the Polish economy is directly dependent on the level of aggregation. The figures presented in this instance apparently result from aggregation on the level of central administrations. In other instances, namely, the transfers of profits or financing of current losses, aggregation may occur at the level of ministries, though not necessarily uniformly.

Saving (item 5). This is the balancing item in the account.

GOVERNMENT SECTOR CAPITAL ACCOUNT (TABLE 3C)

Saving (item 1). This item was transferred from the government sector appropriation account.

Capital transfers from enterprise sector (item 2). See the remarks on the corresponding item in the enterprise sector capital account (Table 2C, item 7).

Borrowing from enterprise sector (item 3). See the remarks on this item under the enterprise sector capital account (Table 2C, item 8).

Government investment (item 4). This represents mainly construction and capital repair of public buildings, prisons, hospitals, schools, and military installations and other government investment. We estimated separately additions to fixed capital and capital repairs. Little is known about government stockpiling of goods of strategic importance and purchases of armaments. This point touches upon a broader question: under what headings are expenditures on armaments and munitions listed in Polish statistics? According to a statement made by S. Jędrychowski, Chairman of the Planning Commission, in 1957, expenditure on current maintenance of the armed forces was considered part of collective consumption whereas the expenditure on armaments was included in accumulation.[25]

This statement raises three questions. First, does the "current maintenance" of armed forces include also expenditure on munitions? It would appear to be so, but the possibility is not entirely excluded that Jędrychowski would treat munitions on the same

[25] Jędrychowski, *Polityka partii i rządu w dziedzinie podziału dochodu narodowego*, p. 4.

footing as armaments, that is, as part of accumulation. Second, under which category of accumulation are purchases of armaments included? Are they treated as additions to fixed capital or to stocks? Finally, it is not clear when the practice described by Jędrychowski was adopted.

Expenditure on munitions is believed to be included under current expenditure on armed forces and hence, according to Jędrychowski, under the Polish statistical category of "collective consumption." If we deduct from the 1956 explicit budget expenditures on national defense our estimates of military subsistence, military pay, wages and salaries, and investment, we obtain an estimate of current purchases other than military subsistence (see Table G2):

		Amount (million zlotys)
Total expenditure		12,682
Less:	Investment	967
	Military pay and subsistence	5,600
Equals:	Current purchases	6,115

Is this residual large enough to account for current purchases of munitions and possibly armaments also? Jędrychowski's statement that expenditure on armaments is included under accumulation does not seem compatible with such a conclusion, and we leave the question open.

Our estimated outlays for military investment in the years 1954–56 (see Appendix Table G2), as well as the corresponding planned figures, are so small [26] that they may refer only to construction of military barracks, airfields, and other installations to the exclusion of purchases of weapons. On the other hand, should purchases of weapons be included under current military purchases, this would invalidate Jędrychowski's statement. A tentative hypothesis may therefore be advanced that expenditure on weapons is included under the heading of increase in inventories and reserves. This would be compatible with Jędrychowski's claim that expenditure on armaments is treated as part of accumulation. Our figures for changes in reserves (see Appendix B, notes to Table 2C, item 6C) were ob-

[26] See *DU 1954,* No. 19, p. 115; *1955,* No. 15, p. 115; *1956,* No. 12, p. 65.

tained by subtracting itemized figures for changes in enterprise inventories (*zapasy*) from the total change in "inventories and reserves" (*zapasy i rezerwy*). The residual thus derived may possibly accommodate armaments.

It goes without saying that this discussion does not preclude the possibility that some types of armaments may also be disguised in Polish statistics under various industrial ministries, for example, as purchases of machinery and equipment. Finally, it may be mentioned that the share of real resources allocated to national defense tends to be understated on another count. Investment in the construction and equipment of defense plants is very probably treated in Polish statistics as an "expenditure on national economy" rather than as a defense expenditure.[27]

Capital transfers to enterprise sector (item 5A). This item covers funds for fixed and working capital, capital repairs, and repayment of debts.

Net capital transfers to foreign sector (item 5B). See the remarks on this item under the foreign sector capital account (Table 4C, item 1).

Net lending to foreign sector (item 6). This was obtained as the balancing item in the foreign sector capital account.

FOREIGN SECTOR PRODUCTION ACCOUNT (TABLE 4A)

Foreign trade operations are recorded in Polish statistics in terms of a special accounting unit, the "foreign-exchange zloty," the official value of which was set at 1 foreign-exchange ruble, or $0.25. The purchasing power of this artificial unit is much higher than that of the domestic zloty, and a fairly complicated equalization mechanism is employed to settle the foreign-trade accounts.

The foreign sector accounts are expressed here in domestic zlotys, and hence they are not to be regarded as indicative of Poland's actual balance with the rest of the world. When we come to making an adjustment to express GNP at factor cost

[27] See Bergson, *Soviet National Income and Product in 1937,* p. 120, for a discussion of the Soviet practice.

and to determine net foreign investment, we shall identify two parts of foreign trade, namely, the part that is exactly balanced in foreign-exchange zlotys and the residual representing the surplus with the rest of the world. Each part will be expressed in domestic zlotys.

We have accepted without adjustment the Polish official figures on foreign trade, including the formal equivalence of the value of exports to the imports they paid for in balanced foreign trade. From the viewpoint of Poland's trade partners there was nothing wrong with this, assuming that trade was voluntary on the part of both sides. (Poland's "reparations" coal deliveries to the USSR was a notable exception.) But from the Polish viewpoint, the level of imports was kept unnecessarily high by the low domestic prices at which imports were sold, with the consequence that exports were provided under great pressure at very high cost to the Polish economy. Indeed, it appeared that exports were handled constantly on an emergency basis as crash programs to provide the foreign exchange needed to finance imports and with scant regard for Poland's possible specialization in the international division of labor.[28]

Commercial imports and exports (items 1 and 3A). Polish foreign-trade organizations record their expenditures on purchases abroad in foreign-exchange zlotys and their receipts from the sale of imports on the domestic market in domestic zlotys. By treating the two kinds of zlotys as formally equal in value, the trade organizations realize huge gross profits. A part of these is used to cover their operating expenses, and the balance is transferred to the state budget in the form of so-called "positive budget differences." The reverse process takes place in the case of exported goods, which are purchased by foreign-trade organizations from domestic producers at relatively high domestic prices and sold abroad at relatively low foreign-exchange zloty prices. The accounting losses to which this method gives rise are covered by the state budget by subsidies called "negative budget differences."

[28] See Józef Krynicki, *Problemy handlu zagranicznego Polski* (Warsaw, Państwowe Wydawnictwo Naukowe, 1958), pp. 314–22.

Weralski points out that in some cases imported goods may be sold domestically at prices lower than their cost in foreign-exchange zlotys and that in the case of some exports their foreign-exchange zloty price may exceed the domestic price.[29] Such cases probably are very rare, if they exist at all, and we made no allowance for them in our estimates.

In addition to positive and negative budget differences, our reconciliation of Polish foreign-trade statistics in foreign-exchange and domestic zlotys must take into account turnover tax on exports and costs of transportation. Polish producers paid turnover taxes on goods sold for export, yet the foreign-trade organization paid only the producer price before tax. In order to recompense the producer, the government refunded the turnover tax,[30] the refund appearing as a negative item among budget revenues.

Beginning in 1952, Polish foreign-trade statistics in terms of foreign-exchange zlotys were reported on an f.o.b. basis for both imports and exports.[31] Accordingly, the import figures exclude freight and other charges arising between the points of origin and the Polish boundary, whereas the export figures include transportation cost between the points of domestic production and the Polish boundary.

We estimated freight and other charges on imports uniformly at 5 percent of their f.o.b. value. In the case of exports, negative budget differences were sometimes paid by the state budget to producers (where the price charged included delivery charges) when a loss would follow from too low an allowance for transportation. Owing to the way in which our estimates were derived (see below), however, these amounts appear to have been merged into our estimate of negative budget differences received by the export organizations, which would be overstated to that extent. Considering the low freight rates prevailing in Poland at that time, no significant bias is likely to result.

Our estimated values of imports in foreign-exchange zlotys

---

29 Weralski, *Finanse i kredyt,* Part I, p. 138.
30 See Alton, *Polish Postwar Economy,* pp. 246–47.
31 Krynicki, *Problemy handlu zagranicznego Polski,* p. 203.

may include some payments that were actually made not to foreign countries but to the Polish merchant marine. We allow for this factor in calculating earnings of the Polish merchant marine so that the gross domestic product is not understated on that account.

The approach adopted in this study may throw some light on little explored problems, such as the relationship between foreign-exchange zlotys and domestic zlotys, the purchasing power parity of the zloty, and the real (as distinct from accounting) benefit or loss derived by Poland from its foreign trade.

Services (items 3B and 3C). Our estimates of service items relate only to the more important items. We did not include, for example, international exchange of technical services, exchange of patents, royalties, some insurance payments, payments for communication services, and foreign travel and tourist expenses. We assumed, therefore, a zero balance on account of these and other omitted items. In fact, however, Poland may have been a net debtor on these items.[32]

The present accounts include specifically transit and maritime services. The former include only earnings on commercial transit services rendered to the Soviet Union, transit credits with other countries being assumed to be exactly offset by transit debits. The latter include transport services, port services, and some insurance services.

Net transit services (item 3B). According to *Trybuna Ludu,* September 30, 1956, the Soviet Union was paying Poland at that time $20 million, or 80 million foreign-exchange zlotys, annually for rail transit. This amount was assumed to apply to each of the years 1954–56. It was converted from foreign-exchange zlotys to current domestic zlotys by conversion factors established for maritime services.

Net maritime services (item 3C). We included under this heading all earnings of the Polish merchant marine. At the same time we made no separate allowance, on the receivables side,

---

[32] See Spulber, *The Economics of Communist Eastern Europe,* pp. 435–37, on technical exchange, and p. 460, on foreign travel.

for the amounts paid to foreign shipping since this is already covered in the value of imports. Polish imports are estimated in the present accounts on a c.i.f. basis. This includes also transport and insurance services rendered by Polish organizations and thus overstates Poland's debits on current account. Consequently, the inclusion, on the payables side, of all earnings of Polish firms rendering maritime services corrects Poland's international payables by those sums that were actually paid to Polish enterprises, while at the same time leaving in the accounts all actual earnings of foreign exchange by Polish maritime enterprises from foreign enterprises. Polish exports are estimated in the present accounts on an f.o.b. basis. This excludes all transportation services between Polish and foreign ports. To the extent that some of them were rendered by Polish enterprises, an additional earning of foreign exchange was realized above those earnings that were determined by the f.o.b. value of exports. This element of additional foreign-exchange earnings is contained within the aggregate of Polish maritime revenues.

In addition to maritime and transit services, Poland was engaging in various other transactions with foreign countries on the service account. For the lack of information we made the assumption that the net balance of all such transactions was zero. Thus, for example, tourist expenditures were not entered in the foreign sector account on the assumption of equal credits offsetting the amounts due to foreign countries.

Foreign Sector Appropriation Account (Table 4B)

This account simply transfers the balance on production account to the capital account. Entries for interest and net factor payments that normally would appear here were omitted because of their unimportance or because of lack of information.

Net factor payments to the nation usually consist of wages and salaries received from abroad, net rents and profits from the foreign sector, and interest received by government from the foreign sector. We assumed that all these items were zero. Some salary payments from abroad did undoubtedly take place, but at the same time a part of the wage bill of various ministries and agencies active abroad consisted of payments to foreign residents. Since no allowance was made for this elsewhere, we assumed that these payments exactly offset each other, leaving net receipts from abroad equal to zero.

Poland apparently had no significant rental property abroad nor enterprises of any importance operating in foreign countries, and, therefore, no significant rents or profits were received from abroad. Similarly, foreign ownership in Poland has been expropriated, and "mixed corporations" of Soviet vintage were never created, so that Polish payments to foreign countries on account of rent and profits probably also are insignificant.

FOREIGN SECTOR CAPITAL ACCOUNT (TABLE 4C)

Net transfers from government (item 1). This item represents turnover tax rebates received from the government by exporters, plus negative budget differences arising in foreign trade minus positive budget differences transferred into the budget by importers. These are the items that relate foreign trade in foreign-exchange zlotys to values in domestic zlotys (see the remarks above under the foreign sector production account, Table 4A, items 1 and 3A), and as such they have significance only for Poland's internal accounting.

Net lending by government to rest of the world (item 2). This is the balancing item between payables and receivables.

Surplus of nation on current account (item 3). This item is transferred from the foreign sector appropriation account.

Transfers to household sector (item 4). This item consists of the two components: (A) gifts delivered through PKO, and (B) cash receipts from abroad. The first component represents the imputed value of goods delivered through PKO, a state enterprise with branches in foreign countries. Under this scheme the sender abroad selects certain items from PKO catalogues of Polish goods and pays PKO for them in foreign exchange. The goods so selected are delivered to gift recipients in Poland thus giving rise to "internal exports" in so far as the goods in question are produced in Poland but are paid for in foreign countries.

The estimated values of "internal exports" in terms of foreign-exchange zlotys were taken from official Polish publications. They were converted into current zlotys by using a commodity rate of exchange of 100 current zlotys to 1 dollar, a rate estimated by comparing the dollar prices of various articles in PKO price lists with Polish retail prices.

The transactions to which "internal exports" give rise were then entered in our accounts, as follows: We debited their values in the foreign sector capital account and credited the household capital account, where their values appear as transfer receipts from abroad. The imputed value of these goods is assumed to be contained in the official statistics of retail sales to households.

The second component includes such items as pensions, bequests, and so forth. Our figure is a very rough estimate taking account of some 1958 data on the value of such receipts and their relation to total net noncommercial transfers.

Consolidated Accounts (Tables 5A, 5B, and 5C)

Upon consolidation certain entries common to pairs of accounts are eliminated. Table 5A shows the consolidated production accounts with imports netted against exports and subsidies deducted from indirect taxes. The result showing GNP at market prices is only an intermediate step in our study of the structure of the economy. In later chapters we shall be interested in the sources and final uses of the product in market prices and, above all, at factor cost. Table 5B showing the consolidated appropriation account provides a summary indication of the sectoral contributions to national income and allocation of the net national product to personal consumption, government consumption, and saving. Like Table 5A, it must also be regarded as a steppingstone to more detailed analyses of national product in the succeeding chapters. Finally, Table 5C shows the consolidated capital accounts. We should point out that this summary statement eliminates the capital flows between sectors that were detailed, sometimes upon tenuous assumptions, in the accounts of the individual sectors. At least one caution should be indicated as regards the net capital transfers from government to the rest of the world. As we have indicated in our discussion of the foreign sector accounts, the results are shown here in a purely formal manner at domestic prices, whereas actual transactions with the rest of the world were based on world prices, which differed widely from domestic prices. We shall return to this problem in our subsequent discussions; for the present, however, the formal character of the entries in question should be kept in mind.

In the chapters that follow we shall provide a more detailed breakdown of GNP at market prices by sectors of origin of product and by final uses and follow this up by parallel factor cost breakdowns. It is worth repeating that the market price structure is of interest in following actual transactions but that because of imperfections in Polish prices the structure that emerges offers a seriously misleading picture of the relative contributions of sectors of production and the relative sizes of final uses at factor cost.

We shall discuss Polish prices in relation to factor cost in Chapter IV. At this point, however, it may be helpful to indicate very briefly, albeit in an oversimplified way, the major imperfections of Polish prices in this regard and to note some of the major consequences for the structure of national product. Under the influence of the Marxist labor theory of value as it was elaborated in the USSR, Polish price formation failed to allow explicitly adequate returns for the services of capital and land. Instead, the major part of what may be regarded as the net return to these factors of production was collected in the guise of turnover tax levied mostly in industry and to a lesser degree in trade. We shall neglect for the present the imperfections under the heading of subsidies and formal accounting profits. Polish official calculations determine the contributions of sectors of production of national income simply by subtracting their material purchases from other sectors from their gross output at market prices. Thus the shares of industry and trade in national income are inflated by their collections of turnover tax, while the shares of agriculture, housing, and transportation, appearing essentially at labor cost, are relatively understated. Similarly, among final uses, personal consumption is greatly overstated in relation to investment.

Our calculations at current market prices are similarly defective as guides to resource allocation, and it is necessary to face explicitly the question of remuneration of nonlabor factors of production to arrive at a more reliable solution. Our eventual adjustments to factor cost are intended to correct for the price distortions. We shall set forth in detail below our reasons for regarding the market price structure of GNP as simply an intermediate step toward a more meaningful analysis of economic structure.

III. GROSS NATIONAL PRODUCT BY SECTOR OF ORIGIN AND BY END USE AT MARKET PRICES

The structure of GNP by sector of origin and by end use at market prices shown in the present chapter is primarily an intermediate stage to the structure at factor cost shown in Chapter IV. Because of the imperfections in system of market prices primarily on account of the skewed incidence of turnover taxes and, to some extent, accounting profits and subsidies, the relative shares of sectors of origin or of end uses are seriously misleading as to the relative importance of these sectors in terms of the services of factors of production used up by the economy. This conclusion will become evident when we compare our findings in Chapter IV with the results shown below in Tables 6 and 7.

Although the structure of GNP at market prices is a bad guide to resource allocation, it is nonetheless interesting in displaying the articulation of economic activities in current prices, and these current market price magnitudes inevitably must serve for international comparisons of national products and their components.

In Table 6 we show Polish GNP by sectors of origin broken down by various charges against the gross value added by sectors. These charges include the conventional categories of wages and salaries, social security contributions, incomes of self-employed persons, interest and profit, indirect taxes, subsidies, and capital consumption allowances. It is worth repeating that the nonlabor returns are not correctly or fully represented in sectoral shares of profit and interest and that in fact we must look to the indirect taxes for the bulk of the return to nonlabor factors. We

TABLE 6

GROSS NATIONAL PRODUCT BY SECTOR OF ORIGIN
IN CURRENT MARKET PRICES

(Billion zlotys)

1954	(1) Wages and Salaries	(2) Social Security Contributions	(3) Income of Self-employed	(4) Profit and Interest	(5) Value Added	(6) Indirect Taxes	(7) Subsidies	(8) Net National Product (5+6−7)	(9) Depreciation Allowances	(10) GNP (8+9)	(11) GNP (Percent Shares)
Industry and handicraft	38.0	5.5	3.4	7.7	54.6	62.3	6.4	110.5	4.7	115.2	46.0
Agriculture	4.8	.7	49.4	.2	55.1		3.1	52.1	.3	52.4	20.9
Forestry	1.0	.1	.4	.0	1.5		.2	1.3	.0	1.3	.5
Construction	11.9	1.8	.0	1.0	14.7		1.0	13.7	.5	14.2	5.7
Transport and communications	7.5	1.1	1.4	1.3	11.3	.8	.8	11.3	1.8	13.1	5.2
Trade and catering	7.9	1.1	1.2	4.9	15.1	5.6	.1	20.6	.3	20.9	8.3
Housing	.3	.0		.0	.3	.7	.4	.6	2.9	3.5	1.4
Other services	3.1	.5	.8	1.0	5.4	3.6	.5	8.5	.3	8.8	3.5
Education	3.4	.5			3.9			3.9		3.9	1.6
Art and culture	.2	.0			.2			.2		.2	.1
Science and research	.4	.1			.5			.5		.5	.2
Public health	2.0	.3			2.3			2.3		2.3	.9
Internal security	2.3	.1			2.4			2.4		2.4	1.0
Administration and justice	3.5	.5			4.0			4.0		4.0	1.6
Quasi-governmental organizations	.5	.1			.6			.6		.6	.2
Defense	6.5	.1			6.6			6.6		6.6	2.6
Domestic services and religious organizations	.7	.1			.8			.8		.8	.3
Total	93.8	12.6	56.6	16.1	179.1	73.1	12.5	239.7	10.8	250.4	100.0

TABLE 6 (Continued)
GROSS NATIONAL PRODUCT BY SECTOR OF ORIGIN IN CURRENT MARKET PRICES
(Billion zlotys)

1955	(1) Wages and Salaries	(2) Social Security Contributions	(3) Income of Self-employed	(4) Profit and Interest	(5) Value Added	(6) Indirect Taxes	(7) Subsidies	(8) Net National Product (5+6−7)	(9) Depreciation Allowances	(10) GNP (8+9)	(11) GNP (Percent Shares)
Industry and handicraft	41.7	6.1	3.6	11.0	62.4	64.7	10.4	116.7	5.6	122.3	45.9
Agriculture	5.3	.8	53.9	.1	60.1		4.4	55.7	.3	56.0	21.0
Forestry	1.0	.1	.5	.0	1.6		.1	1.5	.0	1.5	.6
Construction	12.1	1.8	.0	1.4	15.3		1.1	14.2	.5	14.7	5.5
Transport and communications	8.1	1.2	1.2	2.0	12.5	.5	.2	12.8	2.1	14.9	5.6
Trade and catering	8.4	1.1	1.3	5.8	16.6	6.9		23.5	.3	23.8	8.9
Housing	.3	.1		.0	.4	.8	.3	.9	3.3	4.2	1.6
Other services	3.3	.5	.9	1.0	5.7	2.0	.6	7.1	.3	7.4	2.8
Education	3.8	.5			4.3			4.3		4.3	1.6
Art and culture	.3	.0			.3			.3		.3	.1
Science and research	.5	.1			.6			.6		.6	.2
Public health	2.2	.3			2.5			2.5		2.5	.9
Internal security	2.2	.1			2.3			2.3		2.3	.9
Administration and justice	3.8	.6			4.4			4.4		4.4	1.7
Quasi-governmental organizations	.5	.1			.6			.6		.6	.2
Defense	5.8	.1			5.9			5.9		5.9	2.2
Domestic services and religious organizations	.7	.1			.8			.8		.8	.3
Total	100.0	13.6	61.4	21.3	196.3	74.9	17.1	254.1	12.5	266.6	100.0

TABLE 6 (Continued)

GROSS NATIONAL PRODUCT BY SECTOR OF ORIGIN IN CURRENT MARKET PRICES

(Billion zlotys)

1956	(1) Wages and Salaries	(2) Social Security Contributions	(3) Income of Self-employed	(4) Profit and Interest	(5) Value Added	(6) Indirect Taxes	(7) Subsidies	(8) Net National Product (5+6−7)	(9) Depreciation Allowances	(10) GNP (8+9)	(11) GNP (Percent Shares)
Industry and handicraft	48.8	7.1	3.9	15.5	75.3	56.8	8.3	123.8	11.6	135.4	45.1
Agriculture	6.3	.9	66.9	.2	74.3		5.0	69.3	.4	69.7	23.2
Forestry	1.4	.2	.5	.0	2.1	.5	.0	2.6	.1	2.7	.9
Construction	13.4	2.0	.0	3.3	18.7			18.7	.7	19.4	6.5
Transport and communications	9.6	1.4	1.5	.9	13.4	.4	.2	13.6	3.4	17.0	5.7
Trade and catering	9.9	1.3	1.7	4.3	17.2	2.7		19.9	.3	20.2	6.7
Housing	.4	.0		.0	.4	.9	.2	1.1	3.7	4.8	1.6
Other services	3.8	.5	1.0	1.0	6.3	1.9	.9	7.3	.4	7.7	2.6
Education	4.5	.6			5.1			5.1		5.1	1.7
Art and culture	.3	.0			.3			.3		.3	.1
Science and research	.5	.1			.6			.6		.6	.2
Public health	2.7	.4			3.1			3.1		3.1	1.0
Internal security	2.2	.1			2.3			2.3		2.3	.8
Administration and justice	4.4	.6			5.0			5.0		5.0	1.7
Quasi-governmental organizations	.5	.1			.6			.6		.6	
Defense	5.5	.1			5.6			5.6		5.6	1.9
Domestic services and religious organizations	.8	.0			.8			.8		.8	.3
Total	114.9	15.5	75.5	25.2	231.1	63.2	14.6	279.7	20.6	300.3	100.0

shall go into detail on this question in Chapter IV; here it is our purpose simply to sketch the derivation of Table 6 and to comment on the content of some of the entries.

All of the data shown in Table 6 were drawn from the sectoral accounts and the supporting appendices. Detailed documentation for the breakdown into seventeen sectors of origin of product is given in Appendix H.

Wages and salaries (*column 1*) include cash wages, wages in kind (including food, clothing, cigarettes, and so forth, for the military personnel), and various wagelike payments to employees from special enterprise funds (for example, special incentive funds distributed by directors of enterprises, prizes, and commissions). Our wage figures include the wages paid to the regular employees, the so-called "personal wage bill" according to Polish official sources, as well as the so-called "nonpersonal wage bill," which comprises payments for occasional special services and for work carried out by persons who are not payers of turnover and income taxes, honoraria paid to authors and others, and various miscellaneous payments.

Social security contributions (*column 2*) were estimated as percentages of the personal wage bill at rates given in Polish laws. Details are given in Appendix E.

Income of self-employed (*column 3*) was calculated as the sum of farm income (including income consumed or invested in kind) and nonfarm income. We treated imputed depreciation on private and collective farms as an element of income of self-employed since it is highly unlikely that depreciation allowances were formally set aside by these farms. Income of self-employed outside agriculture was distributed primarily on the basis of data shown in the Polish official national income studies and in tax data. Although a profit element might be considered present in the income of self-employed, we did not attempt to quantify such a refinement, and we shall regard this income as essentially a return to labor. Reasons for our decision as regards farm income will be explained in connection with our factor cost adjustment; they rest on a comparison of average farm income with wages in other sectors. For the remaining sectors where income of self-employed occurs, the amounts that might be classified as profit would be relatively insignificant.

Profit and interest (*column 4*). The total for all sectors was obtained as a residual (column 5 less the sum of columns 1, 2, and 3). Rough estimates were made for the shares of the total contributed by agriculture, passenger transportation, and other services, and the remainder was distributed proportionally to the officially reported profits in sectors of material production. In the category of "other services," there were some profits, but our figures must be regarded as informed guesses.

Here, and in other instances in the breakdown at market prices, we would like to come reasonably close to the actual structure, and we stay within the constraints of totals and identifiable components, but the consequences of some error for our eventual factor cost adjustment are generally negligible. For this adjustment it will become clear that the returns to labor at market prices are crucial (columns 1, 2, and 3), but that non-labor returns and depreciation will be subject to sectoral allocation independently of Table 6, except for the total of such returns. When we shall come to end-use structure of GNP, however, the incidence of profits, indirect taxes, and subsidies will be a basic consideration in our factor cost adjustment.

Value added (*column 5*). The column total was taken from Table 5A, item 8; row entries are sums of columns 1, 2, 3, and 4.

Indirect taxes (*column 6*) were estimated from official data; details are given in Table H1 and supporting notes. The turnover tax is the decisive element in the total and in nearly all of the row entries; positive budget differences and other taxes are relatively minor components. Our distribution of the turnover tax is fairly reliable, being based for the most part on official sources, but a conflict between the official total and a somewhat larger sum of components for 1956 necessitated a compromise solution, a proportional shrinkage of the components. The tax on "other services" was derived as a residual and hence reflects whatever errors the other components may have. Polish statistics on turnover tax, positive budget differences, and turnover tax rebated on exports still represent an area where there is inadequate published information.

Subsidies (*column 7*). The column total was taken from Table 3B; its distribution by rows represents estimates based on official information and other sources for all sectors indicated, except for industry and handicraft, which was obtained as a residual.

Net national product (*column 8*) is to be regarded as having a formal character because of the deficiencies of the capital consumption allowances actually set aside.

Depreciation allowances (*column 9*) in 1956 were based on detailed official information, but only a few sectoral figures were available for 1954 and 1955. We filled in the gaps for these years relying on the 1956 relationships and other information.

Our estimates of GNP by end use at market prices are shown in Table 7. Four main uses are given: (1) personal consumption, (2) government consumption, (3) defense, and (4) gross investment. A number of components under these major headings are given to facilitate regroupings that might be useful for various comparisons. Item 5, "other," represents the loss or gain in domestic zlotys on that part of foreign trade that is exactly balanced in foreign-exchange zlotys; the equivalent in domestic zlotys of the foreign-trade surplus in foreign-exchange zlotys is shown in item 4c, net foreign investment.

We shall have more to say about item 5 below; at this point, however, it may suffice to note its presence as a balancing item between GNP produced (Table 6) and GNP consumed (Table 7). The lack of correspondence between world prices and Polish domestic prices on the items entering foreign trade gives rise to this anomalous category. At domestic prices it might appear that items 4c and 5 should be combined into a single entry denoting net foreign investment, but this result would be specious, for there is no obligation with respect to the rest of the world to correspond to item 5. Alternatively, this item could be shown on the sector of origin distribution (Table 6) as profits (1956) or losses (1954 and 1955) on externally balanced foreign trade, where it would have significance as a balancing item between product originated and product disposed of. In any event, in a comparison of relative proportions of GNP contributed by sectors of origin or allocated to end uses, it would appear expedient to drop item 5 and express the shares of the remaining components in relation to their total taken as GNP. We shall show such percentage compositions of GNP at market prices and at factor cost in Chapters IV and V.

TABLE 7

GROSS NATIONAL PRODUCT BY END USE
IN CURRENT MARKET PRICES

(*Billion zlotys*)

	1954	1955	1956
1. Personal consumption	148.1	158.6	180.9
a. Civilian	144.6	155.5	178.1
b. Military	3.5	3.1	2.8
2. Government consumption	24.2	26.8	30.1
a. Education	6.2	6.7	7.8
b. Art and culture	.6	.7	.8
c. Science and research	.9	1.0	1.0
d. Health	4.9	5.6	6.7
e. Internal security	3.4	3.9	3.9
f. Administration and justice	6.6	7.0	7.8
g. Quasi-governmental organizations	1.7	1.9	2.1
3. National defense	10.4	11.7	11.7
4. Gross investment	58.6	63.4	81.4
a. Fixed capital	43.2	46.4	62.3
b. Increase in inventories	14.7	16.0	14.2
c. Net foreign investment	.6	.9	4.9
5. Other	9.1	6.1	− 3.8
Gross national product	250.4	266.6	300.3

NOTE: Totals may differ slightly from the sums of indicated items because of rounding.

Personal consumption (*item 1*) corresponds to household consumption (item 3) in Table 5B; military consumption (see Table 1B, item 3B7) refers to military pay in kind; civilian consumption is the residual in the total.

Government consumption (*item 2*) represents the value of government services excluding military services. In all instances it covers wage costs, social security contributions by employers, and current purchases from other sectors. Details of the breakdown into subsectors of government are given in Appendix H with references to Appendix Tables G2, G3, G4, and G5.

National defense (*item 3*) refers to the explicit state budget expenditures for military purposes under the Ministry of Defense and omits expenditures by other agencies serving the military program. It appears probable that a part of the expenditure on armaments may be included in state reserves (see the discussion on inventories in Chapter II, p. 45), with implications for item 4b of Table 7. A part of the cost of military research and development and very probably all of the investment in plants supplying military items are carried by the enterprise sector (in item 4a) supported by transfers from the state budget under "financing the national economy." Also a part of the outlays on education, science, and research (items 2a and 2c) may support some research related to defense. On the other hand, special internal security troops and border guards in the 1950 state budget were carried by the Ministry of Defense budget, and this situation may have been continued in later years.

Because of problems of classification of expenditures into those for defense and those for nondefense activities and lack of information as to the character and magnitude of particular expenditures, we did not attempt to augment the figure for defense outlays obtained from the scant reference in state budget data.

Gross investment (*item 4*). Under fixed capital (item 4a) we include fixed capital investment and capital repairs in the enterprise and government sectors. Increase in inventories (item 4b) comprises both changes in stocks (*zapasy*) and in reserves (*rezerwy*), the former presumably referring to business inventories proper and the latter to state reserves.[1] It is within the latter category that purchases of armaments may possibly be included (see the discussion of government investment above, under Table 3C, item 4). Finally, net foreign investment (item 4c) is the estimated equivalent in domestic zlotys of the commodity balance of trade in foreign-exchange zlotys and the net earnings from services.

Other (*item 5*) refers to the balance of exports and imports (both expressed in domestic zlotys) less net foreign investment (item 4c, described above). From the point of view of domestic

---

[1] See Zienkowski, *Jak oblicza się dochod narodowy,* 1st ed., p. 65.

prices alone, the sum of items 4c and 5 represent a formal category akin to net foreign investment, but from the point of view of the rest of the world the content of item 5 apparently is zero (but see below, p. 90). For some Soviet-type economies information may not be available to calculate an item among end uses of GNP corresponding to item 5 in Table 7,[2] but we believe that such an item must exist since it seems improbable that the ratios between values in foreign exchange converted at official exchange rates into national currency and the corresponding values directly based on domestic prices would be the same for both exports and imports.

We have to deal here with at least three sets of exchange rates. First, there is a formal official exchange rate linking the national currency to world currencies. Thus there were 4 zlotys to US $1. In foreign trade statistics these zlotys were referred to as foreign-exchange zlotys (devisa zlotys), but, at the next stage, one devisa zloty in 1954 was equivalent to about 7 domestic zlotys on exports and about 4.3 domestic zlotys on imports, on the average.[3] Although the spread between these implicit rates on imports and exports declined (at the same time as the rates themselves rose) by 1956, the difference still was great enough to give rise to a significant value for item 5 in Table 7. We would expect a comparable situation to exist for other countries, although in countries where there is no foreign trade monopoly and internal prices are not so insulated from world prices as in the Soviet-type economies it would be much less significant.

We have mentioned that there were at least three rates involved in the linking of world trade values to their domestic currency equivalents, and this is the case where we speak of average rates on exports and on imports between devisa zlotys and domestic zlotys. These rates, however, were differentiated by

[2] We have such a figure for Hungary in our 1955 cross section of GNP (see Alton and associates, *Hungarian National Income and Product in 1955*, pp. 58–63), and Hungarian official figures are available for other years. On the other hand, data were inadequate to calculate such a figure for Czechoslovakia in 1955–56 (see Alton and associates, *Czechoslovak National Income and Product in 1947–1948 and 1955–1956*, pp. 45, 172–73).

[3] Ratios derived from Appendix Table D1 and supporting notes relating to comparably defined values of X and of M.

types of commodities and by trade partners, and, in view of the secrecy surrounding foreign trade within the Soviet orbit for much of the postwar period, this mechanism may have been employed by the USSR to exact a form of reparations or unilateral transfers from the East European countries.

Polish deliveries of coal to the USSR at special low prices beginning in 1946 appear to enter here. These deliveries were initially reported to be in compensation for Soviet deliveries to Poland of merchandise from German reparations. Soviet deliveries to Poland, however, ceased in 1948, and, beginning January 1, 1954, all East German reparations were renounced. Apparently coal deliveries at a special low price were stopped at that time.

Coal deliveries to the USSR were scheduled at 8 million tons in 1946, 13 million tons per year for 1947–50, and 12 million tons per year thereafter until the end of the occupation of Germany. In March, 1947, however, the annual quota was reduced to 6.5 million tons.[4] The price was reportedly 1.25 dollars per ton.[5]

Following the Polish riots and demonstrations in 1956 culminating in the return of Gomułka to the leadership of the United Workers' Party and the October confrontation with the Soviet leaders, Soviet exploitation of Poland in the deliveries of coal "in the years 1946–53" was acknowledged by the Moscow declaration of October 18, 1956, and as compensation, the USSR cancelled Polish debts exceeding "2 billion rubles" (US $0.5 billion at the official rate of exchange).[6]

To the extent that Soviet exploitation is concealed in foreign trade statistics, then some part of item 5 may reflect it. Obviously item 5 reflects the lack of correspondence of domestic zloty prices to foreign trade prices in devisa zlotys, whatever may be the influences that shape the latter. Although the values of imports and exports in devisa zlotys on perfectly balanced trade

[4] See the sources cited in Alton, *Polish Postwar Economy*, p. 280, and Spulber, *The Economics of Communist Eastern Europe*, p. 176.

[5] Alton, *Polish Postwar Economy*, citing Margaret Dewar, *Soviet Trade with Eastern Europe, 1945–1949*, pp. 39–40.

[6] *Nowe drogi*, January, 1957, p. 53.

changed only slightly from 1955 to 1956 (see Appendix Table D1), in domestic prices there was a significant shift from a "loss" of some 6.1 billion zlotys in 1955 to a "profit" of some 3.8 billion zlotys in 1956. Some clarification of this change might be gained by an attempt to quantify the changes in values of exports and imports brought about by the upward revision of domestic producer prices in 1956 and similarly by taking account of trends in devisa zloty prices. Here then is an area requiring further investigation.

Our findings on the structure of the Polish GNP by sectors of origin and end uses at market prices shown in Tables 6 and 7 are of interest as regards the articulation of economic activity in current prices, and they may serve as a starting point for international comparisons of magnitudes of product serving end uses. But they are seriously misleading in regard to resource cost allocations. In the following chapter, therefore, we shall adjust the components of GNP at market prices to approximate their values at factor cost.

IV. GROSS NATIONAL PRODUCT AT FACTOR COST

The composition of GNP derived from sectoral accounts obviously reflects both the physical magnitudes of goods and services entering the product and the prices used to make them commensurate. We have already indicated some of the uses of GNP and the supporting sectoral accounts at market prices, for example, in the analysis of sectoral incomes and expenditures, or more generally of the articulation of economic activity, and as a starting point for international comparisons. But where the concern is to study the relative contributions of sectors of production to GNP and the relative importance of final uses, both in terms of the services of factors of production used up by the economy, then Polish market prices are seriously defective. At such prices, one zloty's worth of a typical consumer good represents a relatively smaller resource cost than one zloty's worth of a typical investment good. Similarly at these prices the gross value added by housing and by agriculture is greatly understated in relation to that of industry or trade.

In the present chapter we shall examine the deficiencies in Polish prices that render them delusive guides to resource allocation, and on the basis of this study we shall adjust the values of GNP components at market prices to convert them into estimated factor cost. We shall not be concerned with the theoretical implications of price problems or a discussion of alternative standards of valuation,[1] and we must emphasize at the same time

---

[1] For a discussion of "welfare" and "efficiency" standards of national income valuation, see Hicks, "The Valuation of Social Income," *Economica,* May, 1940, and August, 1948, and Samuelson, "Evaluation of Real National Income," *Oxford Economic Papers,* II, No. 1 (January, 1950). Bergson, *Soviet National Income and Product in 1937,* Chaps. 3 and 4, discusses these standards in relation to his adjustment of Soviet national income to factor cost.

that factor cost as it appears in our tables must be understood
in the sense we define it, including the various practical qualifi-
cations and simplifications described in the text and appendixes.
It is, therefore, only an approximation to the theoretical standard.

THE FACTOR-COST STANDARD

We have already noted that Polish prices offer a poor guide to
resource allocation (see pp. 53–54), and we shall explore the
problem at greater length in the present chapter. This is not a
matter of relatively small consequence as it is in many non-Com-
munist economies, where, despite the incidence of sales taxes,
subsidies, monopoly profits, and other factors causing prices to
diverge from factor costs, the relative structure of GNP at market
prices as regards the contributions of major sectors of origin of
product and the magnitudes of end uses is still reasonably close
to its structure at factor cost. In Poland, however, the consequences of revaluation of GNP at factor cost are indeed striking
—for example, at market prices the share of industry and
handicraft in GNP is around twice as great as that of agriculture,
whereas at factor cost agriculture becomes the larger sector.[2]
The factor-cost structure, aside from showing resource allocation
in meaningful terms, provides some guide to the alternatives
open to the economy in terms of augmenting one sector of production or end use by transfers of factors of production from another sector of production or end use. Clearly these alternatives
must be regarded as limits, for there are difficulties in trans-
ferring factors in the short run, and variable returns from extra-
marginal allocations must be noted.

We must add that Polish economic discussions recognize the
shortcomings of market prices in such matters as the calculation
of the efficiency of invesment and the structure of national income by origin and final use,[3] but the consequences for revaluation of national income have not been carried far enough.[4]

[2] See Table 10.
[3] See Zienkowski, *Jak oblicza się dochód narodowy,* 2d ed., pp. 146–52;
Fiszel, *Prawo wartości a problematyka cen w przemyśle socjalistycznym,* pp.
64–66, 123, 127; *Inwestycje i budownictwo,* February, 1958, pp. 7–14.
[4] Thus in *DN 1956,* pp. 52 ff., the structure of national income in 1955 and

We shall refer in our discussions below to a factor-cost standard of valuation, which we define as follows: [5]

1. All prices of goods and services fully resolve into charges for factors of production, and the national product is equal to the sum of these charges.

2. The charges for labor reflect differences in marginal productivities and in disutilities of labor among the various occupations within each industry. Wage variations are used to distribute labor among industries.

3. The charge for capital covers both capital consumption allowances and a net return at a uniform rate to the present value of fixed and working capital in the various branches of production.

4. The charge for land represents the differential return to superior land.

5. Prices of goods and services are uniform within any given market area.

We shall discuss next Polish prices in relation to this factor-cost standard with a view toward identifying points of divergence and subsequently making adjustments to the GNP aggregates at market prices in order to approximate factor cost.

MARKET PRICE VALUATIONS IN RELATION TO FACTOR COST

Aggregate returns to factors of production. We shall not be concerned in our adjustments with the correction of prices of individual goods and services; instead, we shall be concerned with approximating factor cost for large categories of final uses and for the gross value added by major sectors of production. Our basic assumption is that the magnitude of GNP in zlotys is

---

1956 is given at approximately current labor cost. We shall return to this topic in Chapter 5 where we compare our findings with Polish official figures.

[5] See Bergson, *Soviet National Income and Product in 1937*, Chap. 3, and his *The Real National Income of Soviet Russia since 1928*, Chap. 8, for an extended discussion of standards of national income valuation. Our factor cost standard corresponds to Bergson's, but in its application we differ in some respects. See also Alton and associates, *National Income and Product of Czechoslovakia, 1947–1948 and 1955–1956*, Chap. III, and their *Hungarian National Income and Product in 1955*, Chap. IV, for our factor-cost adjustments in those economies.

the same at market prices as at factor cost. Within this total, we accept the returns to labor as more or less correct as shown in market prices, and the residual is fully attributed to nonlabor factors of production. Whether other assumptions would have greater merit we leave to the reader to consider. If, for the moment, we attribute all the nonlabor returns to the fixed and working capital in production, then the residual aggregate returns, excluding depreciation, amount to about 9 percent of the present value of fixed and working capital.[6] We shall, however, for the sake of illustration show the consequences of likewise arbitrary alternative assumptions establishing a range within which our estimates fall (see below, p. 81).

Wages. At the outset of the Six-Year Plan in 1950, the existing state controls over choice of occupations and geographical locations of employment were augmented by new laws and administrative orders that applied to graduates of vocational schools and higher education institutions, persons trained in professions, engineers, technicians, accountants, tractor drivers, merchant marine officers, and others.[7] By 1954, however, the rigor had weakened; rationing, which tended to restrain labor turnover, had come to an end; and wage differentials appear to have been the principal means for allocating labor among various branches of production. In the years 1954–56, there was in fact a high rate of labor turnover in industry.[8]

Although no definitive answer can be given as to the actual relation of wages to marginal productivity and disutility in various occupations, it was clearly the intent of the economic authorities to use wage policy as a tool for achieving the desired allocation of labor, taking account of the relationship of wages to productivity, effort, and conditions of work.[9] Within occupa-

[6] See Appendix Tables I1 and I2.

[7] Alton, *Polish Postwar Economy,* pp. 70–75.

[8] For example, in 1955, 90,000 workers were recruited for coal mining while over 70,000 left, the total employment for coal mining being on the order of 300,000 (see United Nations, Economic Commission for Europe, *Economic Survey of Europe in 1957* [Geneva, 1958], Chap. VII, pp. 32–33, and *RS 1957,* p. 274) allowing for miners other than in the coal industry.

[9] Alton, *Polish Postwar Economy,* pp. 250–54.

tions, there presumably was a rough correspondence of wages to differences in marginal productivity in view of the prevalence of piecework, the use of bonuses related to productivity, and recognition of labor cost as an element to be minimized for a given level of output. Without doubt the principles of wage policy were poorly approximated by actual practice, but further elaboration would not be helpful at this point. We shall therefore assume that the returns to labor as given in our accounts at market prices more or less correspond to the factor-cost standard.

A glance at Table 6 (pp. 56–58) should make it clear that the same cannot be said about returns to nonlabor factors of production. Keeping in mind the formal character of the entries under profit and interest (and, accordingly, also under value added), the apparent net return, which we shall attribute here only to fixed and working capital, amounts to about 2.7 to 3.4 percent, an extremely low rate. Moreover, the distribution of profits among sectors of production is grossly out of line with the sectoral shares in the total current value of fixed and working capital.[10] Thus, agriculture and housing, two heavily capitalized sectors, show practically no return on capital. As regards capital consumption allowances, although the total was raised by a revision of rates in 1956, the understatement in 1954 and 1955 and the inadequate provision for housing in all years vis-à-vis the other sectors, makes it clear that on this point too the factor-cost requirements were not met at market prices. We have in these instances an illustration of returns to capital in one branch of production being realized in the selling prices of goods and services of other branches. But in view of the low rate of return indicated by the formal profit category, we must look to indirect taxes for the bulk of the return to nonlabor factors of production. We have already indicated that, even within the Soviet-type economies, the turnover tax, which accounts for the preponderant share of the total shown under indirect taxes, is generally regarded as essentially a return to state ownership and control and, hence, a return to capital and entrepreneurship. Here again,

[10] The apparent rate of return was based on column 4, Table 6, and total current values of fixed and working capital as shown in Appendix Table I2.

a glance at Table 6 (column 6) will show that industry and trade realize most of the nonlabor returns of the economy, although these sectors by no means account for a corresponding share of the related services of factors of production. This is what we mean by referring to the formal character of the entries in Table 6 under profits, value added, and net national product. To display economic content in more meaningful terms, adjustments are inescapable. Our main concern will be accordingly with what is formally labeled indirect taxes but essentially represents factor rewards in an aggregate sense.

Indirect taxes. It may be helpful at the outset to offer a few quotations from Polish, Czechoslovak, and Soviet sources as to the nature of "indirect taxes" in the Soviet-type economies. The major item included here is the turnover tax on goods and its counterpart, the tax on noncommodity transactions, that is, on services.

National income is being distributed in the process of its creation in the enterprise. A part of that income goes to . . . wages. The other part remains in the enterprise as the latter's accumulation. Accumulation is subject to further distribution: part of it is appropriated by the state . . . in the form of turnover tax and part of it [is] the enterprise profit.[11]

State enterprises . . . are subject to the concept of the so-called "transfer of profits." The transfers of profits are one of the elements of the distribution of profits conducted by the state as the owner of the enterprise. The economic significance of turnover tax and profit transfers is essentially the same: it means the transfer of part of the enterprise accumulation into the budget.[12]

As to their economic significance, turnover tax and profit represent forms of distributing the net income of the society.[13]

Prices for producer goods in the USSR are planned as a rule at the level of average branch production cost plus a certain planned

[11] Z. Wyrożębski, *Budżety terenowe, dochody państwowe, podatki* (Local budgets, state revenues, taxes), (Warsaw, Polskie Wydawnictwo Gospodarcze, 1954), p. 10.
[12] Reniger, *Dochody państwowe*, pp. 26–27.
[13] *Finanse a úvěr*, 1958, No. 4, p. 205.

percentage of profit, which, as a rule, happens to be significantly lower than the actual value of the producer goods. This means that not all the socially necessary labor is counted into the price of producer goods. . . .

When enterprises of the light and food industries sell goods at their full value, counting all the producer goods value transferred to the goods manufactured, they realize a great deal more accumulation than they themselves have actually created. . . .

The turnover tax received from branches of light industry contains within itself a certain share of the income and surplus product created in both the heavy industrial branches and in agriculture. . . .

In actual fact, the turnover tax in our country long ago ceased to be a tax, a simple addition to the price of consumer goods, determined above their value. It constitutes a definite share of the net income (surplus product) formed by the excess of the value of the product, realized in the prices of goods, over its cost. . . .

This means that under socialism the turnover tax is primary income and is formed as a primary distribution of national income. This, however, is not the main thing which distinguishes the turnover tax from a tax proper. The main thing is that the basis of the turnover tax is the state's ownership of the instruments and means of production, and its source is the net income of state enterprises.

Our economists have often raised the problem that the term, "turnover tax," gives rise to incorrect ideas as to the economic nature of the basic form of the USSR's budget income. Therefore the question of substituting another, more suitable term has long been under discussion.[14]

These quotations, of course, do not prove anything as to the precise identification of turnover tax with returns to nonlabor factors of production even though this seems to be their assertion. Our assumption is simply that we may for the purpose of a factor cost adjustment treat the tax as a return to nonlabor factors of production; obviously, too, equally arbitrary alternative assumptions could be made, taking a higher or lower rate of return in relation to capital than we did. And we shall show that within a considerable range it makes little difference what spe-

[14] D. A. Allakhverdyan, *Finansy sotsialisticheskogo gosudarstva* (Finances of the Socialist State), (Moscow, Izdatel'stvo sotsial'no-ekonomicheskoi literatury, 1961), pp. 122–33.

cific rate is taken so far as the resulting structure of GNP is concerned (see below, p. 81).

In view of the formal character of Tables 6 and 7 and the evident distortion introduced by the turnover tax in relation to factor cost by sectors of origin, little more need be said about the necessity for adjusting GNP components at market prices in order to gain a better insight into the use of resources in the Polish economy.

With some exceptions, such as the relatively unimportant sales by independent artisans and the somewhat more significant sales by farmers on the free market, the prices of goods and services are set by the government. In principle, the prices of goods sold between socialized enterprises should cover the current costs of production. These prices typically fail to provide adequate returns to capital, and often they necessitated subsidies to cover wages and other current costs. Prices of consumer goods were set high enough to absorb the purchasing power of the population after allowing for some relatively unimportant direct taxes and comparatively insignificant savings. In practice, this means that the return to nonlabor factors of production is realized for the most part in the selling prices of consumer goods. Prices of consumer goods, while being affected to some extent by consumer preferences, were changed infrequently by the planning authority; [15] more commonly consumer preferences were manifested in queues and bare shelves for popular goods and in rising stocks of bad quality goods. Clearly, therefore, we must take account of the unequal incidence of the so-called indirect taxes both by sectors in which they are collected and by end uses on which they impinge in adjusting the components of GNP at market prices to factor cost.

Accounting profits and subsidies. What we have said about the turnover tax applies for the most part to accounting profits. Both categories are regarded as a return to state ownership and control; and, though perhaps less so than in the case of the turnover tax, profits do not necessarily originate where they are

15 See *RS 1959*, pp. 347–49.

collected. For example, profits in food processing may arise in agriculture, being suppressed in the latter sector by the device of compulsory deliveries to the state procurement agencies at prices failing to cover costs of production. In our adjustments below we shall lump profits with the so-called indirect taxes and construe the total less subsidies as constituting primarily a net return to nonlabor factors of production. Since the sectoral incidence of profits reflects the convenience of fiscal authorities and aims of economic policy not directly related to the immediate productive contributions of nonlabor factors of production, it is clear that Polish market prices on this count fail to correspond to our factor-cost standard.

Our remarks on the incidence of accounting profits apply in a negative sense to subsidies. The latter tend to make market prices lower than factor cost, and hence their distorting effect must be reckoned with in our adjustments. Their incidence by sector of origin can be identified in a number of instances, but by end use their distorting effect can only be approximated by judgments as to the categories of final goods affected by them.

Nonlabor charges. We include here the returns to capital, land, and entrepreneurship. We have already discussed indirect taxes and the formal profit category as comprising essentially returns to nonlabor factors of production. Interest on capital investment does not enter significantly as such in the Polish economy. The requirements for fixed capital investment and the normal level of working capital are usually met as interest-free grants from the state budget to the socialized enterprises. Short-term loans to expand working capital to meet seasonal peaks do carry interest charges, but the amounts involved are relatively small. We do not attempt to identify interest as a distinct return to capital or to separate it from profits and returns to entrepreneurship in our adjusted returns to capital.

The second form of return to capital, namely, capital consumption allowances, formally enters Polish accounting, although in some sectors of the national accounts, for example, housing and agriculture, the entries are imputations. In 1954 and

1955, depreciation allowances were set too low, but in 1956 they were raised. We have to reckon, therefore, with adjustments for all sectors of origin for 1954–56.

Land rent, considered as a factor charge in agriculture, does not explicitly enter Polish accounting. Our assumption that the actual return to agriculture at market prices consists only of returns to labor is discussed below. By implication, therefore, all nonlabor returns, including rent, are siphoned away from agriculture to appear in other sectors, particularly food processing and trade, as turnover tax or profits. The means to accomplish this consisted of state control over prices of agricultural products and production supplies and of the regimen of compulsory deliveries to state procurement agencies geared to the quantity and quality of land and its location.[16]

Uniformity of prices. It should be clear already that by means of the turnover tax and the discriminating state price policy the prices for given commodities were not the same to all buyers. Within the socialized sector the turnover tax did not apply, but the same goods sold to the private sector generally included a cushion of "accumulation." Such was the case for building materials and farmers production supplies and, of course, for consumer goods generally. The discriminating policy followed on state procurements from agriculture provided low prices on compulsory delivery quotas and higher prices on contractual or above-quota deliveries. A residual portion of the farm output could be sold on the free farm market at prices comparable to those charged in socialized retail stores. Because of the lack of price uniformity, the shares of personal consumption and socialized investment in GNP at market prices are clearly misleading as to the resource costs entailed in their production.

Our discussion of Polish prices in relation to our factor-cost standard shows the need for adjustments to the market-price structure of GNP to convert it into structure at factor cost. We turn now to these adjustments, first, by sectors of origin and, second, by end uses.

16 See Alton, *Polish Postwar Economy,* pp. 193–96.

GNP BY SECTOR OF ORIGIN AT FACTOR COST

The results of our adjustment of GNP at market prices to factor cost by sectors of origin are shown in Table 8 as percentages of the total, and in Appendix Table I1 and supporting tables the corresponding absolute figures and details of the adjustment are given.

TABLE 8

GNP BY SECTOR OF ORIGIN AT FACTOR COST

(*Percentages of total*)

	1954	1955	1956
Industry and handicraft	26.7	27.2	28.1
Agriculture	29.1	29.4	30.0
Forestry	.8	.8	.9
Construction	6.5	6.2	6.2
Transportation and communication	6.4	6.4	6.9
Trade and catering	6.1	6.3	6.1
Housing	12.5	12.3	10.9
Other services	3.0	3.0	3.1
Education	1.6	1.6	1.7
Art and culture	.1	.1	.1
Science and research	.2	.2	.2
Public health	1.0	1.0	1.0
Internal security	1.0	.9	.8
Administration and justice	1.7	1.7	1.6
Quasi-governmental organizations	.2	.2	.2
Defense	2.7	2.3	1.8
Domestic and religious services	.3	.3	.3
Total	100.0	100.0	100.0

NOTE: Totals may differ slightly from the sums of indicated items because of rounding.

In brief, our adjustment to arrive at GNP at factor cost consisted of adding up for each sector of origin the returns to labor, capital consumption allowances, and nonlabor returns. We shall remark on each component in that order.

Returns to labor. On the basis of our discussion above, we concluded that labor as a factor of production was more or less correctly rewarded by the actual wages, salaries, and social security contributions paid or imputed for the various sectors of origin of product. The necessary information was taken directly from Table 6, which referred to Appendix Table E1, except for self-employed occupations, including agriculture. For the self-employed occupations we assumed that all income was a return to labor, leaving no returns to nonlabor factors of production. For the nonagricultural sectors the earnings of self-employed persons were relatively unimportant, the capital requirements were minor, and any explicit separation of capital returns from labor returns would have negligible effect on the eventual shares of GNP by sectors of origin.

Our assumption that the income of all persons engaged in farming represented only returns to labor was based on a comparison of per capita income with average wages paid in other employment. Using the number of persons actively engaged in all of agriculture as the labor force and dividing it into the income realized in all of agriculture (including consumption in kind at average realized prices), reduced by the contribution by nonfarm producers excluded from the labor force figure, we estimated the average income per capita at from 53 to 61 percent of the average wage in socialized industry during the years 1954–56, and at 78 to 89 percent of the average wage, including allowances for clothing, food, and fuel, paid to hired personnel in socialized agriculture.

When we converted the family help on private farms into "man-equivalents" and adjusted income upward to reflect the valuation of income in kind at retail prices excluding trade margins, the resulting average income per man-equivalent in relation to the average wage in socialized industry came to about 77 percent in 1954, 79 percent in 1955, and perhaps as high as 87 percent in 1956 on the basis of a rough extrapolation. In comparison with the average wage in socialized agriculture, the result in all of agriculture was about 12 percent higher in 1955, but this margin would be reduced if account were taken of income derived from garden plots of employees of state farms. These ratios probably exaggerate the relative level of farm income because the official figures on income in kind valued at retail prices on which we based our estimate are considerably higher than subsequent official information would imply. (See notes to Appendix Table I1.)

Because of the government's discriminatory policies toward private agriculture and the fact that as many as 10,000 farmers abandoned farms with a total area of 72,000 hectares between December, 1955, and June, 1956, alone, and let the government expropriate them without compensation rather than continue farming them, it appears that farmers' return on their investment was zero or negative on the margin.[17] Owners could be expected to accept less than they might earn elsewhere as long as they held some hope for the future. In the light of this and other information, as well as our comparisons of earnings, our assumption that the total income of self-employed farmers was a return to labor alone seems reasonable.

Capital consumption allowances. Our estimates for capital consumption allowances were based on the current replacement values of fixed capital by industrial sectors and average rates of depreciation. The latter were derived for each sector as averages of Czechoslovak rates for buildings, machinery, and means of transportation combined by Polish weights representing the sector's composition of fixed capital as of January 1, 1961.

Nonlabor returns. Other returns to nonlabor factors of production were determined as a total by the GNP at market prices less the adjusted value of the domestic zloty figure for the gain or loss on that part of foreign trade that is exactly balanced in foreign-exchange zlotys [18] and less the labor returns and capital consumption allowances already specified. This total was then allocated to the various sectors of origin in proportion to their current (depreciated) values of fixed capital and working capital.

We have already discussed in Chapter III the possible interpretations that might be placed on a singular item in GNP at market prices, namely, item 5 in Table 7, corresponding to the gain or loss in domestic zlotys on that part of foreign trade that is exactly balanced in foreign-exchange zlotys. Even though this item represents a product-originated amount in terms of Polish prices and although we carried it up to the final stage of our adjustments in Appendix Table I6, on the end uses of GNP, in fact it represents an anomalous category on the sector of origin

---

[17] Poland, Rada ekonomiczna przy radzie ministrów, *Główne problemy sytuacji gospodarczej kraju,* p. 46.

[18] See Appendix Table I6 and Chapter III, pp. 61, 63–64.

breakdown of GNP. We decided not to consider it there as a possible balancing item since we are primarily interested in the relative sizes of the conventional sectors of origin. It could, however, easily enough be listed among these sectors and interpreted as a gain or loss from foreign trade.

We have not explicitly provided for a return to land as a factor of production. To some extent it is represented in the figures for fixed capital in the agricultural sector under orchards, drainage and irrigation facilities, and other land improvements. These amounted only to about 10 percent of the value of fixed capital and livestock, and, accordingly, we must take into account some understatement of the return to agriculture in relation to other sectors. If one should regard the average rate of return on capital that we used for all sectors as in some way too high for agriculture, then a part of that return could be attributed to the incomplete coverage of land. As a very rough order-of-magnitude approximation, farm land may be taken as about equal in value to farm fixed capital.

We shall remark briefly here, and more fully in Chapter V, on the share of housing in GNP at factor cost. This depends primarily on the reliability of our capital figures, the estimated rate of depreciation, and the average rate of return by which non-labor factors were compensated in relation to their current values of capital. Some readers may wish to consider a lower than average rate of return on capital in housing, and this, of course, can be readily introduced where considerations of comparability with other countries may require. In the framework of a socialist economy, however, the use of a single rate of return on capital would seem to have merit. As regards the estimated rate of depreciation (2.4 percent), this was based on the rate for buildings in Czechoslovakia. Presumably it includes some provision for capital repairs, which, of course, extends the life of the capital.

Our decision in Table 8 to determine the net return to non-labor factors in the aggregate as equal essentially to the GNP at market prices less the return to labor and the capital consumption allowances was motivated by the desire to keep within values considered in a sense defined by the Polish context. We can, however, readily construct alternative distributions of GNP by sectors of origin by estimating nonlabor returns, inclusive of capital consumption allowances, as percentages of the sum of fixed and working capital. We show here (see the tabulation below), along with our results from Table 8, two such break-downs of GNP for 1956. Under assumption A we took the return to nonlabor factors at 8 percent of the current values of fixed and working capital, and under B at 20 percent, thus establishing a range for the purpose of judging the consequences of selecting various possible rates of return.[19] The figures in the tabulation were based on labor returns as given in Appendix Table I1 and nonlabor returns calculated from the selected rates (8 and 20 percent) applied to the capital values shown in Appendix Table I2.

It seems clear that within a considerable range of rates of return to nonlabor factors based on current values of fixed and working capital there is relatively small variation in the relative shares of GNP originated by the various industrial sectors. The only big changes relate to housing, and this is because of the relatively insignificant labor charges in the sector and its large share in the total capital in the economy. Similar calculations for 1954 and 1955 lead to the same general conclusion.

GNP BY SECTOR OF ORIGIN AT FACTOR COST, 1956,
ON ALTERNATIVE ASSUMPTIONS

(*Percentages of total*)

	A	Table 8	B
Industry and handicraft	27.5	28.1	26.2
Agriculture	32.2	30.0	28.8
Forestry	1.0	.9	.9
Construction	6.7	6.2	6.1
Transportation and communication	6.4	6.9	6.8
Trade and catering	6.5	6.1	6.7
Housing	7.9	10.9	14.6
Other services	2.9	3.1	3.3
Government services	6.4	5.6	4.8
Defense	2.1	1.8	1.6
Domestic and religious services	.3	.3	.2
Total	100.0	100.0	100.0

[19] This range was suggested by Raymond P. Powell, "Industrial Production," in Abram Bergson and Simon Kuznets, eds., *Economic Trends in the Soviet Union*, Cambridge, Harvard University Press, 1963, p. 168.

GNP BY END USE AT FACTOR COST

Table 9 shows our estimates for GNP by end uses at market prices and at factor cost. Details of our calculations are given in Appendix Tables I6 and I7. Here we shall describe briefly our methods of adjustment of components of GNP at market prices to approximate factor cost.

TABLE 9
GNP BY END USE AT MARKET PRICES AND AT FACTOR COST
(*Percentages of total*)

	AT MARKET PRICES			AT FACTOR COST		
	1954	1955	1956	1954	1955	1956
Personal consumption	61.4	60.9	59.5	55.6	56.0	56.5
Gross rent	1.0	1.0	.8	13.1	12.9	11.3
Other	60.4	59.9	58.7	42.5	43.1	45.2
Government	10.0	10.3	9.9	8.2	8.2	8.4
Education	2.6	2.6	2.6	2.2	2.1	2.2
Art and culture	.2	.3	.3	.2	.2	.2
Science and research	.4	.4	.3	.3	.3	.3
Health	2.0	2.1	2.2	1.6	1.6	1.8
Internal security	1.4	1.5	1.3	1.2	1.2	1.1
Administration and justice	2.7	2.7	2.6	2.3	2.3	2.2
Quasi-government services	.7	.7	.7	.5	.5	.5
Defense	4.3	4.5	3.8	4.9	5.4	4.4
Gross investment	24.3	24.3	26.8	31.3	30.4	30.7
Fixed capital	17.9	17.8	20.5	23.3	23.2	23.6
Inventories	5.7	5.8	4.2	7.4	6.7	5.2
Farm investment in kind	.4	.3	.4	.4	.3	.4
Net foreign investment	.2	.3	1.6	.2	.2	1.4
Total	100.0	100.0	100.0	100.0	100.0	100.0

Our adjustment began with the values of components of GNP in market prices as given in Table 7. We adjusted these values, first, by subtracting indirect taxes and accounting profits and adding subsidies, to arrive at what we shall call adjusted base values. These base values roughly represent the labor cost and depreciation charges entering the end uses, but there were some exceptions to be noted below that required special treatment. Next, we identified the sum of indirect taxes and accounting profits less subsidies as the total amount to be redistributed among selected end uses to raise their adjusted base values to approximate factor cost. This amount very roughly corresponds to net nonlabor returns. The augmentation was carried out in three steps.

First, we calculated an average rate of increase of eligible end uses by dividing the total amount to be added to their adjusted base values (that is, indirect taxes plus accounting profit less subsidies) by the sum of these adjusted base values. This average rate, however, was applied only to the gain or loss on that part of foreign trade that was exactly balanced in foreign-exchange zlotys (Table 7, item 5) to arrive at its estimated factor cost value (Appendix Table I6, item 5). Second, we used this estimate to arrive at our GNP at factor cost by sectors of origin because at this stage we needed an estimate of gross rent at factor cost. We estimated the latter as equal to the value of housing services in GNP at factor cost by sector of origin (Appendix Table I1) plus the estimated factor cost value of purchases by housing from other sectors. By this means we in effect raised the value of gross rent from its adjusted base to estimated factor cost by adding a part of the sum of indirect taxes plus accounting profits less subsidies; another part of this amount, we recall, had already been used to arrive at the factor cost value of the profit or loss in domestic prices on that part of foreign trade that was exactly balanced in foreign-exchange zlotys. Third, and finally, the residual in this amount after the two deductions was then added to the adjusted base values of the remaining end uses eligible for upward adjustment in proportion to their adjusted base values.

The end uses that were ineligible for the upward adjustment, which we regarded as primarily for returns to nonlabor factors of production, were those that either consisted entirely of labor services (pay to government employees and members of the armed forces and professional, domestic, and religious services) or those that at their adjusted base values were considered already high enough to approximate factor cost (farm free market sales and farm investment in kind, both of which we assumed were valued at prices high enough to provide full returns to all factors of production).

Our procedure in effect consists of reducing the market price values of end-use categories to what we call adjusted base values representing roughly labor cost and depreciation charges. Polish prices, generally speaking, take account of these basic charges, and when we subtract from market price values the sum of indirect taxes and accounting profits less subsidies, this is roughly what we arrive at in the adjusted base values, use by use, with the exceptions noted above. We then add to those end uses eligible for upward adjustment (on account of a return to non-labor factors of production) their proportionate shares in the total available for that purpose, namely, the sum of indirect taxes and accounting profits less subsidies. Gross rent was then treated as a special case of this type of adjustment. We should ask at this point whether the redistribution of net nonlabor returns proportionately to values of end uses at labor cost plus depreciation is justifiable. Is it not likely that some end uses of GNP reflect more intensive dependence on nonlabor factors of production than the relative adjusted base values consisting primarily of labor cost plus depreciation would imply?

We cannot give a precise reply to these questions in absence of very detailed information on interindustry flows, capital stock, composition of final uses, indirect taxes, profits, and subsidies. But our rough approach, based on the discussion of Polish prices, taking into account the commingling of goods and services from the various sectors of origin in serving aggregate end uses, may be quite reliable, given our special treatment of gross rent, types of labor services, and farm consumption and investment in kind.[20] We may note that among the gross investment categories, construction services would be less capital intensive per zloty of factor cost than producer durables (or, for that matter, consumer durables). Additions to inventories and net foreign investment are mixed categories, which probably would not differ much from the average for the eligible uses that we adjusted at a uniform rate. In view of these and similar considerations, we

[20] Bergson, *The Real National Income of Soviet Russia since 1928*, pp. 145–46, 434–41, presents some U.S. ratios of direct and indirect wage cost per dollar of market value of end-use components (excluding excise taxes on final goods) based on the studies of Wassily Leontief and his associates at Harvard University on the 1947 192-industry model "input-output" table compiled by the U.S. Bureau of Labor Statistics. These ratios show a bunching tendency within a rather narrow range for the uses we adjusted in a uniform manner for nonlabor returns, and by implication the nonlabor factor costs would be clustered also within a narrow range. These labor cost ratios per dollar were slightly higher for gross investment components than for personal consumption.

decided to avoid more differentiated adjustments for the various end uses. Our results, of course, should be more reliable at the higher levels of aggregation than for very detailed end-use categories.

We shall examine some of the implications of our findings in Chapter V.

V. ECONOMIC IMPLICATIONS

Our findings on the structure of the Polish economy in Chapters II, III, and IV provide the basis for a discussion of relative contributions of sectors of production, resource allocation, and the financing of gross investment and government expenditures. In addition to these topics we shall compare briefly our estimates with Polish official national income statistics and with our findings for Czechoslovakia and Hungary.

GNP BY SECTOR OF ORIGIN

In Table 10 we show the relative shares of GNP by sectors of production, both at market prices and at factor cost in order to bring out the differences in structure between the two valuations. Perhaps the most striking result of our adjustment to factor cost is the change in the ratio of industry to agriculture, from industrial predominance at roughly 2 to 1 in market prices to about 1 to 1, slightly favoring agriculture, at factor cost. This statistical conclusion is simply another description of the peculiarities of the Polish price system, which was so devised as to collect, primarily in industry, the returns to state ownership and control in most sectors of the economy.[1]

No doubt some questions might be raised concerning the precision of our estimates, but the change in the proportions shown in Table 10 would not be seriously affected. It will be recalled that our factor-cost estimates represent the sum of labor returns, depreciation, and nonlabor returns, the latter figures for each sector being calculated as shares in the total for the economy in proportion to the sectors' present (depreciated) value of fixed

[1] See above, pp. 53–54.

TABLE 10

GNP BY SECTOR OF ORIGIN AT MARKET PRICES
AND AT FACTOR COST

(*Percentages of total*)

	AT MARKET PRICES			AT FACTOR COST		
	1954	*1955*	*1956*	*1954*	*1955*	*1956*
Industry and handicraft	46.0	45.9	45.1	26.7	27.2	28.1
Agriculture	20.9	21.0	23.2	29.1	29.4	30.0
Forestry	.5	.6	.9	.8	.8	.9
Construction	5.7	5.5	6.5	6.5	6.2	6.2
Transportation and com-						
munication	5.2	5.6	5.7	6.4	6.4	6.9
Trade and catering	8.3	8.9	6.7	6.1	6.3	6.1
Housing	1.4	1.6	1.6	12.5	12.3	10.9
Other services	3.5	2.8	2.6	3.0	3.0	3.1
Education	1.6	1.6	1.7	1.6	1.6	1.7
Art and culture	.1	.1	.1	.1	.1	.1
Science and research	.2	.2	.2	.2	.2	.2
Public health	.9	.9	1.0	1.0	1.0	1.0
Internal security	1.0	.9	.8	1.0	.9	.8
Administration and justice	1.6	1.7	1.7	1.7	1.7	1.6
Quasi-governmental						
organizations	.2	.2	.2	.2	.2	.2
Defense	2.6	2.2	1.9	2.7	2.3	1.8
Domestic and religious service	.3	.3	.3	.3	.3	.3
Total	100.0	100.0	100.0	100.0	100.0	100.0

NOTE: Totals may differ slightly from the sums of indicated items because of rounding.

capital plus working capital. Rent as a return to agricultural land was not explicitly included but was covered to a small extent by the improvements to land (irrigation and drainage facilities, orchards, and so forth) included in our figures for fixed capital.[2] If for some reason one should seek to scale down the rate of return to agricultural capital in proportion to industrial instead of applying the same rate for all sectors as we did, then the question of an explicit rent return should be raised. In a Soviet-type economy the role of the state as owner and entrepreneur is practically all-pervasive. At first sight Polish agriculture with its dominant privately owned farms might seem to be an exception, but upon closer examination it seems clear that the state has managed to leave the owners only the equivalent of wages, taking the nonlabor returns away by means of obligatory sales to socialized procurement agencies at low state-set prices. Thus, with-

[2] See p. 80.

out actual ownership, it succeeded in claiming the nonlabor returns, at least during the period of this study.

The decline in the share of trade upon revaluation to factor cost, like that of industry, reflects the essential arbitrariness of the market-price structure, which realizes in the returns to industry and trade much of the value added in other sectors of production. The vehicles for these transfers are the familiar turnover tax, profit, and subsidy categories.

Sectors showing essentially no change upon revaluation are those consisting primarily of types of labor services: government, defense, professional services, and domestic and religious services. Relatively small changes appear in construction and transportation because of the offsetting character of indirect taxes and profits, on the one hand, and subsidies, on the other, in the market price structure and because of the more or less average character of capital intensity in relation to labor charges in the factor-cost adjustment.

Special note must be taken of the sharp rise in the share of housing, from around 1.5 percent in market prices to 11 to 12 percent at factor cost. Obviously two influences are at work here. First, at market prices, as a matter of state policy, rental rates were set at nominal levels that could barely cover current costs, not to mention adequate depreciation allowances and a net return on the fixed capital investment. Second, we allowed a rather high rate of depreciation (2.4 percent) and a net return to capital at the same rate as in all other sectors, which, taking account of the heavy capitalization of the sector, raised its factor-cost share sharply upward. These methodological considerations may render our factor-cost figures for housing services by origin and for gross rent as an element in personal consumption by end use not strictly comparable with estimates for other countries. One would expect in less-developed countries to find a disproportionately large share of the total capital tied up in dwellings as compared to advanced industrial countries, where investment alternatives are more numerous and the needs for housing less pressing. One should also take into account the existence of rent controls and possible underestimation of services of owner-occupied and rural housing as well as different methodology used in arriving at factor cost in countries with very low shares for housing in GNP.

TABLE 11

GNP BY SECTOR OF ORIGIN AT FACTOR COST IN 1955:
CZECHOSLOVAKIA, HUNGARY, AND POLAND

(Percentages of total)

	Czechoslovakia	Hungary	Poland
Industry	37.4	30.0	27.2
Agriculture	18.0	26.5	29.4
Forestry	1.4	.7	.8
Construction	7.7	6.0	6.2
Transport and communication	9.8	11.4	6.4
Housing	8.0	9.4	12.3
Trade and catering	7.4 *	6.0	6.3
Other	10.3	10.0	11.4
Total	100.0	100.0	100.0

* Includes banking and insurance.

In Table 11 we bring together some of our results for the structure of GNP by sector of origin at factor cost in Czechoslovakia, Hungary, and Poland in 1955.[3] These results were arrived at by essentially the same methodology, although there are minor differences, which are fully described in the sources cited. In the three countries, the relative importance of industry in GNP is highest and that of agriculture and housing is lowest in Czechoslovakia. This finding is, of course, consistent with other information we have on the relative levels of development in these countries. We should caution here that judgments of efficiency and relative levels of production cannot be drawn from this table, as it reflects only the use of factors of production.

RESOURCE ALLOCATION

Our findings on the composition of GNP by end use at market prices and at factor cost have been summarized in Table 9. Details of our factor-cost adjustment are shown in Appendix Tables I6 and I7 and their supporting notes. In this connection we should add that the proportions at factor cost among uses at the

[3] See Alton and associates, *Czechoslovak National Income and Product, 1947–48 and 1955–56*, p. 61, and their *Hungarian National Income and Product in 1955*, p. 76.

more aggregated levels shown in Table 9 are considered more reliable than the more detailed breakdown that might be provided. This is because our assumption of equal capital intensity per zloty of most end uses at factor cost should be more closely approximated where there is more averaging of diverse components; it would obviously be untenable with fine subdivisions of end-use categories. Details of the market-price subcategories of end uses are given in our sectoral tables and supporting notes, and further elaboration may be found in the sources cited there.

As a result of our adjustments, the shares of GNP accounted for by personal consumption and by government declined substantially from market price to factor cost; at the same time the reverse was true for gross investment and defense. These changes simply reflect the character of Polish market prices as the means whereby the state realizes most of its return to ownership of production facilities and control over economic activity on the sales of consumer goods, achieved primarily through the turnover tax and, to a lesser extent, through profits of industrial enterprises.

We recall at this point our decision to drop from the GNP the anomalous category corresponding to the profit or loss in domestic prices on that part of foreign trade that was exactly balanced in foreign-exchange zlotys (Table 7, item 5, and Appendix Table I6). We have already discussed possible interpretations that might be placed on this item.[4] At this point we may note that its inclusion in gross investment would cause the latter's share to rise substantially in 1954 and 1955 and decline somewhat in 1956; concomitantly, the shares of consumption and other end uses would fall in 1954 and 1955 and rise in 1956.

The change in personal consumption as a share in GNP from around 60 to 61 percent at market prices to 55 to 56 percent at factor cost is dampened by the sharp rise in the share of gross rent (from around 1 percent at market prices to around 11 to 13 percent at factor cost). Excluding rent, personal consumption at factor cost (some 43 to 45 percent of GNP) shows a very sharp drop from its share at market prices (around 59 to 60 percent of GNP). Our remarks on the valuation of housing

[4] See above, pp. 61, 63–64.

services at factor cost [5] are relevant here as well as to gross rent. Because we allowed a return to capital in housing at the same rate as in other sectors of production and used a relatively high rate of depreciation on buildings (2.4 percent), the return to housing (and the charge to gross rent) showed a very sharp increase upon adjustment to factor cost. Although this treatment helps to clarify the problem of resource allocation in Poland, it might introduce some problems in international comparisons. As regards the shares in GNP, our remarks above on housing services as a sector of origin of product apply here as well (see pp. 88–89). Accordingly, gross rent as shown here very probably is overstated in comparison with gross rent at factor cost as a share of GNP in Western European and other countries. For more basic comparisons, of course, one could proceed from market-price valuations and market rental ratios for comparable space, or even more directly in terms of space occupied per person, introducing some simplified weights for differences in average quality.

The detail provided under government services is intended to facilitate calculation of alternative measures of consumption and government by suitable choice of components. We should add, finally, that defense as shown here is based directly on the single state budget category that was available and does not take account of some activities supporting the military sectors that doubtless are excluded from the narrow definition of defense used in the state budget.[6]

In Table 12 we bring together some of our results on resource allocation in Czechoslovakia, Hungary, and Poland, together with more or less comparable figures for the USSR given by Bergson.[7] In the present study, however, we cannot undertake a comparative analysis of policies and developments; the figures are offered simply for their own interest. Allowing for some

[5] See above, pp. 88–89.
[6] See above, pp. 44–45.
[7] Soviet figures were given in Bergson, *The Real National Income of Soviet Russia*, p. 245. For other data, see above, Table 9, and Alton and associates, *Czechoslovak National Income and Product, 1947–48 and 1955–56*, p. 70, and their *Hungarian National Income and Product in 1955*, p. 80.

differences because of the methodology followed for the factor-

TABLE 12
RESOURCE ALLOCATION IN
CZECHOSLOVAKIA, HUNGARY, POLAND AND THE USSR
IN 1955
(*In percentages of GNP at factor cost*)

	Czechoslovakia	Hungary	Poland	USSR[a]
Personal consumption	48.2	51.3	56.0	49.2
Government	10.2	8.3	8.2	12.6[c]
Defense	10.7[b]	5.1	5.4	10.3
Gross investment	30.8	35.2	30.4	27.9
GNP	100.0	100.0	100.0	100.0

[a] In 1955 current ruble factor cost.
[b] Includes internal security.
[c] Government administration and communal services.

cost adjustments for these countries, the pattern of resource use
in the USSR and Czechoslovakia is broadly similar. If we com-
bine gross investment and defense, the share of resources in the
four countries supporting these uses falls in a range of roughly
36 to 41 percent of GNP. The high rate of gross investment in
Hungary in 1955 reflects in part a sharp increase in stocks.

SOURCES OF FINANCE

Table 13 shows the sources of revenue used to finance government expenditures, gross investment, and foreign-trade price
equalization. All of the figures were taken from Tables 1–3,
except item 3c, which is given in Appendix Table D1. We should
point out that the financing of price equalization in foreign trade
inflates the totals in Table 13 both in item 3b, where it reflects
turnover taxes on exports, and in item 3c, price equalization
profits on imports. A summary of this accounting is given in
Appendix Table D1.

Enterprise sector payments to government clearly are the
dominant source of finance, accounting for some 70 to 80 percent of the total. But we should note the essentially arbitrary
division between the major items of such payments and enterprise retained earnings and capital consumption allowances. In
the first place, there is little or no economic distinction between

TABLE 13
SOURCES OF POLISH FINANCE
(*Billion zlotys*)

	1954	1955	1956
1. Retained earnings of enterprises	5.1	8.7	8.7
2. Capital consumption allowances	10.8	12.5	20.6
3. Enterprise payments to government	113.9	121.7	125.1
a. Social security contributions	10.8	11.7	13.4
b. Indirect taxes	73.1	74.9	63.2
c. Price equalization profits on imports	12.2	15.4	25.8
d. Direct taxes and other transfers	17.8	19.7	22.7
4. Savings by households	.1	.7	8.8
5. Household payments to government	7.1	8.0	8.8
a. Direct taxes	5.6	6.4	7.3
b. Other	1.5	1.6	1.5
6. Social security contributions paid by government	1.6	1.7	2.0
Total	138.6	153.3	174.0

enterprises' direct and indirect taxes, and the boundary between them is basically a matter of convenience of collection.[8] Second, the dividing line between enterprises' direct taxes and retained earnings of enterprises is also for the most part a matter of central directives concerning the distribution of nonlabor returns to factors of production. Though often loath to speak directly of a return to capital and to draw the necessary inferences from this, economists in the Soviet-type economies go so far as to speak of both profits and turnover taxes as returns to state ownership. The separation of accounting profits into a part retained by enterprises and a part transferred to the state budget reflects mostly the concern of the central planners to guide the directions of new investment and at the same time give some attention to incentive effects. Capital consumption allowances obviously have a distinct significance when they are realistically calculated, but, as was the case in 1954 and 1955, when they are seriously underestimated, then the amount ascribed to profits and turnover taxes will be correspondingly greater. Hence, it would seem desirable in this context to lump together items 1, 2, and 3 in Table 13 and refer to enterprise sources of finance as accounting for some 89 to 94 percent of the total.

[8] See the quotations from Polish, Soviet and Czechoslovak sources above, pp. 72–73.

In any event, household payments to government and personal savings are relatively insignificant sources of finance for non-household expenditures, and this is all the more true of item 6. Obviously this does not mean that households made a correspondingly small contribution toward the cost of government and gross investment. It would seem simplest to attribute the entire product to man and then ask what part of it went to personal consumption. Here the best single indicator at present would be the structure of GNP by end use at factor cost.

The role of the state budget in a Soviet-type economy has many aspects. With respect to private enterprise it serves as an instrument of compression and restraint, aiming to reduce the sector to inconsequential proportions and keep it impotent. For the socialized sector it is a tool of control and redistribution. One index to its dimensions is the ratio of state budget revenues to GNP. For Poland this amounted to about 48 percent in 1954 and 1955 and 45 percent in 1956 (see Appendix Table G1 and Table 7, excluding item 5).

COMPARISON WITH POLISH OFFICIAL STATISTICS

In Table 14 we reproduce some Polish official national income statistics for 1956 for comparison with our findings.[9] We excluded from the sector of origin breakdown the profit or loss on foreign-trade price equalization as it related to externally balanced trade. "Domestic national income" thus defined amounted to 252.9 billion zlotys. By end use, the concept "national income distributed" excludes the value in domestic zlotys of the export surplus in foreign-exchange zlotys, as well as "losses" and a balancing item; its value came to 254.1 billion zlotys. The single comprehensive total, "national income produced," covering all the items we dropped would be the same for both breakdowns; it amounted to 256.7 billion zlotys.

The official national income concept refers to net material product, and in practice it is calculated by sector of origin by subtracting "material costs" (depreciation plus purchases from

[9] See *DN 1956*, pp. 13, 14.

TABLE 14
POLISH OFFICIAL NATIONAL INCOME STATISTICS, 1956

	Billion zlotys	Percent of total
By Sector of Origin		
Industry and handicraft	125.0	49.4
Agriculture	70.6	27.9
Forestry	2.6	1.0
Construction	22.3	8.8
Transport and communication	7.3	2.9
Trade	19.8	7.8
Other material production	5.3	2.1
Domestic national income	252.9	100.0
By End Use		
Consumption	202.7	79.8
Individual	189.2	74.5
Collective	13.4	5.3
Accumulation	51.4	20.2
Net investment	37.2	14.6
Increment to working		
capital and reserves	14.2	5.6
National income distributed	254.1	100.0

other material production sectors) from gross production. The result is something grosser than the concept of net value added because it includes purchases from nonmaterial sectors of production that are reflected in gross production but not in material costs. Thus, in the official statistics showing national income distributed to various charges (wages, profit, and so forth), we find an item labeled "other nonmaterial costs" amounting to 7.6 percent of national income in 1955 and 7.5 percent in 1956.[10]

Obviously our figures referring to GNP at market prices by sector or origin are not directly comparable to the Polish national income statistics, also in market prices, because GNP includes the so-called "nonmaterial" production sectors (passenger transportation, government, and other services) and it includes capital consumption allowances. We can, however, on a sector-by-sector basis subtract depreciation from our figures for GNP at market prices (see Table 6) and compare our results with the Polish official figures for the material production sectors. There was close agreement when we did this for 1956, the official figures usually exceeding ours by a small margin, pre-

[10] *DN 1956*, p. 13.

sumably because they included purchases from nonmaterial sectors. We observed lesser agreement in 1954 and 1955, probably because statistics for those years were less complete and more estimates were necessary for the profit and subsidy categories. In general, however, the relative sizes of sectors agreed reasonably well in all years. What is more important is that essentially the same statistics for returns to labor stand behind both representations of economic activity for the years 1954–56. We had no basis for disagreeing with the official statistics in this area, and they were reasonably complete. Cleared of the obfuscations of indirect taxes, profits, and subsidies, they provided the basis for our eventual factor-cost adjustments.

As regards the official concept of national income by end use, again reference is to material product only, excluding nonmaterial services as contributing product to serve end uses but including such services as consumers only to the extent of their consumption of goods and services originating in material production sectors. For example, government services are included in collective consumption to the extent of material product used up in providing government services; pay of government employees is excluded. We have referred above to the treatment of material expenditures of the military establishment, a part of the cost falling under collective consumption (pay in kind to personnel), and a part (armaments) apparently being counted under accumulation.[11]

Because of the incomplete coverage of the official concept, and, above all, because of the deficiencies of Polish prices, the breakdown shown in Table 14 is of little value. We would expect that, by cutting down our figures of end uses (see Table 7) and rearranging components to match the Polish official categories of consumption and accumulation, substantial agreement should emerge. Such was the case for 1956, particularly in the accumulation categories when we took account of depreciation, including the imputed depreciation on private and collective farms, that was used to arrive at the Polish figures of net fixed capital investment. Similarly, by dropping (see Appendix Table

[11] See pp. 44–46.

I6) such service items as wages and salaries in government and domestic and religious services and adding up the commodity components, we arrived at a total close to the official figure for consumption, but the breakdown between individual and collective consumption was less close.

But, aside from the formal aspect of reconciliation of estimates, there is little point in carrying out such comparisons in detail when clearly both the official figures and ours in current market prices convey a seriously misleading picture of the relative contributions of sectors of production and the resource cost of final uses, and, to a Western reader unfamiliar with Soviet-type national income concepts, the official figures are doubly misleading. Some recognition of the inadequacy of these concepts is appearing even in Polish publications.[12]

The fact that Polish market prices convey a deceptive picture of the allocation of resources is also recognized by some Polish economists. In this connection, an interesting appendix to the official national income study for 1956 [13] points out that "the structure of the actual selling prices of material goods does not correspond to the structure of the amounts of socially necessary labor spent on their creation. This leads to deformation of the structure of origin and uses of national income and its trends." For this reason the study undertook, with some apologies for lack of precision and with the caution that the results must be treated as materials for discussion, to estimate "national income" and net global product (*produkt globalny netto,* an approximation to gross value added in material production but still including purchases from nonmaterial sectors) at so-called *"ceny umowne"* (conventional prices) of 1956.

These prices are intended to approximate "own costs of production" (*koszty własne*) less material costs. Essentially the calculation consisted of subtracting from the value of production in current prices the turnover tax, income tax, and positive

[12] See Włodzimierz Brus, "Liczyc czy nie liczyc" (To Calculate or Not to Calculate), *Zycie Gospodarcze,* June 3, 1962, pp. 1–2. Brus refers to the so-called "nonproductive" services thus far excluded from the Polish definition of national income.

[13] *DN 1956,* pp. 52–55.

budget differences and adding negative budget differences, in this way deriving "the value of production corresponding to own costs plus insignificant profit." Agriculture was an exception; here it was assumed that for comparability to other sectors the value of total agricultural production ought to be established at average weighted realized market prices. The statement added that the "internal structure of agricultural prices was based on the proportions of average prices of above-quota procurements and free market prices." The end-use composition of national income at "conventional prices of 1956" was estimated in "an analogous manner." No absolute figures or details of the calculation were given; results were shown only as percentages, which we reproduce in Table 15 for 1955 and 1956, both years based on 1956 "conventional prices." Foreign-trade price equalization and net foreign investment were excluded from the calculation.

TABLE 15

POLISH NATIONAL INCOME AT 1956 "CONVENTIONAL PRICES"

	NATIONAL INCOME		NET GLOBAL PRODUCT	
	1955	*1956*	*1955*	*1956*
By Sector of Origin				
Industry and handicraft	40.2	40.1	41.6	41.5
Agriculture	33.1	32.5	32.6	32.0
Forestry	1.0	1.1	0.9	1.0
Construction	11.6	11.6	10.9	11.0
Transport and communication	3.7	3.7	4.1	4.2
Trade	7.5	8.2	7.1	7.7
Other material production	2.9	2.8	2.8	2.6
Total	100.0	100.0	100.0	100.0
By End Use				
Consumption	70.8	73.2	63.7	65.9
Individual	65.9	68.5	59.8	62.2
Collective	4.9	4.7	3.9	3.7
Accumulation	29.2	26.8	36.3	34.1
Net investment	20.2	19.4	27.9	27.2
Stocks and reserves	9.0	7.4	8.4	6.9
Total	100.0	100.0	100.0	100.0

A glance at Tables 14 and 15 will show that revaluation at 1956 "conventional prices" has resulted in a decline of the share of industry and handicraft and an increase in the shares of most other sectors of production, but trade and forestry were scarcely affected. In the end-use breakdowns, consumption categories decline as accumulation categories rise correspondingly.

Although the revaluation at conventional prices is a step in the right direction, it does not go far enough. Its end result is a rough approximation to the labor-cost shares in the total labor cost for the material production sectors as regards national income, and to labor cost plus depreciation as regards net global product. Agriculture, however, is an exception, as we have indicated above.

Failure to take explicit account of returns to fixed and working capital and to extend the coverage to include nonmaterial production obviously reduces the significance of this attempt to introduce resource cost notions into Polish national accounting. Even so, the fall of the share of consumption in national income from 80 percent at market prices to 73 percent at conventional prices and the fall in the share of industry and handicraft from 49 percent to 40 percent, with offsetting changes in other end uses and sectors of origin, goes a substantial part of the way toward correcting the deficiencies of Polish prices.

Our factor-cost shares in GNP (see Tables 8 and 9) are not comparable to the official figures shown in Table 15, although the formal resemblance is closer to the notion of net global production in the sense that both concepts include capital consumption. Our revaluation to factor cost took account of net returns to capital, as well as labor costs and depreciation, whereas the Polish official figures refer roughly to "own costs," which provide little or no net return to capital. The shares by sector of origin at conventional prices in national income are very close to those in net global product (see Table 15); some small increase occurring in industry and transportation and communications and the offsetting declines in the remaining sectors presumably are caused by taking into account capital consumption.

In comparison with our figures in Tables 8 and 9, the percentages as such should be disregarded since our GNP includes nonmaterial sectors omitted from the Polish net global product. What is more important is the ratio of pairs of sectors or uses. Thus, our results show agriculture slightly larger than industry and handicraft, whereas the official figures show the latter sector about one third larger than the former. Since transportation and communications in the official figures refer only to material production excluding passenger transportation, while our figures cover the entire sector, direct comparisons of the unadjusted figures are proscribed. Among the end uses, we again face problems of definition of sectors in addition to the different basis of valuation. The decline in the share of consumption in Table 15 from 73.2 percent in national income to 65.9 percent in net global product on account of the inclusion of capital consumption allowances suggests that a further decline would occur if provision were made also for a net return to nonlabor factors of production as represented by the values of fixed and working capital, such as we provide in our estimated factor-cost distributions.

Given the different bases of valuation, there is little to be gained by attempting a detailed comparison of percentage shares in our Tables 8 and 9 and the official figures in Table 15. To readers unfamiliar with Polish official national income concepts and unaware of the problems inherent in valuation at Polish market prices, our estimates within the framework of more comprehensive concepts of national product and with adjustments to approximate factor cost should provide welcome insights into the structure of the Polish economy.

The economic implications of our findings on the structure of Polish national income will become more complete when we conclude the study, now in progress, of Polish economic growth during the years 1937–1962. These findings will provide weights for combining indexes of sectoral growth.

APPENDIX A: NOTES TO HOUSEHOLD SECTOR ACCOUNTS (TABLES 1A, 1B, AND 1C)

NOTES TO TABLE 1A

Item 2. Value added by sector
See Appendix Table E1, rows IA and IB, columns *4* and *7*.

NOTES TO TABLE 1B

Item 1. Valued added by household sector
Transferred from Table 1A.

Item 2A1a. Wages and salaries
See Appendix Table E1, Row II, column *5*.

Item 2A1b. Income of self-employed
See Appendix Table A1 and notes thereto.
Row 1, a and b. 1954: Industry was assumed equal to the rounded figure for 1955. According to the official estimates shown in *DN 1954–55,* p. 7, value added in private industry was practically equal in 1954 and 1955. Handicraft was assumed to represent roughly the same share of gross output of handicraft as in 1955 (38 percent). Gross output in 1954 and 1955 was estimated by raising the total shown in *DN 1954–55,* p. 7, by 57 percent to account for admitted underestimation of total output in the private sector (see *DN 1956,* pp. 17, 20). 1955–56: See *DN 1956,* p. 20, for totals and the values for handicraft; industry was derived as a residual.
Row 2. Construction. 1954: This was assumed to represent one

APPENDIX TABLE A1
INCOME OF SELF-EMPLOYED OUTSIDE AGRICULTURE
(*Million zlotys*)

	1954	1955	1956
1. Industry and handicraft	2,945	3,220	3,559
a. Industry	280	281	267
b. Handicraft	2,665	2,939	3,292
2. Construction	24	4	0
3. Transport and communications	1,350	1,212	1,444
a. Transport of goods	1,171	1,017	1,227
b. Passenger transport	179	195	217
4. Trade	970	1,138	1,595
a. Retail trade	170	114	193
b. Other	800	1,024	1,402
5. Other services	680	750	844
a Commercial	50	50	50
b. Professional	630	700	794
6. Forestry	441	460	528
Total	6,410	6,784	7,970

half of value added (*DN 1954–55,* p. 16), which was roughly the ratio in 1955. 1955–56: See *DN 1956,* p. 32.

Row 3a. Income in this category was derived from registered transport and horse carting, as follows (in million zlotys):

	1954	1955	1956
Registered transport	665	427	586
Horse carting	506	590	641
Total	1,171	1,017	1,227

The 1954 figure for motor transport was estimated at two thirds of value added (*DN 1954–55,* p. 18), which was roughly the ratio in 1955; the figures for 1955–56 are from *DN 1956,* p. 38. Net income from horse carting in 1954 and 1955 was assumed to have accounted for roughly the same percentage share of "other household income" as in 1956. The income figures were taken from *DN 1954–55,* p. 22, and *DN 1956,* p. 43.

Row 3b. Income in this category was derived by cab drivers. It was estimated as the product of the number of cabs and the average net income per cab. The number of private cabs (both motor and horse) for 1954–56 was taken from *RS 1956,* p. 396, and *RS 1960,* p. 458; their number in 1954 was assumed equal to the 1955 figure. Average income per motor cab was obtained from total expenditure on cabs (Appendix Table A3) reduced by the cost of inputs and taxes, assumed to represent the same shares of gross and net revenue as in the case of private freight transport (*DN 1956,* p. 38). The 1955 breakdown was assumed applicable also to 1954. The average income per horse cab was assumed to equal one half that of a motor cab.

Row 4a. Retail trade and catering income in this category was derived from the net trade margin by subtracting from it wages, social security contributions, and taxes. The net margin in 1954–55 was taken from *DN 1954–55,* p. 20; that for 1956 was assumed to represent roughly the same share of total turnover in private trade (*RS 1960,* p. 271) as in 1955 (20 percent). Wages and social security contributions were taken from Appendix Table E1, row II E2. Taxes for 1954 were assumed to represent roughly the same share of net margin as in 1955; those in 1955–56 were taken from *DN 1956,* p. 42.

Row 4b. This item represents sales by households of scrap metal, bottles, and so forth. For 1954, see *DN 1954–55,* p. 4; for 1955–56, see *DN 1956,* p. 43. We treat this income in the same manner as wages.

Row 5a. Net income originating in such commercial services as laundries, hotels, and so forth, is estimated very roughly at 50 million zlotys per year throughout 1954–56, on the basis of the numbers of private retail merchants shown in *RS 1960,* p. 458, and their estimated average earnings.

Row 5b. Income from professional services was estimated from gross income shown in Appendix Table A3, row 6, after deduction of tax payments shown in *RS 1957,* p. 301. The percentage of gross income paid out as taxes in 1954 was assumed to be the same as in 1955.

Row 6. This item consists of sales of nonwood forestry products (400 million zlotys each year estimated at the 1956 figure given in *DN 1956,* p. 43) and value added by private forestry (see *DN 1954–55,* p. 15 and *DN 1956,* p. 28).

Item 2A1c. Farm income
See Appendix Table F1. The figures we show here include depreciation, since the latter apparently is an imputed item, and we seek to show actual money flows.

Item 2A2a. Wages in kind
See Appendix Table E1, row II, column 6.

Item 2A2b. Farm consumption in kind
See Appendix Table F3.

Item 2A3. Profits distributed to members of nonagricultural cooperatives

Members were entitled to 20 percent of net profits earned by the labor cooperatives in 1954 and 1955 (Polskie towarzystwo ekonomiczne oddział w Poznaniu, *Problemy gospodarcze drobnej wytwórczości,* p. 184). They were entitled to receive 300 million zlotys in 1955 (*ibid.*). We assumed this sum was actually distributed, and we used the same figure for 1954. Distributed profits in 1956 were estimated at 50 percent of net profits earned by the cooperatives (*ibid.*). Net profits were estimated from total sales (21 billion zlotys), less cost of goods and services sold (17.9 billion zlotys), less tax (930 million zlotys) (see *ibid.,* pp. 94–95).

Item 2A4. Interest received from enterprise sector
See *RS 1957,* p. 310.

Item 2B1. Government sector: Cash wages and salaries
See Appendix Table E1, row III, column 5.

Item 2B2. Income in kind
See Appendix Table E1, row III, column 6.

Item 2B3a. Transfer payments from government

Total transfers from government consist of cash and imputed transfers. Imputed transfers are equal to the total amount of wages (including social security) received by clergy and other members of religious organizations. We considered the latter as belonging to, and being paid by, the household sector. In fact, however, clergymen and other employees of religious organizations received remuneration directly from government funds. In order to satisfy all of the above conditions, we imputed a transfer from the government to the household sector for that specific purpose. See Appendix Table G2, item 4a, for cash transfers and Appendix Table E1, item IB, for imputed.

Item 2B3b. From quasi-governmental organizations
See Appendix Table G5.

Item 3A. Purchases of goods and services from households
See Table 1A and Appendix Table E1.

Item 3B1. Retail purchases for consumption

Retail trade sales to households for consumption are shown in Appendix Table A2 and explained in the notes that follow.

APPENDIX TABLE A2
RETAIL TRADE SALES FOR CONSUMPTION
(*Million zlotys*)

	1954	1955	1956
1. Total retail sales	123,858	132,525	150,931
Less:			
2. Purchases by state enterprises and government	8,389	9,026	10,341
3. Miscellaneous purchases for production and investment	6,200	6,616	8,849
4. Wages in kind	781	849	981
5. Intrahousehold sales	1,268	1,152	1,215
a. Pawnshops	478	442	575
b. Private trade	790	710	640
6. Purchases by private trade for resale	2,375	2,138	1,870
7. Per diem travel allowances	2,163	2,073	2,278
8. Protective clothing and equipment	1,373	1,644	1,773
9. Equals: Total retail sales for consumption	101,309	109,027	123,624

Row 1. *RS 1960,* p. 271.

Row 2. This item was assumed to represent 7 percent of socialized retail sales (*RS 1960,* p. 271), which was the ratio in 1957 (*RS 1958,* p. 241). In the period 1957–60 the range for this ratio was from 7 to 12 percent (see *ibid.* and *RS 1962,* p. 264).

Row 3. This item includes purchases by farmers for production and investment (fertilizers, seed, feed, machinery, building materials) as well as purchases by private industry and handicraft (*DN 1956,* p. 44). 1954: It was assumed to represent about the same share of sales through the socialized trade network as in 1955. The resulting figure was rounded to the nearest hundred million zlotys. 1955–56: *RS 1958,* p. 243.

Row 4. Some wages in kind were included in the official estimate of socialized retail sales (*RS 1960,* p. 271). We assumed, however, that subsistence of armed forces, internal security, fire brigades, and prison guards were not included in this estimate. Consequently, total wages in kind to be subtracted include wages in the enterprise sector, health, education and welfare, administration and justice, and quasi-governmental organizations (see Appendix Table E1 and notes thereto for appropriate entries).

Row 5. This item represents that part of trade turnover in socialized pawnshops and private retail trade which represents also household incomes.

Row 5a. It was assumed that socialized pawnshops earn a 25 percent commission on their retail sales shown in *RS 1956,* p. 222, and *RS 1957,* p. 219. We show the remaining 75 percent here.

Row 5b. According to *DN 1956*, p. 44, private trade acquires its goods primarily in socialized retail trade in addition to goods bought from the population. We assumed that the value of goods acquired from households accounted for about 25 percent of the total value of goods purchased by private traders for resale. The value of the latter for 1954–55 was shown in *DN 1954–55*, p. 20 (total sales minus gross margin). Its value in 1956 assumed to represent roughly the same percentage share of private retail trade turnover as in 1955 (*RS 1960*, p. 271). The resulting estimates were rounded to the nearest ten million zlotys.

Row 6. This item represents purchases by private retail trade from socialized retail trade and individual farmers for resale to the population. 1954–55: This is the residual in total purchases by private trade after subtraction of purchases from households (see Row 5b, above). 1956: This equals the total turnover in private retail trade (*RS 1960*, p. 271), less purchases from households (see Row 5, above), less net margin (estimated in notes to Appendix Table A1), less material cost met through nonretail sources.

Row 7. This item represents expenditure on meals and other items financed out of per diem allowances paid by enterprises and government to employees traveling on official business. The totals for each year were estimated at 75 percent of the total annual allowances shown in Przelaskowski, "Rozwój indywidualnego oszczędzania w krajach socjalistycznych," p. 42. The remaining 25 percent was attributed to services.

Row 8. This item represents enterprises' purchases of protective clothing and equipment for their employees. 1954–55: It was assumed to represent roughly the same share (50 percent) of total expenditure on work safety and hygiene (*RS 1956*, p. 289) as in 1956. 1956: *RS 1957*, p. 287.

Item 3B2. Farm market purchases

These sales were estimated as equal to two thirds of total farm market sales as shown in Appendix Table F1, row 1c. We excluded one third as an order-of-magnitude allowance for purchases by private trade, private carters (fodder for horses), institutions (hospitals, and so forth), and cafeterias and plants operated by certain state farms (see Poland, Główny urząd statystyczny, *Produkcja globalna i brutto rolnictwa przed wojną i w latach 1946–1958*, pp. ix, xii. Total farm market sales as given in various official statistics are clearly very rough estimates with a considerable margin of error, being derived as residuals in total estimated supply (see *ibid.*). Our estimate of household purchases on the farm market may err on the low side since we were guided to some extent by the total income available on the household sector appropriation account and the sum of outlays other than farm market purchases. We believe that the income items are generally more reliable than the outlay items in the account. If we should wish to raise the estimated purchases on the farm market, we could accommodate such an increase by reducing retail purchases (item 3B1). The latter item was derived from total retail sales by deducting, among other items, purchases by socialized enterprises and institutions, estimated at 7 percent of the socialized retail sales. Since the range of such nonhousehold purchases was from 7 to 12 percent in the period 1957–61 (see *RS 1960*, p. 271; *RS 1961,* p. 252; *RS 1962,* p. 264) and no figure was available for the years 1954–56, we could have chosen something higher than the 7 percent deduction we allowed.

Item 3B3. Services (excluding domestic)

Our estimates of household purchases of services include seven major categories of services, shown in detail in Appendix Table A3. The estimates exclude purchases of handicraft services as well as gross cash rent, which are shown as separate categories of household expenditure.

The estimates for 1954 and 1955, explained in detail below, were derived for the most part by extrapolating 1956 estimates obtained from a detailed percentage distribution of the values of services purchased by households and an estimate of the absolute value of one of the components, namely, cash rent. The resulting 1956 figures were subsequently checked by comparing estimates of household purchases of electricity, urban transport, and motion picture entertainment obtained with figures taken directly from official statistics. The two sets of estimates were in substantial agreement.

Selected services purchased by households in 1956 (see *SC 1957,* p. 11) were distributed in percentages as follows (the list in the cited source was both more comprehensive and more detailed than the selected portion shown here):

Transport	63.4
Communications	5.3
Recreation and holidays	1.7
Entertainment	13.0
Rent	7.6
Utilities	9.0
Total	100.0

Our estimate of 1956 cash rent at 742 million zlotys (see Appendix Table A4) implies a total value of 9,763 million zlotys for the listed services. The following checks comparing the values of specific items as derived from our estimate of cash rent and the detailed percentage distribution of expenditures given in *SC 1957*, p. 11, and as derived from other official statistics support our estimated total:

a. The value of electricity consumed by households in 1956 based on the detailed distribution given by *SC 1957* (693 million zlotys) is very close to an estimate compiled on the basis of official statistics (679 million zlotys; see notes to Appendix Table A4 below).

b. The expenditure on motion pictures in 1956 based on the above distribution (517 million zlotys) is practically identical with the officially stated receipts of movie theaters in 1956 (518 million zlotys; see *SK 1958*, p. 44).

c. The total value of services purchased by households, including rent, repairs, and goods purchased from handicraft, estimated on the basis of the distribution shown in *SC 1957*, p. 11, 12,531 million zlotys, was equal to 7.6 percent of household purchases of goods and services (*ibid.*). This was also equal to the share of free-market sales of farm products. The value of the latter was estimated separately from *DN 1956*, pp. 25 and 46, and from *SC 1957*, pp. 4–5, at 11,899 million zlotys, which is fairly close to the estimated value of services.

It may also be mentioned that our estimate of services, excluding rent and handicraft services and including professional and other services, equal to 9.9 billion zlotys, is only slightly above the figure of 9.6 billion zlotys, derived from Bogusławski, "Kilka słów o równowadze rynkowej." The extent of coverage of the latter estimate is not stated, and there is a good chance that differences in coverage may be responsible for the discrepancy.

The sales of services to households in 1956, except where stated, were estimated from the total value of services (see above) by applying to it the percentage distribution shown in *SC 1957*, p. 11. The estimates for 1954–55 were derived for the most part from 1956 figures by deflating the latter by appropriate quantity indexes. This procedure appears to be correct in view of the fact that, according to *SC 1957*, p. 2, and *RS 1960*, pp. 404 and 406, the price level of services remained practically constant in the period 1954–56.

The estimated total value of services purchased by households (see Appendix Table A3) was reduced by the value of purchases of some services (transportation, lodging) from travel allowances received by

APPENDIX TABLE A3
PURCHASES OF SERVICES BY HOUSEHOLDS
(*Million zlotys*)

	1954	1955	1956
1. Transport	5,705	5,962	6,190
2. Communications	441	477	517
3. Recreation and holidays	165	162	166
4. Entertainment	757	861	955
5. Utilities	658	751	879
6. Professional services	709	788	894
7. Other services	230	253	275
Total	8,665	9,254	9,876
8. Less: Per diem allowances	721	691	759
9. Equals: Total purchases	7,944	8,563	9,117

enterprise and government employees. The deductions we show are residuals in the total allowances (Przełaskowski, "Rozwój indywidualnego oszczędzania w krajach socjalistycznych," p. 42) after subtraction of purchases from retail trade (see Appendix Table A2, item 7, above). Detailed documentation of rows 1–7 of Appendix Table A3 follows.

Row 1. Transport was estimated as follows (in million zlotys):

	1954	1955	1956
a. Railroads	3,840	3,919	3,983
b. Air	17	22	29
c. Bus	687	745	830
d. Urban transport	693	763	810
e. Taxicabs	404	440	459
f. Other (sea, inland water)	64	73	79
Total	5,705	5,962	6,190

Rows a, b, c, and f. 1954–55 figures were estimated by extrapolating the 1956 figure by the index of passenger-kilometers derived from *RS 1960*, p. 261.

Row d. 1954–55 were estimated by extrapolating the 1956 figure by an index of passengers based on *RS 1956*, p. 262, and *RS 1960*, p. 313.

Row e. The 1956 figure was extrapolated by an index of private taxi cabs (*RS 1956*, p. 369, and *RS 1957*, pp. 211 and 410) on the assumption that the average number of passengers per taxi and average expenditure per passenger remained constant during 1954–56. Privately owned cabs accounted for over 90 percent of all cabs in 1957 (*RS 1960*, p. 313), and it was assumed that a similar ratio existed also during 1954–56.

Row 2. Communications figures were estimated as follows (in million zlotys):

	1954	1955	1956
Letters	173	193	215
Parcels	103	111	117
Money orders	60	63	68
Telegrams	72	74	78
Telephone			
Conversations	18	19	20
Rentals	15	17	19
Total	441	477	517

All of the 1954–55 figures were extrapolated from the 1956 figures by indexes obtained from *RS 1956,* pp. 218–19, *RS 1957,* p. 216, and *RS 1960,* p. 269. All telephone conversations were assumed to show the same trend as long distance conversations alone. The number of telephones rented by households was assumed to show the same trend as the total number of phones.

Row 3. The amounts for recreation and holidays were estimated as follows (in million zlotys):

	1954	1955	1956
Holidays organized by			
state travel agency	42	28	29
Workers' Holiday Fund	47	51	49
Health resorts	18	19	20
Tourism	58	64	68
Total	165	162	166

1954–55: These amounts were extrapolated from 1956 figures by indexes based on *RS 1955,* p. 257, *RS 1956,* pp. 360, 361, 374, and *RS 1957,* pp. 370, 371, 383. For tourism the number of overnight accommodations given was used for the index.

Row 4. The figures for entertainment were estimated as follows (in million zlotys):

	1954	1955	1956
a. Movies	416	455	517
b. Theaters	184	195	185
c. Circuses	26	28	29
d. Radio and television	301	346	410
Transferred to budget	260	264	314
Other	41	82	96
e. Sports	90	101	128
Total	1,017	1,125	1,269

Rows a–c. 1954–55: These amounts were extrapolated from 1956 figures by indexes based on *RS 1956,* pp. 347, 349, and *RS 1957,* pp. 360–64. Theaters in this context includes ballet, concerts, and other stage performances.

Row d. We assume that the primary expenditure on radio and television was for annual license fees that are shown separately in the category "payments to government" (see Appendix Table G1, notes to row 3B). Consequently, only those fees not transferred directly to the budget were considered as belonging to the category "purchases of services" in Appendix Table A3. The estimates for 1954–55 were extrapolated from 1956 figures by indexes based on *RS 1956,* p. 354, and *RS 1957,* p. 368.

Row e. 1954–55: These amounts were extrapolated from 1956 figures by indexes based on *RS 1956,* p. 363, and *RS 1957,* p. 373, on the assumption that expenditure on all sport events showed the same trend as the number of spectators at events organized by the central sports agency to which the above data pertain.

Row 5. Utilities were estimated as follows (in million zlotys):

	1954	1955	1956
a. Electricity	509	582	693
b. Gas	149	169	186
Total	658	751	879

Row a. 1954–55: These amounts were extrapolated from the 1956 figure by an index of electricity consumption by urban households (*RS 1956,* p. 260, and *RS 1957,* p. 253) and rural households. Consumption of rural households on farms of less than 2 hectares was taken from Poland, Głowny urząd statystyczny, *Elektryfikacja wsi 1950–1959,* p. 3, after subtraction of electricity used for production. The latter was estimated as equal to 15 percent of total consumption, based on the average annual consumption of 50 kilowatt hours per farm (Thor, "Stan elektryfikacji wsi w Polsce oraz wydatki ludności wiejskiej związane z elektryfikacją," p. 157). The amount consumed by farm households with more than 2 hectares was estimated as the product of the number of farms with electricity (*Elektryfikacja wsi 1950–1959,* p. 3) and the average consumption per household (183 kilowatt hours). Average total consumption per farm in 1958 was 233 kilowatt hours (*ibid.,* p. xxv), but average consumption for productive purposes was 50 kilowatt hours (see above). We assumed that per farm both total consumption and consumption for productive purposes remained fairly constant in the period 1954–58, and thus the figure of 183 kilowatt hours was used for the period 1954–56.

Row b. Gas consumption was extrapolated from the 1956 figure by an index based on *RS 1956,* p. 259, and *RS 1957,* p. 252.

Row 6. 1954: This amount was assumed equal to 90 percent of the 1955 figure, which was roughly the ratio between 1955 and 1956 values. 1955: This was estimated from the 1956 figure on the assumption that the income tax paid by professionals in 1955 represented the same share of gross income as in 1956 (*RS 1957,* p. 301). 1956: See Cegielski and Kucharski, "O niektórych zagadnieniach rozwoju prywatnej gospodarki miejskiej w Polsce Ludowej," p. 114.

Row 7. Other services were estimated as follows (in million zlotys):

	1954	1955	1956
1. Laundries, dry cleaning, dyeing	77	92	107
2. Hotels	109	115	121
3. Public baths	44	46	47
Total	230	253	275

Row 1. These figures were estimated roughly as the product of weight and average price per ton (see *RS 1960,* p. 315). The volume in 1954 was estimated from data shown in *RS 1956,* p. 265. We assumed there was no change in average price between 1954 and 1957.

Row 2. These amounts were estimated as the product of number of nights' lodging given by hotels (*RS 1955,* p. 183, and *RS 1960,* p. 314) and price per night averaged at 20 zlotys. The share of the private sector in 1954 was insignificant.

Row 3. These figures were estimated as the product of the number of customers in public baths (*RS 1956,* p. 264, and *RS 1960,* p. 314) and the average price, which was assumed to equal the price of a haircut (5 zlotys).

Item 3B4. Purchases from handicraft

1954–55: These amounts were estimated at 52 percent of the value of gross output in each year (*DN 1954–55,* pp. 7, 43–44).

1956: This was obtained as the difference between the value of all services, including handicraft (12,531 million zlotys) and the value of services, excluding handicraft (9,763 million zlotys; see p. 108, above). This estimate was equal to about one third of the gross output of private handicraft in 1956, a lower share than that given for 1954–55 because of the indicated underestimate of gross output in the earlier years (see *DN 1956*, p. 17).

Item 3B5. Farm consumption in kind
See Appendix Table F3.

Item 3B6. Wages in kind
See Appendix Table E1, column 6, rows II, III A, III B, III C, and III E.

Item 3B7. Military subsistence
See Appendix Table E1, column 6, row III D.

Item 3B8. Housing: cash and imputed gross rent
Cash and imputed gross rentals are shown in Appendix Table A4 and explained in the notes thereto. They were estimated by multiplying space occupied at the end of each year by average annual rentals. A more refined procedure would be to use the average space for year, but, while requiring additional assumptions, this refinement would result in relatively insignificant changes in the derived rent figures.

Columns 1–3. Area
Row 1. The figures for 1954–55 are residuals after subtracting from the total area the space occupied by farm population. The figure for 1956 is the sum of residential housing proper (151.0 million square meters; see Litterer, "W sprawie czynszów źródeł finansowania gospodarki zasobem mieszkaniowym," p. 2), plus dormitories, and so forth (4.0 million square meters; Litterer, "Szacunek zasobów mieszkaniowych użytkowanych przez ludność pozarolniczą," p. 2).

Rows 1a(1) and 1a(2). This item refers to housing supervised by local national councils, government institutions, enterprises, and social and political organizations. For 1954–55 this was the residual in total area occupied by nonagricultural population. The same result in 1955 is obtained as the product of the number of rooms (*RPG 1958*, p. 688) and the average area (17.5 square meters; Litterer, "Szacunek zasobów mieszkaniowych użytkowanych przez ludność pozarolniczą," p. 2). For 1956, see Litterer, "W sprawie czynszów i źródeł finansowania gospodarki zasobem mieszkaniowym," p. 2.

Row 1a(3). 1954–55: These figures were estimated from 1955 and 1956 figures, respectively, by subtracting new construction dur-

APPENDIX TABLE A4
GROSS RENT, CASH AND IMPUTED

	(1)	(2)	(3)	(4)	(5)	(6)
		AREA (million square meters)			GROSS RENT (million zlotys)	
	1954	1955	1956	1954	1955	1956
1. Nonagricultural population	148.4	151.5	155.0	1,208	1,229	1,255
a. Socialized sector	68.3	71.1	74.0	436	453	470
(1) National councils	64.1*	66.5*	59.2	419*	435*	382
(2) State enterprises and institutions			9.6			68
(3) Cooperatives	1.0	1.1	1.2	17	18	20
(4) Workers' hostels, etc.	3.2	3.5	4.0			
b. Private sector	80.1	80.4	81.0	772	776	785
(1) Non-owner-occupied	40.2	40.2	40.0	273	273	272
(2) Owner-occupied	39.9	40.2	41.0	499	503	513
2. Agricultural population	104.1	104.5	105.0	1,246	1,248	1,248
a. State farm sector	4.4	4.7	5.2			
b. Private and cooperative sectors	99.7	99.8	99.8	1,246	1,248	1,248
3. Total	252.5	256.0	260.0	2,454	2,477	2,503
a. Cash				709	726	742
b. Imputed (1b(2) and 2b(2))				1,745	1,751	1,761

* Includes 1a(2); see table notes for rows 1a(1) and 1a(2).

ing 1955 and 1956 (*RS 1959,* p. 163) converted at the ratio of 17.5 square meters per room. Since cooperative housing was a relatively recent phenomenon, it was assumed that no significant retirement of housing occurred. 1956: See *RS 1959,* p. 269, and Litterer, "W sprawie czynsów i źródeł finansowania gospodarki zasobem mieszkaniowym," p. 2.

Row 1a(4). 1954: This was estimated from 1955 figures by subtracting new construction during 1955 (*RS 1959,* p. 162) on the assumption that no significant retirement of space occurred. 1955: See *RPG 1958,* p. 686. 1956: See Litterer, "Szacunek zasobów mieszkaniowych użytkowanych przez ludność pozarolniczą," p. 2.

Row 1b(1). 1954: This was assumed equal to the 1955 figure. 1955: *RPG 1958,* p. 688, showed private non-owner-occupied housing accounting for 2.3 million rooms. We converted this at the ratio of 17.5 square meters per room (Litterer, "W sprawie czynszów i źródeł finansowania gospodarki zasobem mieszkaniowym," p. 2). 1956: *Ibid.*

Row 1b(2). 1954: This was estimated from the 1955 figure by subtracting new construction during 1955 (*RS 1959,* p. 163) converted at the ratio of 17.5 square meters per room. We assumed that retirement of space was insignificant. 1955: *RPG 1958,* p. 688, shows private owner-occupied housing space equal to non-owner-occupied housing space (row 1b(1) above). 1956: Litterer, "W sprawie czynszów i źródeł finansowania gospodarki zasobem mieszkaniowym," p. 2.

Row 2. 1954: This was estimated from the 1955 figure by subtracting new construction during 1955 (98.9 thousand rooms; *RS 1959,* p. 163) and adding retired space (41.8 thousand rooms; see Skałuba, "Sytuacja mieszkaniowa na wsi w końcu 1955," p. 14) and rooms in rural areas incorporated into cities during 1955 (33.0 thousand rooms, the annual average during 1950–55 derived from Litterer, "Szacunek zasobów mieszkaniowych użytkowanych przez ludność pozarolniczą," p. 2). We converted rooms at 17.5 square meters per room. 1955: This figure represents the total space in rural areas (132.5 million square meters; *RPG 1958,* p. 686) less space occupied by the nonfarm population (1.6 million rooms, *RPG 1958,* pp. 686, 688), converted at 17.5 square meters to a room. 1956: This is the residual in total occupied space after subtraction of space occupied by nonfarm population.

Row 2a. This category was estimated as follows:

	Resident Employment (thousand persons)	Dependents (thousand persons)	Space Occupied (million square meters)
1954	230.1	271.5	4.4
1955	243.9	287.8	4.7
1956	270.9	319.7	5.2

Resident employment was assumed to represent the same share of total employment on state farms as in the case of state farms (*PGR*) supervised by the Ministry of Agriculture (Poland, Główny urząd statystyczny, *Statystyka rolnictwa 1946–1957*, p. 189). Total employment (permanent and seasonal) on all state farms was obtained by subtracting employment in state and communal MTS (*ibid.*, p. 237) from employment in socialized agriculture (*RS 1961*, p. 44).

Dependents were estimated by means of the 1950 ratio of dependents per farm employee (1.18) as shown in *RS 1957*, p. 27.

Space occupied was estimated on the basis of 2.0 persons per room (see Skałuba, "Sytuacja mieszkaniowa na wsi w końcu 1955," p. 12) and 17.5 square meters per room.

Row 2b. This represents the total space occupied by the farm population less the state farm sector.

Row 3. 1954: This was estimated from the 1955 figure by subtracting new construction during 1955 (*RS 1959*, p. 162) and adding retirement of urban housing (17.0 thousand rooms, equal to the 1950–55 average, shown in Litterer, "Szacunek zasobów mieszkaniowych użytkowanych przez ludność pozarolniczą," p. 2) and rural housing (41.8 thousand rooms, Skałuba, Sytuacja mieszkaniowa na wsi w końcu 1955," p. 14), converted at 17.5 square meters per room. 1955: See *RPG 1958*, p. 686. 1956; Computed from the 1955 figure by adding new construction during 1956 (*RS 1959*, p. 162) and subtracting retirement of space, taken equal to 1955 (see above).

Columns 4–6. Gross rent

Gross rent was obtained by multiplying individual categories of housing by the respective average annual rents per square meter. From among several official and other sources giving rental rates, we chose those having the most comprehensive coverage (given implicitly by Andrzejewski, *Polityka mieszkaniowa*, p. 328). Although these rates refer to urban socialized housing in 1957, it appears that during the period 1953–57 they did not change (see *RS 1960*, p. 404).

The average annual rates in zlotys per square meter were as follows:

National councils	6.45
State enterprises and institutions	7.06
Cooperatives	16.67
Private non-owner-occupied	6.80
Private owner-occupied	12.50

Gross rent in the state sector in 1954–55 was estimated by using the weighted average rent in state housing in 1956 (6.54 zlotys per square meter for the combined national councils and state enterprises and institutions).

We used 12.50 zlotys per square meter for the imputation of gross rent in farm dwellings.

We excluded state farm housing, hostels, and so forth, from our estimate of gross rent, either because this space was taken into account in connection with wages in kind in the household sector appropriation account or because the amounts were nominal.

Item 3C1. Dues paid to quasi-governmental organizations
See Appendix Table G5, row 5.

Items 3C2. Direct taxes and 3C3. Transfers
See Appendix Table G1, rows 1B and 3B.

Item 3C4. Social security contributions
See Table 1A, item 2C.

Item 4. Saving
This is the balancing item between receivables and payables.

NOTES TO TABLE 1C

Item 1. Saving
This item was transferred from the household appropriation account.

Item 2. Transfers from foreign sector
See Table 4C, item 4.

Item 3. Lending to enterprise sector
This item represents increments in savings deposits (see W.

Przełaskowski, "Rozwój indywidualnego oszczędzania w krajach socjalistycznych," p. 24).

Item 4. Transfers to enterprise sector
This is the balancing item between payables and receivables.

APPENDIX B: NOTES TO ECONOMIC ENTERPRISE SECTOR ACCOUNTS (TABLES 2A, 2B, AND 2C)

NOTES TO TABLE 2A

Item 1A. Sales to household appropriation account
See Table 1B, item 3B.

Item 1B. Sales to government production account
See Table 3A, item 4.

Item 1C. Sales to government capital account
See Appendix Table G2, row 7.

Item 1D. Sales to enterprise sector capital account
See Table 2C, items 6A and 6B.

Item 1E. Sales to foreign sector
See Table 4A, item 3.

Item 2. Inventory changes
See Table 2C, item 6C.

Item 3. Subsidy receipts, excluding foreign trade
See Table 3B, item 4, and notes thereto.

Item 3A. State farms
Subsidy receipts of state farms were estimated as follows (in million zlotys):

	1954	1955	1956
1. State farms proper (PGR)	2,303	3,502	
2. Plus: Other state farms	100	122	
3. Equals: All state farms	2,403	3,624	3,865

Row 1. Poland, Główny urząd statystyczny, *Państwowe gospodarstwa rolne w 1956 roku*, p. xv.

Row 2. 1954: This is a round figure taken roughly on the same order of magnitude as the 1955 figure. 1955: This is the residual in total state farm subsidies.

Row 3. 1954: Sum of rows 1 and 2. 1955–56: Poland, Główny urząd statystyczny, *Produkcja globalna i brutto rolnictwa przed wojną i w latach 1946–1958*, p. 27.

Item 3B. MTS
MTS subsidies were estimated as follows (in million zlotys):

	1954	1955	1956
1. State MTS (POM)	609	670	962
2. Plus: Communal MTS (GOM)	102	114	161
3. Equals: All MTS	711	784	1,123

Row 1. Total expenditure (Appendix Table G2, row 3A) less total revenue (Appendix Table G1, row 2A).

Row 2. Poland, Główny urząd statystyczny, *Państwowe i gminne ośrodki maszynowe w 1956 roku*, p. 22.

Item 3C. Other enterprises
This represents the residual in total subsidies.

Item 4. Purchases from foreign sector
See Table 4A, item 1.

Item 5A. Turnover tax and positive budget differences, excluding foreign trade
This is the sum of rows 1A(1)a1, 1A(1)a3, 1A(1)a4, and 1A(1)b1 in Appendix Table G1 and turnover tax paid by enterprises on exported goods (see Appendix Table D1).

Item 5B. Other indirect taxes
This is the sum of rows 1A(1)a5, 1A(1)b2, 1A(1)b3, 1A(1)b4 and 1A(1)b5 in Appendix Table G1.

Item 6. Capital consumption allowances
These figures were estimated on the basis of the official Polish formula in which capital consumption allowances are equal to gross investment plus capital repairs less net investment (see *DN 1956*, p.

45). From the total capital consumption figure thus derived we subtracted estimated capital consumption on private and collective farms, since the latter apparently is an imputed figure that does not correspond to actual money flows. There is good reason to believe that private farmers and the collective farms on the whole made no formal provision for capital consumption but instead used all their income for current consumption and saving. Our estimate is shown in detail below (in million zlotys):

	1954	1955	1956
1. Gross investment	36,990	39,041	51,686
2. Capital repairs	6,259	7,404	10,650
3. Net investment	28,452	29,505	37,251
4. Capital consumption	14,797	16,940	25,085
5. Imputed capital consumption on private and collective farms	3,951	4,442	4,453
6. Other capital consumption	10,846	12,498	20,632

Row 1. *SIB 1956,* p. viii.

Row 2. 1954: This amount was estimated by deflating the 1955 estimate by the index linking the value of capital repairs in the socialized sector in both years in 1956 prices (118.3, as shown in *SIB 1958,* p. 7). There was no change in the average cost of investment between 1954 and 1955 (see *SIB 1956,* pp. viii and 2). 1955: This represents total expenditure on gross investment and capital repairs (*DN 1956,* p. 51) less gross investment shown in row 1. 1956: *DN 1956,* p. 46.

Row 3. 1954: This amount was estimated by deflating the 1955 estimate by the index linking net investment in both years in 1956 prices (103.7, as shown in *Wiadomości statystyczne,* III, No. 1 [January-February, 1958], p. i). The index of investment costs remained unchanged between 1954 and 1955. 1955–56: *DN 1956,* p. 14.

Row 4. Row 1 less the sum of rows 2 and 3.

Row 5. See Appendix Table F1.

Row 6. Row 4 less row 5.

Items 7A1. Cash wages and salaries; 7A2. Social security contributions; 7A3. Wages in kind

See Appendix Table E1, row II, columns 5 to 7.

Item 7B. Interest payments to households

See Table 1B, item 2A(4).

Item 7C. Profits and incomes of self-employed
This was obtained as the balancing item between receivables and payables.

NOTES TO TABLE 2B

Item 1. Value added by sector
Transferred from enterprise production account.

Item 2. Transfer receipts from government
See Appendix Table G2, row 4b.

Item 3. Compensation of employees (cash and in kind)
See Appendix Table E1, row II, column *4*.

Item 4. Social security contributions
See Appendix Table E1, row II, column *7*.

Item 5. Interest payments to households
See Table 1B, item 2A(4).

Items 6. Direct Taxes; 7. Transfers to government
See Appendix Table G1, rows 1A(2) and 3A.

Items 8. Incomes of self-employed; 9. Farm consumption in kind; 10. Farm income; 11. Profits distributed to members of nonagricultural cooperatives
See Table 1B, items 2A(1)b, 2A(2)b, 2A(1)c, and 2A(3).

Item 12. Retained earnings
This is the balancing item between receivables and payables. It includes the increment to livestock in agriculture; see *DN 1956,* pp. 23, 25, for 1955–56 values at free market prices (in million zlotys): *1955,* 831; *1956,* 1,319. Our rough estimate for *1954,* 950, was derived by applying price and quantity indexes to the 1955–56 data and rounding the result (indexes based on *SIB 1958,* p. 186, and Poland, Główny urząd statystyczny, *Produkcja globalna i brutto rolnictwa przed wojną i w latach 1946–1958,* p. 9). There are two components in these increments: (i) the change in the basic, or reproductive, stock, which is included in the Polish official figures on fixed capital investment, and (ii) the change in the turnover, or

fattening, stock, which is included in the official figures on changes in inventories. In millions of zlotys, current prices, the former amounted to: *1954,* 593; *1955,* 797; and *1956,* 489 (*SIB 1958,* p. 186), and the latter (obtained as the residual in each year) to: *1954,* 357; *1955,* 34; and *1956,* 830.

NOTES TO TABLE 2C

Item 1. Retained earnings
See Table 2B, item 12.

Item 2. Capital consumption allowances
See Table 2A, item 6.

Item 3. Capital transfers from government
See Appendix Table G2, rows 8 and 9a.

Item 4. Borrowing from households
See Table 1C, item 3.

Item 5. Capital transfers from households
See Table 1C, item 4.

Item 6A. Additions to fixed capital
These amounts were estimated as follows (in million zlotys):

	1954	1955	1956
1. Total fixed capital investment	36,990	39,041	51,686
2. Less: Fixed capital investment in government sector	3,837	4,063	5,159
3. Equals: Fixed capital investment in enterprises	33,153	34,978	46,527

Row 1. *SIB 1956,* p. viii.
Row 2. Appendix Table G2, row 7a.

Item 6B. Capital repairs
These were estimated as follows (in million zlotys):

	1954	1955	1956
1. Total expenditure on capital repairs	6,259	7,404	10,650
2. Expenditure on capital repairs in government sector	992	1,130	1,574
3. Expenditure on capital repairs in enterprises	5,267	6,274	9,076

Row 1. See notes to Table 2A, item 6.
Row 2. See Appendix Table G2, row 7b.
Row 3. Row 1 less row 2.

Item 6C. Increase in inventories
1954–55: *DN 1954–55,* p. 3; 1956: *DN 1956,* p. 14. The change
in inventories for 1954 and 1955 was calculated at "average prices"
and for 1956 at prices in effect at the beginning of the year according
to the indicated sources. The figures we show are changes in stocks
(*zapasy*) and reserves (*rezerwy*), the former presumably representing business inventories and the latter apparently state reserves (see
Zienkowski, *Jak oblicza się dochód narodowy,* 1st ed., p. 65). Zwass,
"Rola bodźców ekonomicznych w prawidłowym kształtowaniu zapasów," *WNBP,* 1958, No. 3, p. 112, gives the increase in business
inventories as follows (in million zlotys): *1954, 9,900; 1955, 11,000;
1956, 7,600.* State reserves apparently account for the balance of
the total changes in inventories.

Item 7. Capital transfers to government
This is the balancing item between payables and receivables.
Within this sum we can identify transfers of working capital and
surplus depreciation funds shown in Appendix Table G1, row 6. The
residual is unidentified and is considered an imputed transfer to
balance the account.

Item 8. Lending to government
See Appendix Table G1, row 5A.

APPENDIX C: NOTES TO GOVERNMENT SECTOR ACCOUNTS (TABLES 3A, 3B, AND 3C)

NOTES TO TABLE 3A

Item 1. Value of government services
This is the sum of the cash items on the payable side of the account.

Item 2. Compensation of employees
See Appendix Table E1, row III, columns *4, 5,* and *6.*

Item 3. Social security contributions
See Appendix Table E1, row III, column 7.

Item 4. Current purchases from enterprises
This is the sum of purchases by government (Appendix Table G2, row 6A, column 6) and of purchases by quasi-governmental organizations (Appendix Table G5, row 4).

Item 5. Net purchases from foreign sector
In the absence of more complete information, we assumed that government purchases from the foreign sector (Appendix Table G2, row 6b, column 6) were exactly offset by government sales to the foreign sector.

NOTES TO TABLE 3B

Item 1A. Indirect tax receipts
The totals shown in Appendix Table G1, row 1A(1) were adjusted by adding the estimated turnover tax rebated on exports and sub-

tracting the positive budget differences realized from foreign trade (see Appendix D, Notes to Table 4A, item 1, and summary, Appendix Table D1) as follows (in million zlotys):

	1954	1955	1956
Indirect taxes	75,258	80,271	80,931
Turnover tax rebates on exports	10,000	10,000	8,100
Positive budget differences from foreign trade	12,200	15,400	25,800
Adjusted indirect tax receipts	73,058	74,871	63,231

Items 1B. Direct tax receipts; 1C. Social security contributions
See Appendix Table G1, rows 1B, 1A(2), and 4.

Item 1D. Dues paid to quasi-governmental organizations
See Table 1B, item 3C1.

Item 1E. Transfers
See Appendix Table G1, rows 3A and 3B.

Item 2. Purchase from government production account
See Table 3A, item 1.

Item 3A. Transfers to households
See Table 1B, item 2B(3) and notes thereto.

Item 3B. Transfers to enterprises
See Appendix Table G2, row 4b, column 6.

Item 4. Subsidies to enterprise sector, excluding foreign trade
These subsidies were estimated as follows (in million zlotys):

	1954	1955	1956
1. Subsidies to budget enterprises	1,059	1,165	1,562
2. Subsidies to other enterprises	11,500	15,924	13,127
Total	12,559	17,089	14,689

Row 1. These figures represent total expenditure (Appendix Table G2, row 3) less total revenue (Appendix Table G1, row 2).
Row 2. See Appendix Table G2, row 2b.

Item 5. Saving
This is the balancing item between receivables and payables.

NOTES TO TABLE 3C

Item 1. Saving
See Table 3B, item 5.

Item 2. Capital transfers from enterprise sector
See Table 2C, item 7.

Item 3. Borrowing from enterprises
See Appendix Table G1, row 5A.

Item 4. Government investment
See Appendix Table G2, row 7, column 6.

Item 5A. Capital transfers to enterprise sector
See Appendix Table G2, rows 8 and 9a, column 6.

Items 5B. Capital transfers to foreign sector (net); 6. Net lending to foreign sector
See Table 4C, items 1 and 2.

APPENDIX D: NOTES TO FOREIGN SECTOR ACCOUNTS (TABLES 4A, 4B, AND 4C)

NOTES TO TABLE 4A

Item 1. Imports

We present here and in summary form in Appendix Table D1 below estimates of commercial imports and exports in domestic zlotys and the related figures of turnover tax and budget differences. Because the data are more complete for 1956, we shall begin with that year and use our results to guide our calculations for 1955 and 1954, which follow in that order.

1956: Unfortunately the Polish sources of data on foreign trade are often conflicting; no single choice of figures can be consistent with the values and relationships appearing in all of these sources. Our solution was chosen with a view toward consistency with some of the firm figures and relationships at the cost of conflict with other data. The range of conflict, however, is small. We shall discuss the devisa (foreign-exchange) zloty values of imports to illustrate the problem.

The values of 1956 imports and exports in devisa zlotys differ in the Polish official sources. Thus *BS 1957,* No. 2, p. 23, and the official announcement of foreign trade plan fulfillment given in *Handel zagraniczny,* 1957, No. 2, p. 27, show (in billion zlotys) exports and imports equal to 3.9 and 3.6, respectively, while the official statistical yearbooks, beginning with *RS 1957,* p. 243, give figures of 3.9 and 4.1, respectively. Hence, an export surplus apparent in the first instance becomes an import surplus in the second. It is interesting to note that the Polish official national income calculations, *DN 1954–55,* p. 3, and *DN 1956,* p. 14—the latter published in July, 1958—show an export surplus based on the values in devisa zlotys, and the 1957 statistical yearbook (*RS 1957*) on p. 56, gives the same figures as *DN 1956* but on p. 240 shows an import surplus. Clearly there was either some failure to coordinate the two sections of the yearbook or there was some revision of import statistics that was not considered relevant to the national income calculations.

An examination of the detailed statistics as they appear in *BS 1957* and *RS 1957* shows that the major change in figures was in machinery imports from the USSR and, to a much lesser extent, from Czechoslovakia. Export statistics were changed only slightly. We are at a loss to explain the increase in value of machinery imports (439 million foreign-exchange zlotys, of which 391 million zlotys was in Soviet trade), particularly since the communiqué on 1956 plan fulfillment issued by the Ministry of Foreign Trade (*Handel zagraniczny*, 1957, No. 2, pp. 27–28) makes specific mention of the decline of imports of machinery and other investment goods as occurring with the agreement of the investors. A comparison of the content of the machinery, equipment, and transportation equipment category, where the total change in the value of imports occurred (see *BS 1957*, No. 2, p. 24, and *RS 1957*, p. 242), shows no change in values in the incomplete list of detailed subcategories. Evidently either some *ex post facto* adjustment was made in total values without any real change in goods received, or some actual—also perhaps *ex post facto*—additional transfers of goods occurred to account for the difference in total values.

Lacking information, we can only speculate on the cause of the upward revision of the value of machinery imports. It may well be connected with the Moscow Agreement of November, 1956, following the Polish October demonstrations against the USSR. Krynicki (*Problemy handlu zagranicznego Polski*, note to Table 5) mentions taking account of changes in realized prices in Polish trade statistics for 1947–55, brought about by the Moscow Agreement. How this Agreement might cause a rise in the value of 1956 Polish imports is not clear; perhaps it involved a transfer of military equipment or other machinery or investment goods as a concession to Polish economic claims against the USSR. Such information as we have suggests that the adjustments were made in 1957.

Normally we would choose the more recent official sources, but, in view of the conflicts, we chose the figures given in *BS 1957*, No. 2, and *Handel zagraniczny 1957*, No. 2, as reflecting the actual current 1956 transactions in devisa zlotys. These figures are consistent with the export surplus indicated in *DN 1956*. We return now to our estimates for 1956.

We took 28.4 billion zlotys as the value of exports in current domestic prices from E. Krzeczkowska, *et al.*, in *Ekonomista*, 1958, No. 1, p. 116. *DN 1956*, pp. 13–14, shows for externally balanced, or compensating, trade that the domestic value of imports exceeds that of exports by 3.8 billion zlotys and, at the same time, that the surplus of exports over imports in foreign-exchange zlotys is equivalent to 2.4 billion domestic zlotys. Taken together, these data imply that in domestic prices total imports exceeded total exports by 1.4 billion zlotys. Thus, total imports were estimated at 28.4 plus 1.4, or 29.8, billion domestic zlotys, a figure slightly lower than that given by Krzeczkowska, *et al.*

In order to relate the foreign trade estimates to the state budget, we needed estimates of turnover tax rebates and budget differences arising from the profits and losses of the foreign-trade organization in connection with differences in prices expressed in devisa zlotys and domestic zlotys. Because of lack of information, our estimates based on the preceding estimates of imports and exports and on certain assumptions spelled out below may have a substantial margin of error; yet these estimates are essential to an analysis of the government budget.

In calculating the positive foreign-trade budget differences accruing to the revenues of the state budget, we assumed that these differences appeared as the result of the high domestic prices at which imports were sold and the low devisa zloty costs of the imports and transportation and other charges. Zienkowski (*Jak oblicza się dochód narodowy*, 1st ed., pp. 89–94) sketched the method of calculation but did not indicate whether imports and exports were valued in devisa zlotys at c.i.f. or f.o.b. Essentially the calculation treats a domestic zloty and a devisa zloty on a 1 to 1 basis, and the difference between the domestic and the "world" price level leads to profits or losses in the form of budget differences that enter the state budget on a gross basis.

We assumed that the above estimated 29.8 billion zlotys of imports in domestic prices was equal to the sum of 3.6 billion devisa zlotys, given by *BS 1957*, No. 2, p. 23, plus estimated freight and other costs (see below) plus the gross profits realized on the sale of the imports in Poland.

Freight charges were estimated as follows. Krynicki (*Problemy handlu zagranicznego Polski*, p. 202) stated that beginning in 1952 all foreign-trade statistics compiled by the Ministry of Foreign Trade recorded the value in devisa rubles (equal 1 to 1 to devisa zlotys) at prices f.o.b. for both imports and exports. Also *Handel zagraniczny*, 1957, No. 2, p. 19, indicated that Polish transactions were concluded c.i.f. as of the port of destination and that the settlement of freight charges took place partly in free foreign currencies and partly on the basis of clearings. This would seem to imply that Polish shipping entered the calculation on the basis of devisa zlotys; see also *ibid.*, 1957, No. 5, p. 29. Freight and other charges on imports were estimated roughly at 5 percent of the f.o.b. value of imports on the basis of the Hungarian Central Statistical Office import statistics given in its *Statisztikai Évkönyv* 1949/55, p. 255, and its *Adatok és Ádalékok a népgazdaság fejlödésének tanulmányozásához 1949–55*, pp. 255, 297, 318–32.

Subtracting the devisa-zloty values of imports and freight from the domestic value of the imports, we obtained 26 billion zlotys gross profit on imports. We reduced this amount by 0.2 billion zlotys as a rough allowance for the operational costs of the foreign-trade organizations on the basis of the net margin in 1955 shown in *DN 1954–55*, p. 20, and considered the balance, 25.8 billion zlotys, as representing positive budget differences received by the state budget. This figure accounts for about 92 percent of the 28.1 billion zlotys total positive budget differences received by the budget in 1956 as given in *RS 1957*, p. 290.

Similarly, from the 28.4 billion zlotys domestic value of exports we subtracted 3.9 billion devisa zlotys representing the receipts from the sale of the exports abroad (see *RS 1957*, p. 240) and obtained a residual of 24.5 billion domestic zlotys covering 8.1 billion of rebated turnover tax on industrial products exported (see below) and balance of 16.4 billion of negative budget differences.

Our figure for turnover-tax rebates is based on data given in *DN 1954–55*, p. 9, and *DN 1956*, p. 19. In the earlier publication the net value of socialized industrial production for 1955 is given exclusive of turnover tax on exports, whereas in the later publication it is given including this tax. A detailed comparison of the components of total value shown in these sources, particularly budget differences and profits, indicated that the 9.9 billion zlotys labeled "profit-loss (balance)" was accounted for almost entirely by turnover-tax rebates. A small amount of loss also appeared to enter the figure, and accordingly we rounded it to 10 billion zlotys. For lack of better means, we assumed that the corresponding figure for 1956, 8.1 billion zlotys (also rounded), shown in a parallel column in *DN 1956,* p. 19, was a fair approximation to turnover-tax rebates for that year.

1955: DN 1954/55, p. 20, shows the foreign-trade turnover in 1955 equal to 34.5 billion zlotys, in which (according to *DN 1954 /55* p. v) imports were valued in domestic sale prices (*ceny zbytu*) which include turnover tax, whereas industrial exports were valued at factory prices, which exclude turnover tax. Transportation costs on exports, probably the costs from the factory to the Polish customs boundary, were added to the factory price of exports in the calculation of the so-called "balance of trade," which refers to the difference in domestic prices of the externally equal, or compensating, imports and exports, and in the determination of the so-called "credit balance of foreign trade" (shown in *DN 1954/55,* pp. vi, vii, 3), which refers to the externally unbalanced import and export surplus converted into domestic prices.

The trade turnover, 34.5 billion zlotys, less the "credit balance of foreign trade," 0.4 billion zlotys import surplus (*DN 1954/55,* p. 3), gave 34.1 billion zlotys as the sum in domestic zlotys of externally balanced imports and exports. Moreover, these imports minus exports equals 3.9 billion domestic zlotys (*DN 1954/55,* p. 3). Taken together, these equations representing the externally compensating trade imply that imports in sale prices were equal to 19 billion zlotys and that exports in factory prices were equal to 15.1 billion zlotys. Adding from *DN 1956,* p. 14, 0.5 billion zlotys import surplus (which is slightly higher than in *DN 1954/55,* possibly on account of more complete coverage), we obtained 19.5 billion zlotys as the total imports in domestic prices.

The value for exports in 1955, 15.1 billion zlotys, was increased by 10.0 billion zlotys of turnover tax on industrial products (see the discussion for 1956 above) to give 25.1 billion zlotys as the value of exports at domestic sale prices. Within this total, besides the turnover tax, we identified 3.7 billion zlotys as the yield in foreign-exchange zlotys on exports (*RS 1956,* p. 249) and the balance of 11.4 billion zlotys as negative budget differences.

Following the same procedure as we used in our estimates for 1956, we equated the 19.5 billion zlotys of total imports in domestic prices to 3.7 billion devisa zlotys of imports f.o.b. as of the port or boundary of the supplier (as shown in *RS 1956,* p. 249), plus 0.2 billion devisa zlotys (about 5 percent of the f.o.b. value of the imports, the same figure as in 1956, above) for freight and other charges, plus 15.6 billion zlotys of gross profit realized on the imports. We allowed 0.2 billion zlotys of these profits to operational costs of the foreign-trade enterprises and considered the balance, 15.4 billion zlotys, as positive budget differences paid into the state budget in 1955. There is room for such a sum in the 19.3 billion zlotys total positive budget differences shown among budget revenues for 1955 in *RS 1956*, p. 296.

1954: Our estimates for 1954 follow the methods applied for 1955 and 1956 insofar as the available data permit. *DN 1954/55*, p. 20, shows 31.3 billion zlotys total turnover, imports apparently in sale prices and exports in factory prices plus internal transportation costs, but excluding turnover tax. The "credit balance" of trade, 0.3 billion zlotys (shown in *DN 1954/55*, p. 3), signifying an import surplus, was subtracted from this figure, leaving 31.0 billion domestic zlotys as the sum of the externally compensated imports and exports. This relationship, together with the 0.9 billion zlotys difference in the domestic value of the externally compensated imports and exports given in *DN 1954/55*, p. 3, implies that the domestic value of the externally compensated imports was about 15.9 billion zlotys, and of exports, 15 billion zlotys. Total imports in domestic sale prices, 16.2 billion zlotys, were obtained by adding the 0.3 billion zlotys of the import "credit balance" of trade to the 15.9 billion zlotys internal value of the imports compensated externally by exports.

Positive budget differences, estimated at 12.2 billion zlotys, were obtained by subtracting from the 16.2 billion zlotys of total imports, a total of 4 billion zlotys covering (*a*) 3.6 billion devisa zlotys of imports shown in *RS 1955*, p. 177, (*b*) 0.2 billion devisa zlotys for transportation and other charges on imports estimated as in 1955–56 at 5 percent of the f.o.b. value, and (*c*) 0.2 billion zlotys operational costs of the foreign trade enterprises (the same figure as in 1955–56).

Negative budget differences on exports were estimated at 11.5 billion zlotys by subtracting the devisa zloty value of exports, 3.5 billion (given in *RS 1955*, p. 177), from the domestic value at factory prices plus transportation, which was derived above. Turnover tax rebates, in the absence of information, were estimated at 10.0 billion zlotys, the same level as in 1955, since the domestic value of exports in 1954 before the tax was about the same as in 1955. The value of exports at sale prices therefore was estimated at 25.0 billion zlotys.

Our estimates of imports and exports and the related budget differences and turnover tax rebates are summarized in Appendix Table D1.

APPENDIX TABLE D1
POLISH FOREIGN TRADE ESTIMATES
(*Billion zlotys*)

	1954	1955	1956
Devisa zloty totals, f.o.b.			
Imports	3.6	3.7	3.6
Exports	3.5	3.7	3.9
Domestic zloty totals			
Imports, sale prices, c.i.f.	16.2	19.5	29.8
Exports, sale prices, f.o.b.	25.0	25.1	28.4
Positive budget differences	12.2	15.4	25.8
Negative budget differences	11.5	11.4	16.4
Turnover tax rebates on exports	10.0	10.0	8.1

Item 2. Balance on production account
This is the balancing item between receivables and payables.

Item 3A. Commercial exports
This was estimated in item 1, above, in connection with imports.

Item 3B. Transit services (net)
According to *Trybuna ludu,* September 30, 1956, the USSR was paying Poland a sum of $20 million (80 million devisa zlotys) annually for transit services rendered by Poland. We converted this amount into domestic zlotys by using for each year the conversion factor established below (see note on item 3C, maritime services). We assumed that there were no net earnings from transit services exchanged with other countries.

Item 3C. Maritime services
Service earnings of the Polish merchant marine for 1954 and 1955 were estimated on the basis of Wesołowski, "Usługi morskie w bilansie rozrachunkowym i płatniczym," p. 22. The following items from Wesołowski's tables were included (in million devisa zlotys):

	1954	1955
Port fees	9.6	10.7
Loading, unloading and storage	7.8	8.9
Commissions	3.9	4.3
Repairs	.4	.3
Other port services	4.8	4.6
Transport services	50.1	68.6
Other services, including insurance	47.3	88.1
Total	123.9	185.5

To estimate service earnings of the Polish merchant marine in 1956 we used information from *Handel zagraniczny,* 1957, No. 5, p. 29, where the actual earnings on transportation in Polish ships were given at 119.4 percent of their 1955 level. We assumed that total credits on maritime services calculated by us rose between 1955 and 1956 by 19.4 percent, or by the same ratio as earnings from transportation in Polish ships. We thus obtained for 1956 a figure of 221.5 million devisa zlotys as income on maritime service account.

To convert the devisa zloty figures estimated above into current domestic zlotys we used the ratios of devisa zlotys to domestic zlotys manifested in imports of goods, as derived in our calculation of Polish foreign trade (see Appendix Table D1). Thus, in domestic zlotys (millions) these maritime earnings were estimated as follows: *1954,* 558; *1955,* 983; and *1956,* 1,838.

NOTES TO TABLE 4B

Item 1. Surplus of nation on current account
   See Table 4A, item 2.

Item 2. Balance on production account
   See Table 4A, item 2.

NOTES TO TABLE 4C

Item 1. Net transfers from government
   Our calculation is based on figures (in billion zlotys) derived in the foreign sector production account (see Appendix Table D1):

	1954	*1955*	*1956*
Turnover tax rebates on exports	10.0	10.0	8.1
Plus: Negative budget differences on exports	11.5	11.4	16.4
Less: Positive budget differences on imports	12.2	15.4	25.8
Net capital transfers to foreign sector	9.3	6.0	− 1.3

Item 2. Net lending to rest of the world by government
   This was obtained as the balancing item between payables and receivables.

Item 3. Surplus of nation on current account
   This item was transferred from the foreign sector appropriation account (Table 4B, item 1).

Item 4. Transfers to household sector
This item was estimated as follows (in million zlotys):

	1954	*1955*	*1956*
Gifts delivered through PKO	370	618	998
Cash payments received from abroad	180	307	502
Total	550	925	1,500

The values of gifts delivered through PKO (see above, p. 31) in foreign-exchange zlotys, found in *Handel zagraniczny,* 1957, No. 2, p. 22 and No. 4, p. 18, were converted into domestic prices at the rate of 1:25, roughly estimated by comparing PKO price lists with Polish retail prices.

Cash payments received by Polish citizens from abroad include such items as pensions, bequests, honorariums. They were estimated at roughly one third of total transfers shown above. In 1958 gifts were valued at 10.9 million dollars (Frankel, "Lekceważone źródło dewiz," p. 6) and accounted for slightly more than one half of all net noncommercial transfers, 18.6 million dollars (Wyźnikiewicz, "O dalszy rozwój eksportu niewidocznego," p. 19). Since these included also transfers other than personal, the share of gifts in total transfers to households was likely to be considerably higher than one half.

APPENDIX E: NATIONAL WAGE BILL

Wages and salaries paid to employees in each of the major sectors —households, enterprises, and government—consisted of three components:

a. Personal wage fund (*osobowy fundusz płac*) defined in Polish statistics as embracing regular payments of wages and salaries in cash and in kind, remuneration of paid vacations, and other payments resulting from collective work agreements.

b. Nonpersonal wage fund (*bezosobowy fundusz płac*) embracing author's fees and honorariums, as well as various lump-sum payments for commissioned work to personnel not regularly employed by a given enterprise or institution, such as consultants and research workers.

c. Other wage-like payments, including military pay and subsistence pay of internal security troops, secret police, and prison guards, and such items as commissions earned by employees of state trading enterprises, prizes, payments out of director's fund, and other payments not otherwise specified that, in the official Polish sources, are included in the total wage bill in the economy.

The estimate of the total wage bill in the economy is shown in Appendix Table E1 and explained in the notes and tables.

NOTES TO APPENDIX TABLE E1

In view of the often involved estimating procedures, the entries in columns *1* to *4* were computed separately for each sector of the economy: households, enterprises and government. The totals in columns *5* to *7* were obtained for the most part as percentages of column *1* and for that reason no separate computations were necessary.

APPENDIX TABLE E1
TOTAL WAGE BILL
(Million zlotys)

1954	(1) Personal Wage Bill	(2) Nonpersonal Wage Bill	(3) Other Wage-like Payments	(4) Total 1 + 2 + 3	(5) Cash	(6) In Kind	(7) Social Security
					TOTAL WAGE BILL		
I. Household sector	601		121	722	601	121	120
A. Domestic services	121		121	242	121	121	24
B. Religious services	480			480	480		96
II. Enterprise sector	69,453	1,861	3,026	74,340	73,651	689	10,839
1. Socialized	68,943	1,861	2,601	73,405	72,716	689	10,686
2. Private	510		425	835	835		153
A. Industry and handicraft	35,574	704	1,690	37,971	37,617	354	5,545
1. Socialized	35,359	704	1,265	37,331	36,977	354	5,481
2. Private	215		425	640	640		64
B. Agriculture	4,617	49	123	4,789	4,743	46	716
1. Socialized	4,617	49	123	4,789	4,743	46	716
2. Private							
C. Forestry	774	173	19	966	958	8	120
1. Socialized	774	173	19	966	958	8	120
2. Private							
D. Construction	11,398	185	341	11,924	11,810	114	1,770
1. Socialized	11,376	185	341	11,902	11,788	114	1,763
2. Private	22			22	22		7
E. Transportation and communications	7,190	99	204	7,494	7,423	71	1,123
1. Socialized	7,130	99	205	7,434	7,363	71	1,105
2. Private	60			60	60		18

APPENDIX TABLE E1 (*Continued*)

TOTAL WAGE BILL

(*Million zlotys*)

1954	(1) Personal Wage Bill	(2) Nonpersonal Wage Bill	(3) Other Wage-like Payments	(4) TOTAL WAGE BILL Total 1 + 2 + 3	(5) Cash	(6) In Kind	(7) Social Security
F. Trade and catering	6,736	552	563	7,851	7,785	66	1,065
1. Socialized	6,597	552	563	7,712	7,646	66	1,023
2. Private	139			139	139		42
G. Housing	254	3	8	265	263	2	48
1. Socialized	194	3	8	205	203	2	30
2. Private	60			60	60		18
H. Other services	2,910	93	77	3,080	3,051	29	453
1. Socialized	2,896	93	77	3,066	3,037	29	449
2. Private	14			14	14		4
III. Government sector	10,382	573	7,830	18,785	14,993	3,792	1,609
A. Public health, education, welfare	5,421	480	136	6,037	5,983	54	840
1. Art and culture	151	77	4	232	230	2	23
2. Science and research	374	48	9	431	427	4	58
3. Health, physical culture	1,883	22	47	1,952	1,933	19	292
4. Education	3,013	332	76	3,421	3,391	30	467
B. Administration and justice	3,305	93	83	3,481	3,448	33	512
1. Administration	3,145	88	79	3,312	3,281	31	487
2. Justice	160	5	4	169	167	2	25
C. Internal security	609		1,691	2,300	2,100	200	94
D. National defense	591		5,909	6,500	3,000	3,500	92
E. Quasi-governmental organizations	456		11	467	462	5	71
IV. Total	80,436	2,434	10,977	93,847	89,245	4,602	12,568

APPENDIX TABLE E1 (Continued)
TOTAL WAGE BILL
(Million zlotys)

1955	(1) Personal Wage Bill	(2) Nonpersonal Wage Bill	(3) Other Wage-like Payments	(4) Total 1+2+3	(5) Cash	(6) In Kind	(7) Social Security
				TOTAL WAGE BILL			
I. Household sector	614		130	744	614	130	96
A. Domestic services	130		130	260	130	130	20
B. Religious services	484			484	484		76
II. Enterprise sector	75,171	2,018	3,165	80,354	79,607	747	11,724
1. Socialized	74,675	2,018	2,708	79,401	78,654	747	11,575
2. Private	496		457	953	953		149
A. Industry and handicraft	39,114	781	1,777	41,672	41,283	389	6,096
1. Socialized	38,883	781	1,320	40,984	40,595	389	6,027
2. Private	231		457	688	688		69
B. Agriculture	5,142	55	131	5,328	5,277	51	797
1. Socialized	5,142	55	131	5,328	5,277	51	797
2. Private							
C. Forestry	837	187	20	1,044	1,036	8	130
1. Socialized	837	187	20	1,044	1,036	8	130
2. Private							
D. Construction	11,577	189	336	12,102	11,986	116	1,795
1. Socialized	11,574	189	336	12,099	11,983	116	1,794
2. Private	3			3	3		1
E. Transportation and communications	7,817	108	215	8,140	8,062	78	1,217
1. Socialized	7,776	108	215	8,099	8,021	78	1,205
2. Private	41			41	41		12

APPENDIX TABLE E1 (*Continued*)
TOTAL WAGE BILL
(*Million zlotys*)

1955	(1) Personal Wage Bill	(2) Nonpersonal Wage Bill	(3) Other Wage-like Payments	(4) TOTAL WAGE BILL Total 1+2+3	(5) Cash	(6) In Kind	(7) Social Security
F. Trade and catering	7,232	593	598	8,423	8,352	71	1,142
1. Socialized	7,090	593	598	8,281	8,210	71	1,099
2. Private	142			142	142		43
G. Housing	290	4	8	302	300	2	55
1. Socialized	225	4	8	237	235	2	35
2. Private	65			65	65		20
H. Other services	3,162	101	80	3,343	3,312	31	492
1. Socialized	3,148	101	80	3,329	3,298	31	488
2. Private	14			14	14		4
III. Government sector	11,204	639	7,075	18,918	15,541	3,377	1,736
A. Public health, education, welfare	6,073	538	148	6,759	6,698	61	941
1. Art and culture	171	87	4	262	260	2	26
2. Science and research	427	55	10	492	488	4	66
3. Health, physical culture	2,172	25	53	2,250	2,228	22	337
4. Education	3,303	370	81	3,754	3,721	33	512
B. Administration and justice	3,601	101	87	3,789	3,753	36	558
1. Administration	3,430	96	83	3,609	3,575	34	532
2. Justice	171	5	4	180	178	2	26
C. Internal security	563		1,587	2,150	1,975	175	87
D. National defense	508		5,242	5,750	2,650	3,100	79
E. Quasi-governmental organizations	459		11	470	465	5	71
IV. Total	86,989	2,657	10,370	100,016	95,762	4,254	13,556

APPENDIX TABLE E1 (Continued)
TOTAL WAGE BILL
(Million zlotys)

1956	(1) Personal Wage Bill	(2) Nonpersonal Wage Bill	(3) Other Wage-like Payments	(4) Total 1+2+3	(5) TOTAL WAGE BILL Cash	(6) In Kind	(7) Social Security
I. Household sector	618		132	750	618	132	24
A. Domestic services	132		132	264	132	132	5
B. Religious services	486			486	486		19
II. Enterprise sector	86,690	2,111	4,747	93,548	92,686	862	13,441
1. Socialized	86,151	2,111	4,256	92,518	91,656	862	13,353
2. Private	539		491	1,030	1,030		88
A. Industry and handicraft	45,384	781	2,626	48,791	48,340	451	7,071
1. Socialized	45,129	781	2,135	48,045	47,594	451	6,995
2. Private	255		491	746	746		76
B. Agriculture	6,036	63	234	6,333	6,273	60	936
1. Socialized	6,036	63	234	6,333	6,273	60	936
2. Private							
C. Forestry	1,147	203	43	1,393	1,382	11	178
1. Socialized	1,147	203	43	1,393	1,382	11	178
2. Private							
D. Construction	12,699	178	537	13,414	13,287	127	1,968
1. Socialized	12,698	178	537	13,413	13,286	127	1,968
2. Private	1			1	1		
E. Transportation and communications	9,094	104	364	9,567	9,477	90	1,402
1. Socialized	9,034	104	369	9,507	9,417	90	1,400
2. Private	60			60	60		2

APPENDIX TABLE E1 (Continued)
TOTAL WAGE BILL
(Million zlotys)

1956	(1) Personal Wage Bill	(2) Nonpersonal Wage Bill	(3) Other Wage-like Payments	(4) Total 1+2+3	TOTAL WAGE BILL		
					(5) Cash	(6) In Kind	(7) Social Security
F. Trade and catering	8,444	664	788	9,896	9,813	83	1,293
1. Socialized	8,302	664	788	9,754	9,671	83	1,287
2. Private	142			142	142		6
G. Housing	352	4	13	369	366	3	47
1. Socialized	286	4	13	303	300	3	44
2. Private	66			66	66		3
H. Other services	3,543	114	137	3,785	3,750	35	546
1. Socialized	3,519	114	137	3,770	3,735	35	545
2. Private	15			15	15		1
III. Government sector	13,201	678	6,691	20,570	17,551	3,019	2,046
A. Public health, education, welfare	7,287	547	189	8,023	7,950	73	1,129
1. Art and culture	195	100	5	300	298	2	30
2. Science and research	443	56	12	511	507	4	69
3. Health, physical culture	2,631	27	68	2,726	2,700	26	408
4. Education	4,018	364	104	4,486	4,446	40	623
B. Administration and justice	4,135	131	107	4,373	4,332	41	641
1. Administration	3,911	124	101	4,136	4,097	39	606
2. Justice	224	7	6	237	235	2	35
C. Internal security	670		1,530	2,200	2,050	150	104
D. National defense	647		4,853	5,500	2,750	2,750	100
E. Quasi-governmental organizations	462		12	474	469	5	72
IV. Total	100,509	2,789	11,570	114,868	110,855	4,013	15,511

I. Household sector

  Column 1. Personal wage bill

  Row I A. Domestic services. The wage bill for the years 1954–56 was estimated as the product of employment and average wages. According to *Przegląd zagadnień socjalnych,* 1957, No. 6, p. 78, there were about 20 thousand full-time domestic servants in 1957; the same number was also assumed for 1954–56. Their cash wages in 1956 were taken as equal to average wages paid in the private sector, or 548 zlotys a month (*BS,* March, 1958, p. 30). Since the official data refer only to wages that form the basis for assessing social security contributions, they presumably exclude income in kind in the form of food and lodgings. The 1954 and 1955 average wages were obtained by deflating the 1956 wage by the index linking average wages paid in the so-called "unproductive services" (*RS 1956,* p. 279; *RS 1957,* p. 269). Owing to lack of data, no attempt was made to estimate the wage bill of part-time domestic servants.

  Row I B. Religious services. The wage bill for the years 1954–56 was estimated as the product of employment and average wages. According to *Słowo powszechne,* January 6, 1958, the number of clergy and members of religious orders in 1957 was about 42,000. We rounded this figure to 40,000 for the period 1954–56 as a rough adjustment for an assumed increase after 1956. The average wages in each year were assumed to equal average wages paid in a residual category of quasi-governmental and religious organizations, estimated by dividing their personal wage bill by employment. These figures were residuals: total wage bill in the socialized sector (*RS 1959,* p. 331) less indicated components (*ibid.*) and less nonproductive services (*RS 1956,* p. 279, for 1954; *RS 1959,* p. 331, Table 4, for 1955–56); and total employment (*RS 1959,* p. 45) less indicated components (*ibid.*) and less administration and nonproductive services (*RS 1956,* p. 279, for 1954; *RS 1959,* p. 46, for 1955–56).

  Column 2. Nonpersonal wage bill

  This did not exist in the household sector.

  Column 3. Other wage-like payments

  Row I A. Domestic services. These payments were estimated as the product of employment (see column *1,* above) and average wages in kind (food and lodging), assumed to equal the amount of cash wages in each year.

  Row I B. Religious services. It was assumed that there were none in this category.

II. Enterprise sector

The total is the sum of the components, Rows A through H.

Column 1. Personal wage bill

Row II A1. Industry and handicraft: Socialized. In addition to wages paid to employees of socialized industry (*RS 1961*, p. 371), we include here wages paid to workers in cottage industries (*chałupnicy*) under contract to socialized enterprises. Their wage bill was included in the official estimate of the personal wage bill in the national economy, and they were subject to social security (*RS 1961*, p. 370). Also included were wages paid to employees of the publishing industry, which are included in the official statistics within the category "social and cultural institutions" (*RS 1957*, p. 267).

The personal wage bill of workers in cottage industries was estimated as the product of employment and average wages. We estimated employment very roughly at 40,000 during 1954–56, taking account of a figure of 20,000 peasant cottage workers presumably for 1957–58 (given by S. Szatyński, in *Życie gospodarcze*, April 12, 1959, p. 8) and allowing for some urban cottage workers and a progressive decline over the years (*DN 1947*, p. 8, estimated 80,000 for 1947).

The average monthly wage was estimated (in zlotys) at 1,000 in 1955 and 1,070 in 1956. These were average wages in cooperatives engaged in manufacture of leather articles, embroidery, and basket weaving where presumably most of the workers were employed (see Poland, Główny urząd statystyczny, *Statystyka przemysłu: statystyka produkcji, zatrudnienia i płac, 1956*, pp. 22–23). The 1955 average wage was assumed to have been 3 percent above the 1954 wage as was the case in all cooperative industry and handicraft (*RS 1956*, p. 279).

The personal wage bill in the publishing industry was taken from *RS 1957*, p. 369, for 1955–56. The 1954 wage bill was assumed to account for the same share of the personal wage bill in social and cultural institutions as it did in 1955 (see *RS 1956*, p. 279).

Row II A2. Industry and handicraft: Private. The 1954 estimate was based on the 1955 wage bill, 1954–55 employment (*RS 1956*, p. 122), and 1954 average wages were derived by deflating the 1955 average wages by an index of 103, the same as in cooperative industry (*RS 1956*, p. 279). The 1955–56 figures were estimated on the assumption that social security contributions (*DN 1956*, p. 20) were equal to 30 percent of the personal wage bill (*DU 1951*, No.

9). After 1955 apprentices in private handicraft were subject to lower rates, equal to 15.5 percent of the personal wage bill (*DU 1955*, No. 3), and hence the personal wage bill in private industry is slightly understated in the later years.

Row II B. Agriculture. 1. Socialized. *RS 1961*, p. 371. 2. Private. None.

Row II C. Forestry. 1. Socialized. *RS 1961*, p. 371. 2. Private. None.

Row II D. Construction. 1. Socialized. *RS 1961*, p. 371. 2. Private. 1954: This is the product of employment in private construction enterprises (*RS 1956*, p. 206) and average wages, which were assumed equal to wages in construction cooperatives (*RS 1955*, p. 144). 1955–56: *DN 1956*, p. 32.

Row II E1. Transportation and communications: Socialized. This was taken as the sum of wages paid to employees of the socialized transport and communications system (*RS 1961*, p. 371) and of urban transportation, which the official employment statistics consider as part of communal services. The 1955 wage bill in urban transportation was given in *BS*, April 1957, p. 23, and the 1956 wage bill in *BS*, May 1958, p. 29. The 1954 wage bill was obtained by deflating the 1955 wage bill by 119, the index linking personal wage bills in communal services in 1954 and 1955 (*RS 1956*, p. 279).

Row II E2. Transportation and communications: Private. It was assumed that private transport enterprises were engaged only in freight transport and as such they belonged to the "material" sector of the economy. The remuneration of private taxicab owners was considered as falling under the category of "income of self-employed." The personal wage bill in 1954 was taken to represent 6 percent of total net product in private transport (*DN 1954–55*, p. 18), which was roughly the same percentage as in 1955. The 1955–56 figures were taken from *DN 1956*, p. 38.

Row II F. Trade and catering. 1. Socialized. *RS 1960*, p. 391. 2. Private. For 1955–56, see *DN 1956*, p. 42. The 1954 estimate was based on implicit employment (*DN 1954–55*, p. 20) and on 1955 average wages estimated from *ibid.*, and *DN 1956*, p. 42, and deflated to the 1954 level by an index of 102, taken from cooperative trade (*RS 1956*, p. 279).

Row II G1. Housing: Socialized. The estimate refers to employees of state and cooperative housing. Employment in housing belonging to industry, transportation, and other economic sectors was omitted on the assumption that it was included in the latter sectors. The personal wage bill in state housing was estimated as follows:

	Employment (thousand persons)	Average Annual Wage (zlotys)	Personal Wage Bill (million zlotys)
1954	18.9	9,850	186
1955	20.6	10,508	216
1956	23.0	11,902	274

Employment in 1954–55 was taken from Ginsbert, *Ekonomika gospodarki komunalnej,* Part III, p. 115. The 1956 figure was obtained from the number of employees in 1959 (47.5 thousand, from *RS 1960,* p. 321), less the increase during 1957–58 (16.5 thousand, from *RPG 1959,* pp. 637–38), less the increase in 1959 (assumed to be roughly one half of the increase in 1957–58). The average annual wage was assumed to equal 90 percent of the average wages paid in communal services in 1954–56 (*RS 1960,* p. 391), that being roughly the ratio in 1959 (*RS 1960,* p. 321).

The wage bill in housing cooperatives was estimated as equal to the same share of gross rent paid in cooperative housing as in the case of state housing (see Appendix Table A4). This results in the following wage bills (in million zlotys): *1954, 8; 1955, 9; 1956, 12.*

Row II G2. Housing: Private. The number of janitors was estimated at 10,000 throughout the period 1954–56 by subtracting the estimated number of domestic servants, 20,000 (see row I A, above) from the total number of janitors and domestic servants (*BS,* March, 1958, p. 30). Janitors' average wages were assumed to equal those paid to domestic servants (see row I A, above).

Row II H1. Other services: Socialized. The personal wage bill in other services was estimated as a residual in the total personal wage bill in the socialized economy. "Other services" include the services of those working in, among other places, financial institutions, entertainment, communal services, barbershops, beauty parlors, and medical and legal cooperatives. The estimates were as follows (in million zlotys):

	1954	1955	1956
Communal services	717	863	1,092
Finance and insurance	642	613	684
Entertainment	305	342	412
Other socialized services	1,232	1,330	1,331
State	0	6	12
Cooperative	1,232	1,324	1,319
Total	2,896	3,148	3,519

The personal wage bill in communal services was estimated by subtracting wages paid in urban transportation and in state-owned housing (see notes to rows II E1 and II G1, above) from the figures shown in *RS 1960,* p. 391. Wages in finance and insurance were taken from *RS 1961,* p. 371. The wage bill in entertainment was estimated from the wage bill in entertainment and publishing (see notes to row III A, below) by subtracting the wage bill in publishing (see notes to row II A1, above). The wage bill in "other socialized services" was obtained as the sum of wages paid in state and cooperative barbershops, beauty parlors, chimney sweeping, and other service enterprises (*RS 1956,* p. 279; *RS 1959,* p. 331) and in cooperative scientific, educational, and administrative services. The latter for 1955–56 were taken from *RS 1961,* p. 372. The estimate for 1954 was obtained by deflating the wage bill in 1955 with the index of 117, linking unaccounted wage bills in the cooperative sector between 1954 and 1955 (*RS 1956,* p. 279). The totals in all three years were reduced by subtracting the wages paid in cooperative housing (see notes to row II G1 above). It was assumed that the wage bill in state service enterprises in 1954 was insignificant.

Row II H2. Other services: Private. The 1954–55 estimates were based on the assumption that this series showed the same trend during the period 1954–56 as the personal wage bill in the private enterprise sector excluding services. The 1956 figure is a residual in the total wage bill in the private sector of the economy (*BS,* March, 1958, p. 30), left after subtraction of wages of domestic servants (Row I A1, above) and wages in sectors listed in Rows II A2 to II G2, above.

Column 2. Nonpersonal wage bill

In 1954 this was assumed to represent the same percentage share of the personal wage bill in each sector as in 1955. Estimates for 1955 and 1956 were obtained as follows. Industry and handicraft: nonpersonal wage bill in industry (*RS 1961,* p. 380) plus nonpersonal wage bill in publishing, assumed to represent the same share of personal wage bill as in the case of industry excluding publishing and workers in cottage industries. Agriculture, forestry, construction, trade and catering: *RS 1961,* p. 380. Transport and communications: nonpersonal wage bill in nonurban transport and communications (*RS 1961,* p. 380) plus nonpersonal wage bill in urban transport, which was assumed to represent the same share of nonpersonal wage bill in communal services shown in *RS 1961,* p. 380, as was its share in the personal wage bill in that sector. Housing: estimated in the same manner as in urban transport. Other services: estimated below (in million zlotys); the sources follow.

	1955	1956
1. Communal services	16	16
2. Finance and insurance	44	55
3. Entertainment	41	43
Total	101	114

1. This was calculated as the total nonpersonal wage bill in communal services (*RS 1961,* p. 380) less the components in urban transport (4 million zlotys each year) and housing (8 million zlotys in 1955 and 9 million zlotys in 1956) as estimated above.

2. *RS 1961,* p. 380.

3. It was assumed that this represented the same percentage of the personal wage bill (see p. 147, above) as in "education, science, and culture" (*RS 1961* pp. 371, 380).

Column 3. Other wage-like payments

Other wage-like payments in the enterprise sector are shown in Appendix Table E2 and explained in the notes thereto (see p. 160).

III. Government sector

The documentation of columns *1* and *2* follows below. In column *3* we allocated proportionately to the personal wage bills the total of other wage-like payments falling to the government sector, namely (in million zlotys): *1954,* 260; *1955,* 272; *1956,* 342 (see notes to column *4* of Appendix Table E2, below). In addition, in rows III C and III D, column *3,* we included pay and allowances of noncivilian personnel in internal security and defense (see notes to rows for details). We shall show first, row by row, the derivation of columns *1* and *2.* Column *3* is determined when column *1* is completed for all rows and account is taken of defense and security.

Row III A. Health, education and welfare

Column *1.* The personal wage bill was estimated as follows (in million zlotys):

	1954	1955	1956
1. Official personal wage bill	5,909	6,620	7,926
2. Less: Personal wage bill in entertainment and publishing enterprises	488	547	639
3. Equals: Personal wage bill in state health, education and welfare	5,421	6,073	7,287

1. 1954: This represents the total official personal wage bill in socialized health, education, and welfare institutions (*RS 1956*, p. 279) less the personal wage bill in cooperative institutions. The latter figure was obtained by deflating the wage bill in 1955 (*RS 1960*, p. 391) by the index of 117, connecting the residual wage bill in the cooperative sector in 1954 and 1955 (*RS 1956*, p. 279). 1955–56: *RS 1960*, p. 391.

2. This item includes wages paid in publishing houses, theaters, orchestras, circuses, the movie industry, and cinemas, which we regard as part of the enterprise sector although they are included in the official category "health, education, and welfare." 1954: This amount was estimated by deflating the wage bill in 1955 (*RS 1957*, p. 369) by the index of 112, connecting the wage bill in social and cultural institutions in 1954 and 1955 (*RS 1956*, p. 279). 1955–56: *RS 1957*, p. 369.

Column *2*. The nonpersonal wage bill was estimated as follows (in million zlotys):

	1954	1955	1956
1. Total official nonpersonal wage bill	n.a.	582	594
2. Less: Nonpersonal wage bill in entertainment and publishing	n.a.	45	47
3. Equals: Adjusted nonpersonal wage bill	479	537	547

1. 1954: No official figures were available. 1955–56: *RS 1961*, p. 380. We assumed that nonpersonal wage bill was paid only in the state sector.

2. This was estimated above in connection with the nonpersonal wage bill in industry and services (see notes to column 2 of the enterprise sector).

3. 1954: This was assumed to represent the same percentage of the personal wage bill as in 1955. 1955–56: This is the residual.

Row III A1. Art and culture

The total wage bill was obtained as the sum of wages paid by libraries (excluding scientific), museums, archives, cultural and educational centers, the radio network, and the official press agency.

Column *1*. In 1954, total wages, including social security contributions but excluding per diem travel allowances and other payments, were assumed to account for 27 percent of the sum of current expenditures, outlays on capital repairs (including grants), and working capital transfers—the same share as in 1955 (see Appendix Table

G3). Their percentage breakdown between the personal wage bill, social security contributions, and the nonpersonal wage bill was also assumed to have been the same as in 1955.

In 1955 and 1956, the personal wage bill data, with the exception of the press agency, were given directly in *SK 1956,* pp. 51–52. The personal wage bill in the press agency was estimated roughly at 10 million zlotys in 1955 and 12 million in 1956 on the basis of analogy with state budgets in 1957–58.

According to the 1958 and 1959 state budgets (*DU 1958,* No. 16, and *DU 1959,* No. 16), the personal wage bill in art and culture accounted for about 60 percent of the total wage bill. We applied this rate to expand the personal wage bill obtained above to the total wage bill. Social security contributions were estimated at 15.5 percent of the personal wage bill.

Column 2. The nonpersonal wage bill was estimated as the residual in the total wage bill after subtraction of the personal wage bill and social security contributions, both of which were estimated as indicated above.

Row III A2. Science and research

Column 1. The personal wage bill, the nonpersonal wage bill, and social security contributions are estimated by analogy with the 1957, 1958, and 1959 state budgets (*DU 1957,* No. 25; *DU 1958,* No. 16; *DU 1959,* No. 16). On this basis we assumed that total wages and social security contributions for the years 1954–56 accounted for about 55 percent of the current expenditures plus capital repairs (shown in Appendix Table G3) and that the personal wage bill accounted for 78 percent of the total wage bill.

Column 2. The nonpersonal wage bill was estimated as a residual in the total wage bill after subtraction of the personal wage bill and social security contributions (estimated at 15.5 percent of the personal wage bill).

Row III A3. Health and physical culture

The wage bill data refer to the health service, tourism, and physical culture, and homes for the aged. Homes for the aged are financed from the social welfare budget.

Column 1. For the personal wage bill, see *RS 1961,* p. 371.

Column 2. The nonpersonal wage bill for 1954 was assumed to be in the same proportion to the personal wage bill as in 1955. For 1955–56, see *RS 1961,* p. 380.

Row III A4. Education

Columns 1 and 2 were obtained as residuals in the total personal and nonpersonal wage bills after the subtraction of wages in the subsectors estimated above.

Row III B1. Administration

We show here the wages paid in central and local administrations, excluding the Ministries of the Interior and National Defense.

Column *1*. The personal wage bill for 1954 was estimated as the total official wage bill in socialized administration and justice (*RS 1961*, p. 371) less the estimated wage bill in cooperative administration (see notes to row II H1, above) and less the wage bill in justice (estimated in row III B2, below). The amounts for 1955–56 were obtained by subtracting the wage bill in justice (*BS*, April, 1957, p. 23) from the total for administration and justice (*RS 1961*, p. 372).

Column *2*. The nonpersonal wage bill for 1954 was estimated from the personal wage bill in the same proportions as in 1955. In 1955–56 the nonpersonal wage bill in administration and justice (*RS 1961*, p. 380) was divided between the two categories in proportion to their personal wage bills.

Row III B2. Justice

This item includes wages paid in the administration of justice (in the courts and in the office of the state prosecutor and attorney general). Control over prisons was transferred from the Ministry of Interior to the Ministry of Justice in September, 1956 (*DU 1956*, No. 41). For the sake of comparability, however, we kept prison wages together with those for internal security.

Column *1*. The personal wage bill for 1954 was estimated by deflating the 1955 wage bill by the index of wage bills in administration in 1954 and 1955 (*RS 1956*, p. 279). For 1955–56, see *BS*, April, 1957, p. 23.

Row III C. Internal security

Columns *1* and *2*. The personal wage bill of the civilian employees of the Ministry of Internal Security (after 1956 called the Ministry of the Interior) was identified very roughly with the unexplained residual in the total personal wage bill in the economy. The nonpersonal wage bill (column *2*) was asumed to be nonexistent.

In deriving the personal wage bill as a residual in the total personal wage bill in the economy (*RS 1957*, p. 267), we subtracted (*a*) the total personal wage bill in the socialized sector (*RS 1960*, p. 391), (*b*) the total personal wage bill in the private sector (rows I A and II2), (*c*) our estimates of the personal wage bill in cottage industries (see notes to row II A1, above), and (*d*) our estimates of the personal wage bill in the professional fire protection services, calculated as the product of employment (*RS 1956*, p. 398, for 1954; *RS 1957*, p. 412, for 1955–56) and average annual cash wages (taken as the same as for administration and justice, *RS 1961*, p. 371), plus average annual wages in kind (assumed equal to rounded figures for the militia, excluding housing; see below). The remaining balance was split between the personal wage bills of civilian employees in the Ministry of Defense and the Ministry of Internal Security in the ratio of 3 to 1, more or less as an informed guess. The figures for internal security (row III C, column *1*) are the sum of this residual plus the personal wage bill in the fire protection services (see above). These services were apparently controlled by the Ministry of Internal Affairs (*DU 1954*, No. 54, pp. 441–42; *DU 1955*, No. 28, p. 272).

Column *3*. Other wage-like payments are intended to cover wages and salaries paid to the militia and the secret police, and to prison guards, as these are presumably excluded from the official estimate of the total wage bill in the economy. We included the pay of the so-called Internal Security Troops and Frontier Guards, administered by the Ministry of the Interior under military pay (row III D., column *3*).

Wage payments to the militia were estimated as the product of the number of militiamen and their average wages in cash and in kind. Radio Warsaw, September 22, 1957, put the number of militiamen at 50,000. In view of the general trends in internal security policies, we estimated accordingly the numerical strength of the militia at: 80,000 in 1954, 70,000 in 1955, and 60,000 in 1956. The general order of magnitude of these estimates is supported by the fact that the number of party members employed in internal security agencies, militia, and prisons, amounted to 61,200 as of January 1, 1956 (*Nowe Drogi*, June, 1956, p. 104). In the 1947 state budget, the strength of militia, secret police, and prison guards was put at 90,000 (*DU 1947*, No. 50, p. 799).

Militiamen were assumed to receive an average cash wage equal to that paid to administration personnel (*RS 1961*, p. 371). Wages in kind consisted of uniforms and free lodging (*DU 1954*, No. 34, p. 274). Their imputed value was estimated, in zlotys per capita, at 1,650, 1,600, and 1,575 in 1954, 1955 and 1956, respectively. These estimates were arrived at on the basis of detailed calculations of amounts distributed (*DU 1948*, No. 47), their useful life (assumed to be the same as for firemen's and foresters' uniforms; see *DU 1952*,

No. 52; *DU 1954,* No. 57; and *DU 1959,* No. 4), and the retail prices of comparable items of clothing (see *SC 1957,* p. 14).

The strength of the secret police was taken to be some 10,000 in each of the three years, with an estimated average pay of 36,000 zlotys a year. These estimates are token figures to make some allowance for this group of employees.

We estimated the pay of prison guards on the basis of employment and average wages. Employment in 1954 and 1955 was set roughly at 16,200 and in 1956 at 11,700. We estimated these figures from the total employment in the administration of justice as planned on December 31, 1957, namely, 31,900, less the employment in non-prison administration, 19,600 (see *DU 1957,* No. 25, p. 246, and *BS,* No. 5, 1958, p. 29). The resulting figure for 1957, 12,300, was adjusted to 1954–56 on the basis of the ratio of prison employees to prisoners in 1957 (1 to 5; see *RS 1958,* p. 473) and the average number of prisoners in 1955 and 1956 (*RS 1957,* p. 404); 1954 was taken equal to 1955. Average wages in cash and in kind were taken the same as for the militia (see above).

To complete the entry in column *3* we added (in million zlotys), 15, 14, and 17, for 1954, 1955, and 1956, respectively, arising from wage-like payments described in notes to Appendix Table E2, column *4,* below, plus rounding elements of 16, 14, and 17 million zlotys in these years in order to arrive at rounded figures for the total wage bill in column *4* (which is the sum of columns *1, 2,* and *3*). We did this rounding to avoid giving an impression of precision in the figure for the total wage bill.

Row III D. National defense

This item covers only the pay and subsistence of the armed forces and the wages and salaries of civilian employees of the Ministry of Defense. We included here the internal security troops and the frontier guards, although they were under the control of the Ministry of the Interior (see *DU 1954,* No. 34, pp. 269 ff., and No. 54, pp. 441–45; *DU 1958,* No. 36, p. 527; *RPG 1958,* p. 140). At the same time, however, it is known that they were a part of the military establishment (see *RPG 1960,* pp. 147, 149). They were financed by the budget of the defense ministry in the early 1950s (see *DU 1950,* No. 16, p. 26), and we assumed that this was true for 1954–56.

Column *1.* The personal wage bill is assumed to have been paid to civilian employees of the Ministry of National Defense, who were employed in schools, libraries, museums, archives, publications, print-

ing shops, sport clubs, and administrative positions (see *RPG 1958,*
pp. 329–31). In the absence of any data, no attempt was made to
estimate the number of employees. The personal wage bill was estimated from a residual in the total wage bill (see notes to Row III C,
above).

Column 2. It was assumed that there was no nonpersonal wage
bill.

Column 3. Other wage-like payments include military pay and
subsistence of the armed forces and certain payments to civilian
employees. The latter payments were estimated as described in the
introductory remarks to row III (see p. 149, above). Armed forces
pay and subsistence were based on the estimated strength of the
forces and average wages.

On the basis of scattered sources, some of which are indicated below, we estimated the strength of the armed forces very roughly as
follows: *1954,* 500,000; *1955,* 450,000; *1956, 400,000.* A figure of
500,000 for 1954 is given by the New York *Times,* August 24, 1954.
The Minister of Finance in his budget speech in 1956 indicated that
the 10 percent cut in the forces ordered in 1955 amounted to 47,000
men (*Finanse,* March, 1956, p. 6). If we round the total strength
to 450,000 and take account of a reduction of 50,000 during 1956
(New York *Times,* August 18, 1956), we obtain the figure for
1956. All of these figures must be regarded as rough approximations.
They are, however, broadly consistent with other bits of information.
For example, a Polish radio broadcast of March 27, 1957, mentioned a reduction of forces of 141,000 men during the preceding
eighteen months; and the New York *Times* (March 28, 1957) gives
the strength of the forces at 350,000. Year-end census data for 1950
and 1960 by comparison with the 1931 census categories implicitly
give figures of about 394,000 and 370,000 for 1950 and 1960, respectively (*RS 1959,* p. 36; *RS 1961,* p. 13; Poland, Główny urząd
statystyczny, *Polska (dane skrócone)* [Poland (Summary Data)],
Statystyka Polski, Series C, Vol. 62 [Warsaw, 1933?], p. ix). An
increase of 100,000 between 1950 and 1954 would not be surprising
in view of the international tension following the Korean War.

The number of officers and senior noncommissioned officers was
taken roughly at 20 percent of the total strength of the armed forces.
Their average basic monthly wage was taken roughly as equal to that
received by engineers and technicians in socialized industry, that is,
1,800 zlotys for 1954–55 (*RS 1956,* p. 110) and 2,000 zlotys in
1956 (*RS 1957,* p. 83).

The average monthly cash pay of the remaining military personnel was assumed to have been 50 zlotys throughout the period. Their wages in kind covering food, clothing, and so forth, were taken roughly as follows (in zlotys): *1954,* 8,700; *1955,* 8,550; *1956,* 8,500. These estimates were based on 1956 consumption of food, regular uniforms taken at the same value as for militiamen, fatigue uniforms approximated by the cost of civilian work uniforms, and an allowance for soap, cigarettes, and miscellaneous items taken at about one third of the value of food. The 1956 estimates were deflated by price indexes in socialized retail stores to arrive at the figure for 1954–55. The sum of average income in cash and in kind, some 9,000 zlotys per head, is equal to that for some of the more poorly paid occupations—a rough check of its reasonableness.

In column *3* we show the total of column *1,* the other wage-like payments of civilian personnel (see introductory remarks to row III, p. 149, and the notes to Appendix Table E2, p. 160), the military pay and subsistence, and rounding elements (in million zlotys, *1954,* + 14; *1955,* – 8; *1956,* +4) to get the figures shown in column *4.* The round totals in column *4* were preferred in this area of incomplete information and rough estimates.

Row III E. Quasi-governmental organizations

We include here wages paid to employees of political parties, youth organizations, trade unions, and other organizations listed in Poland, Główny urząd statystyczny, *Klasyfikacja gospodarki narodowej,* p. 32.

Column *1.* The personal wage bill was estimated as a residual in the total wage bill (*RS 1959,* p. 330, and Appendix Table E1; see also notes to row I B, above).

Column *2.* According to *RS 1957,* p. 270, the nonpersonal wage bill apparently did not exist in nonproductive service enterprises or in quasi-governmental organizations during 1955–56, and we assumed, therefore, that none existed in 1954.

Column *3.* For other wage-like payments see the introductory remarks to row III, p. 149.

Row IV. Totals (columns 1–3)

Column *1.* Personal wage bill. *RS 1959,* p. 330.

Column *2.* Nonpersonal wage bill. 1954: Sum of totals in rows I to III. 1955–56: *RS 1960,* p. 400.

Column *3.* Other wage-like payments. Sum of totals in rows I to III.

Total wage bill (columns 4–6) and Social security (column 7)

We have completed the documentation of columns *1 to 3* for all sectors, and we turn now to the distribution of the total wage bill between wages in cash and wages in kind and to the distribution of social security contributions.

Column *4*. For all rows this total is the sum of columns *1, 2,* and *3*.

Column *5*. For all rows the amount of cash wages is column *4* less column *6*.

Column *6*. Wages in kind (all rows).

According to *RS 1960,* p. 390, the values of commodities (*deputaty*) distributed to employees in 1959 as wages in kind amounted to about 0.8 percent of the personal wage bill of which they form a part. The personal wage bill includes also the value of free uniforms and housing (lodging, heat, light). Taking the latter in account, we placed the value of wages in kind at 1.0 percent of the personal wage bills in the socialized sectors during 1954–56. Except for domestic services, we made no estimates of wages in kind in the private sectors because of the insignificant magnitudes involved. In addition, some special cases of wages in kind are noted below.

In the household sector we took the value of other wage-like payments of domestic services, row I A, column *3,* as the value of wages in kind. The remaining special cases were rows III C and III D, where we used particular estimates of wages in kind developed for column *3* plus a part of the values in column *1*.

In the internal security subsector the pay of the fire protection service included in column *1* has components of wages in kind as follows (in million zlotys): *1954,* 40; *1955,* 35; *1956,* 35. Civilian personnel other than firemen accounted for only about 2 million zlotys of wages in kind according to our 1.0 percent rule of calculation in each of the years 1954–56, on the basis of their personal wage bills. The figures in column *6* were rounded for 1954.

In view of the rounding of the figures for wages in kind, column *6* of row III D (national defense), only the wages in kind of the armed forces developed for column *3* were significant.

Column *7*. Social security contributions in the socialized sector were estimated at 15.5 percent of personal wage bill (*DU 1951,* No. 9), and those in the private sector at 30.0 percent of personal wage bill (*ibid.*), with the exceptions stated below.

The total amount of social security contributions in 1954 and 1955 (shown in *RS 1959,* p. 359) was allocated among the sectors according to these percentages, except in the household sector where the amount was taken as the residual. Some employers within the private sector paid 15.5 percent rather than 30 percent of the personal wage bill (see *RPG 1958*, p. 854). Although we assumed a flat rate of 30 percent for all the enterprise sector private employers, the contributions of the household sector, estimated as the residual in total contributions after subtraction of those paid by the enterprise and government sectors, amounted to less than 30 percent of total personal wage bill in that sector. We allocated this residual between domestic servants and religious services in the ratio of their personal wage bills.

In 1956 the official total (*RS 1959*, p. 359) is barely sufficient to cover the socialist sector if the presumption is that social security contributions were equal to 15.5 percent of personal wage bill. We made, therefore, the following adjustments: social security contributions in the socialized sector were computed at 15.5 percent of personal wage bill; those in private industry were estimated at 30 percent of the personal wage bill; and the residual in total social security contributions was allocated among the remaining sectors in proportion to their respective personal wage bills. The underlying assumption was that the socialized sector and private industry were more likely to adhere strictly to the letter of the law than the rest of the private sector. Moreover, the magnitudes involved were negligible so that no serious error was introduced by our procedure.

Notes to Appendix Table E2

Appendix Table E2 provides the data for the enterprise sector rows of column *3* of Appendix Table E1. Its sources are indicated below.

Column *1*. Director's fund (*fundusz zakładowy*). For each of the years 1954–55 payments out of director's funds were assumed equal to the amount paid out in 1956. For 1956, see Poland, Rada ekonomiczna przy radzie ministrów, *Sytuacja gospodarcza kraju w roku 1958,* p. 144. The intersectoral allocation was assumed to have been roughly the same as in 1957, as shown in *RS 1960,* p. 400. The total for communal services was divided roughly between housing and other services.

Column *2*. Other prizes. In 1954 these were assumed equal to the amounts paid out in 1955. For 1955–56, see *RS 1957,* p. 287, payments in industry being obtained as a residual. The list of exclusions from the personal wage fund suggests that these prizes were distinct from payments out of the director's fund (see *RS 1957*, p. 266).

Column *3*. Deferred payments, commissions and other wage-like payments. This item includes payment of wages owed for periods prior to 1956, which were paid in the second half of 1956, commissions received by employees of state retail trade establishments, and

APPENDIX TABLE E2

WAGE-LIKE PAYMENTS IN ENTERPRISE SECTOR

(*Million zlotys*)

	(1) Director's Fund	(2) Other Prizes	(3) Deferred Payments, Commissions, and Other Wage-like Payments	(4) Other Wage-like Payments Not Otherwise Specified	(5) Total
1954					
Industry and handicraft	308	64	425	893	1,690
Agriculture	6			117	123
Forestry				19	19
Construction	48	6		287	341
Transport and communi-cations	21	5		179	205
Trade and catering	10		386	167	563
Housing	3			5	8
Other services	4			73	77
Total	400	75	811	1,740	3,026
1955					
Industry and handicraft	308	64	457	948	1,777
Agriculture	6			125	131
Forestry				20	20
Construction	48	6		282	336
Transport and communi-cations	21	5		189	215
Trade and catering	10		415	173	598
Housing	3			5	8
Other services	4			76	80
Total	400	75	872	1,818	3,165
1956					
Industry and handicraft	308	90	1,058	1,170	2,626
Agriculture	6		72	156	234
Forestry			14	29	43
Construction	48	9	152	328	537
Transport and communi-cations	21	7	107	234	369
Trade and catering	10		564	214	788
Housing	3		3	7	13
Other services	4		42	91	137
Total	400	106	2,012	2,229	4,747

unspecified wage payments in private industry. Overdue wages paid out in 1956 were estimated at 1,056 million zlotys (Poland, Rada ekonomiczna przy radzie Ministrów, *Główne problemy sytuacji gospodarczej kraju,* p. 111), of which 567 million zlotys was allocated to socialized industry (Poland, Główny urząd statystyczny, *Statystyka przemysłu, statystyka produkcji, zatrudnienia i płac,* 1956, p. vii). The residual, 489 million zlotys, was allocated among the remaining socialized enterprise subsectors in proportion to their respective personal wage bills.

Commissions in socialized retail trade were estimated on the assumption that they represented roughly the same share of nonpersonal wage bill in retail trade (70 percent) as in 1958 (*RS 1960,* p. 400).

Wage-like payments in private industry in 1954 were assumed to represent the same share of total labor income as in 1955. The estimates for 1955–56 were obtained as a residual in the total wage-like income (*DN 1956,* p. 20) after subtraction of the personal wage bill (see above, Appendix Table E1).

Column 4. Other wage-like payments not otherwise specified. The total amount of such payments in 1954 was assumed equal to 2,000 million zlotys, or roughly the 1955 amount. The figures for 1955 and 1956, 2,090 and 2,571 million zlotys, respectively, were calculated as residuals in the total wage bills paid out in the socialized sector, 92,000 million zlotys in 1955 and 107,225 million zlotys in 1956 (as shown in *RPG 1958,* p. 824, and Poland, Rada ekonomiczna przy radzie ministrów, *Sytuacja gospodarcza kraju w roku 1958,* p. 144). The residuals were obtained by subtracting (*a*) the personal wage bill (*RS 1957,* p. 267) excluding domestic services and private enterprise (Appendix Table E1); (*b*) nonpersonal wage bill (*RS 1960,* p. 400); (*c*) payments out of the director's fund and other prizes (Appendix Table E2); and (*d*) commissions in retail trade and deferred payments (Appendix Table E2).

The totals for each year were divided between the socialized enterprise and government sectors in the ratio of their respective personal wage bills (shown in Appendix Table E1, column *1*). The percentage composition of the personal wage bills served as the basis for allocating unspecified wage-like payments among the subsectors within the socialized enterprise sector, with industry obtained as a residual.

APPENDIX F: SELECTED ESTIMATES IN AGRICULTURE

In view of their lengthy and involved character, we present here our estimates of (i) the net money income of individual farms and producer cooperatives and (ii) farm consumption in kind. In other instances, when there was no need for extensive calculations, we estimated the necessary items directly in the documentation of particular entries in the sectoral accounts.

Net money income of individual farms and producer cooperatives

Our estimates of net income of individual farms and producer cooperatives are summarized in Appendix Table F1 and explained in the supporting notes. Laborers employed by state farms also sold part of the produce grown on their household plots (see Poland, Główny urząd statystyczny, *Produkcja globalna i brutto rolnictwa przed wojną i w latach 1946–1958,* p. 19), but, in view of the relatively small gross revenue from sales during 1954–56, the net income available for consumption was considered insignificant and has been omitted.

In so far as producer cooperatives were concerned, apparently no distinction was made in the official sources between income accruing to the cooperatives as enterprises and to members of cooperatives as individuals in 1955–56. In other words, it was implied that all residual income in cooperatives was distributed among members and was available for consumption and saving. Although formally incorrect, since part of the net income of cooperatives was not distributed among the members (see *DN 1954–55,* p. 14), this approach has the advantage of simplicity without detracting in the least from the final estimates of income originating in agriculture.

Appendix Table F1
FARM INCOME
(*Million zlotys*)

	1954	1955	1956
1. Revenue from sale of farm products	31,751	35,150	41,751
a. Centralized procurements ⎫	23,051	24,256	29,651
b. Decentralized procurements ⎭		1,252	1,455
c. Farm market sales	8,700	9,642	10,645
2. Current expenditure	15,301	16,464	16,601
a. Purchases of inputs from other sectors	6,476	7,106	7,901
b. Depreciation	3,951	4,442	4,453
c. Land tax	4,066	4,096	3,683
d. Transfers and other taxes	407	489	484
e. Net insurance payments	401	331	80
3. Net income	16,450	18,686	25,150

Notes to Appendix Table F1

1. Revenue from sale of farm products

Rows 1a. Centralized procurements, and 1b. Decentralized procurements. The 1954 rounded total for centralized and decentralized procurements was taken from Przełaskowski, "Rozwój indywidualnego oszczędzania w krajach socjalistycznych," p. 45. Our independent estimates of centralized procurements based on quantities delivered to, and prices paid by, the state procurement agencies confirm the above estimate.

The 1955–56 figures were taken from *RS 1960,* p. 244. The decentralized procurements relate to purchases by retail trade, hospitals, nurseries, and so forth, from private and cooperative farms. This is evident from *RS 1960,* p. 244, and implicitly from *Finanse,* February, 1959, p. 43.

Row 1c. Farm market sales. Free market sales in 1954 were assumed to represent roughly the same percentage share of total procurements as in 1955. The 1955–56 figures were taken from "Dochody realne ludności chłopskiej z produkcji rolniczej w latach 1956–58," p. 4.

2. Current expenditure

Row 2a. Purchases of inputs from other sectors.

Figures shown for 1955–56 were taken from "Dochody realne ludności chłopskiej z produkcji rolniczej w latach 1956–58," p. 4. Our estimates for 1954 are explained below, estimated as follows (in million zlotys):

1. Artificial fertilizers	1,071
2. Current repairs	1,778
3. Fuel and power	194
a. Coal	126
b. Other fuels	41
c. Electricity	27
4. Industrial feed and seed	978
5. MTS services	383
a. State (POM)	255
b. Communal (GOM)	128
6. Other inputs	2,072
7. Total	6,476

1. This is the product of quantities (*RS 1956*, pp. 175–76) and retail prices of calcium cyanamide ($CaCN_2$), superphosphate (P_2O_5), potash salts (K_2O) and lime (CaO), based in *SC 1957*, p. 17, allowing for differences in percentage content of active ingredients.

2. This was assumed to represent roughly the same ratio with respect to depreciation as in 1955, that is, about 45 percent. See "Dochody realne ludności chłopskiej z produkcji rolniczej w latach 1956–58," p. 4, and the depreciation figure in Appendix Table F1.

3. Net income

3a. According to Kołodziej, "Zaopatrzenie rolnictwa w środki dla produkcji rolnej," pp. 8–9, coal deliveries to farmers amounted to about 65 percent of total rural deliveries, or 2,332 thousand tons. Lacking detailed information, we allowed 20 percent of this to cover such uses as heating of brooders for young poultry, drying of grain, and heating potatoes for feed. In many instances production needs were served concurrently with household uses so that a more precise determination of the share serving production would be difficult. The price of coal was taken from *SC 1957*, p. 16.

3b. This was taken as equal to the 1955 figure estimated from data on rural trade in petroleum products other than for lighting (shown in *RS 1960*, pp. 273, 282), assuming that prices and quantities did not change significantly from 1954. Most retail prices in fact did not change, and the number of combustion engines and other machinery using fuel and lubricants did not change significantly.

3c. According to Thor, "Stan elektryfikacji w Polsce oraz wydatki ludności wiejskiej związane z elektryfikacją," pp. 156–57, the average consumption of electricity for production purposes in 1957 was estimated at 50–55 kilowatt hours per farm. Since the number of electric motors did not change significantly between 1954 and 1957 (Fiutowski and Kozłowski, "Szacunek wyposażenia gospodarstw indywidualnych w maszyny rolnicze," pp. 70–71) and their intensity of use was unlikely to have changed much in the same period, the average consumption per farm in 1954 was estimated at 50 kilowatt hours. The number of individual farms supplied with electricity was 848,700, while 115,000 such farms belonged to cooperatives (Poland, Głowny urząd statystyczny, *Elektryfikacja wsi 1950–1959*, p. 2). The average fee per kilowatt hour was estimated at .57 zlotys (*ibid.*, p. xxvi), based on 1959 rates that were assumed to be unchanged since 1954, paralleling urban rates (see *RS 1960*, p. 404).

4. *RS 1956*, p. 224.

5a. Outlays for services of machine-tractor stations were estimated on the assumption that the share of producer cooperatives and individual farms (about 75 percent) in total receipts of state MTS (POM) was the same as in 1955. The POM receipts are shown in Appendix Table G1, row 2A, and the 1955 payments by cooperatives and individual farms in Poland, Główny urząd statystyczny, *Państwowe i gminne ośrodki maszynowe w 1956 roku*, p. 16.

5b. This was estimated on the assumption that the payments of cooperatives and individual farms to communal MTS (GOM) was equal to their share of GOM dues in MTS (GOM) in 1954. See Poland, Główny urząd statystyczny, *Państwowe i gminne ośrodki maszynowe w 1956 roku*, pp. 22, 23.

6. This item includes such inputs as insecticides, veterinary service, administrative costs, and various other costs not otherwise specified. We estimated this item together with fuel and power costs at 35 percent of the total purchases from other sectors roughly on the basis of 1955 ratios (see "Dochody realne ludności chłopskiej z produkcji rolniczej w latach 1956–58," p. 4). Fuel and power and other components of the total for 1954 are shown above, items 1–5.

Row 2b. Depreciation. The 1954 figure was assumed to represent roughly the same share of total depreciation in agriculture (see Appendix Table H3) as in 1955, that is, 93 percent. The 1955–56 estimates for individual farms were obtained as the difference between the total depreciation in the private material sector of the economy (*DN 1956*, p. 51) and depreciation in private industry and handicraft and private transport (*DN 1956*, pp. 20, 37).

Depreciation in producer cooperatives in 1955 was estimated at 250 million zlotys and in 1956 as insignificant, on the assumption that the increase in depreciation allowances in private agriculture between 1955 and 1956 was roughly equal to depreciation allowances in cooperatives, which after dissolution during 1956 became part of the private sector.

Row 2c. Land tax. See Appendix Table G1, rows 1A2a3 and 1A2b2.

Row 2d. Transfers and other taxes. This item includes payments connected with land reform and with rural electrification and various other fees listed in the notes to Appendix Table G1, row 3A. The 1954 figure was estimated on the assumption that these payments were roughly 10 percent of the figure for land tax, a ratio somewhat lower than in 1955. The 1955–56 data were taken from "Dochody realne ludności chłopskiej z produkcji rolniczej w latach 1956–58," p. 4.

Row 2e. Net insurance payments. These were estimated as follows (in million zlotys):

	1954	1955	1956
Insurance premiums	965	1,038	1,025
Less: Indemnity payments	564	707	945
Equals: Net payments	401	331	80

For 1954, see *RS 1956,* p. 299 (includes socialized farms, but their share was insignificant; see *RS 1957,* pp. 310–11).

For 1955–56, see "Dochody realne ludności chłopskiej z produkcji rolniczej w latach 1956–58," p. 1.

Farm consumption in kind

Estimating farm income in kind in Poland presents a difficult problem, which may be mentioned briefly. Ideally, consumption of farm income in kind should be estimated as the sum of all the commodities entering into it, each valued at its appropriate price. In actual practice, however, the amounts involved are not easily determinable. They may be obtained on the production side as residuals of gross output of each commodity left after subtraction of sales, losses, and amounts used on the farm for feed, seed, and additions to inventories. Such residuals are subject to errors in all the other components. This has to be borne in mind when appraising the reliability of official Polish estimates of farm income in kind for 1954 and 1955, as these appear to have been derived in this way (see *DN 1954–55,* p. 30).

An even more serious problem is posed by the prices at which these amounts should be valued. The usual approach implies valuation of farm income in kind at prices received by farmers for the marketed part of their produce, since these prices correspond to the farmers' marginal rates of substitution between money income and income in kind derived from a given product. This method is widely adopted and is recommended by the Food and Agriculture Organization of the United Nations (FAO) to its member states (FAO, *Agriculture Sector, Accounts and Tables, A Handbook of Definitions and Methods,* pp. 28–29). According to a Polish expert, this method implies, in the case of Poland, valuation of consumption in kind at average realized prices of farm marketings (Płowiec, "Koncepcja dochodów realnych ludości wiejskiej," p. 36). This follows from the existence of different prices for compulsory deliveries, decentralized procurements by state agencies, and free market sales.

It might appear that the free market price best expresses the farmers' marginal rates of substitution. In fact, however, this price depends upon quantities and prices under government procurements. Its use for valuation of farm income in kind would result in an unrealistically high figure. Valuing farm income in kind at retail prices, as is done in some Polish official sources (*DN 1954–55,* p. 3), is even less defensible, since these prices bear no direct relationship to prices actually received by farmers. Moreover, this procedure ignores the basic economic fact that a commodity is "a bundle of utilities"; even apart from differences in physical quality, a pound of butter in retail stores is not the same commodity as on the farm, since services performed by the transportation and distribution systems have added to its value.

In Polish official statistics, three different approaches have been used at various times. Consumption of farm income in kind in 1954 and 1955 is valued both at adjusted retail prices and at average realized farm prices (*DN 1954–55,* p. 3). The latter is computed as a weighted average of prices received by farmers for various types of marketings. Consumption of farm income in kind in 1955 and 1956 is valued at prices received by farmers for above-quota deliveries (*DN 1956,* p. 23).

No serious reservation attaches to the use of Polish official figures for the years 1954 and 1955 in average realized farm prices. They are consistent with figures on alternative allocations of farm produce, such as marketings, farm inputs, and increase in livestock, which are all valued at the same prices. In 1956, however, the official figures value farm consumption in kind and farm inputs into production at prices paid for above-quota deliveries (in the case of inputs, these prices are reduced by 5 percent to allow for lower quality). Marketings are valued at average realized prices, while the increase in livestock is valued at free market prices (*DN 1956*, p. 23).

For the sake of internal consistency of our 1956 estimates and to make them readily comparable with those of other years, we decided to recompute the 1956 farm income in kind and express it in the average realized prices received by farmers for agricultural marketings. For this purpose we constructed a price index based on twelve main products. This index has the form: $I = \Sigma p_1 q / \Sigma p_0 q$, where p_1 = price per unit of above-quota deliveries of a given product in 1956, p_0 = average realized price per unit in 1956, and q = quantity consumed by the rural population in 1955. The use of 1955 quantities as weights was necessitated by the lack of data for 1956.

The calculation of the price index for 1956 is shown in Appendix Table F2. Sources, detailed by columns, are shown below.

APPENDIX TABLE F2

DERIVATION OF THE INDEX OF REALIZED FARM PRICES FOR 1956

(1)	(2)	(3)	(4)	(5)	(6)
					Value
		1956 Price		(million zlotys)	
	Quantity (q)	Above-Quota (p_1)	Average Realized (p_0)	Above-Quota (qp_1)	Average Realized (qp_0)
In thousand tons		(*zlotys per ton*)			
1. Grains	3,213	2,631	1,809	8,453	5,812
2. Pulses (edible)	35	8,853	6,633	309	232
3. Potatoes	3,605	781	455	2,816	1,640
4. Vegetables	766	1,803	1,456	1,381	1,115
5. Fruit	58	2,290	3,538	133	205
6. Pork	412	15,000	13,190	6,180	5,434
7. Veal	15	6,700	5,460	101	82
8. Mutton	21	4,844	3,948	102	83
9. Poultry	15	15,007	18,081	225	271
10. Beef	28	8,000	6,500	224	182
In million liters		(*zlotys per thousand liters*)			
11. Milk	4,467	2,150	2,150	9,604	9,604
In millions		(*zlotys per thousand*)			
12. Eggs	1,889	1,200	1,263	2,267	2,386
Total				31,795	27,046
Index				117.6	100.0

NOTES TO APPENDIX TABLE F2

Columns 1 and 2

See Płowiec, "Przyczynek w sprawie badania spożycia ludności chłopskiej," p. 16.

Columns 3 and 4

Row 1. Grains. Average prices of grains were derived from prices of wheat, rye, and barley (Chlebowczyk, Beskid, and Felbur, *Materiały do badania relacji cen,* p. 329, using as weights amounts consumed on farms in 1958 (Poland, Główny urząd statystyczny, *Produkcja globalna i brutto rolnictwa przed wojną i w latach 1946–1958,* p. 23).

Rows 2, 4, and 5. Pulses, vegetables, and fruits. Above-quota prices were estimated by multiplying 1955 above-quota prices (Płowiec, "Przyczynek w sprawie badania spożycia ludności chłopskiej," p. 16) by the index of farm market prices linking 1955 and 1956 (*RS 1957,* p. 239) on the assumption that above-quota prices moved parallel to farm market prices. Average realized prices were estimated on the assumption that the relative prices of pulses, vegetables, fruit, and potatoes remained unchanged between 1954–55 and 1956. The 1954–55 prices are shown in Gorzelak and Kozłowski, "Zagadnienie cen porównywalnych produktów rolnych w planie 5-letnim," p. 81. Starting with the price of potatoes in 1956 (Chlebowczyk, Beskid, and Felbur, *Materiały do badania relacji cen,* p. 239), we constructed prices for the other items in 1956.

Rows 3, 6, 7, 10, and 11. Potatoes, pork, veal, beef, and milk. For both sets of prices see Chlebowczyk, Beskid, and Felbur, *Materiały do badania relacji cen,* pp. 329–30. The meats refer to animals for slaughter.

Row 8. Mutton. Both prices were estimated on the basis of 1954–55 price relatives between calves and sheep for slaughter. The 1954–55 prices came from Gorzelak and Kozłowski, "Zagadnienie cen porównywalnych produktów rolnich w planie 5-letnim," p. 82; the 1956 prices of calves came from Chlebowczyk, Beskid, and Felbur, *Materiały do badania relacji cen,* p. 330.

Row 9. Poultry. The above-quota price was assumed equal to the average delivery price received by individual farmers, shown in the special insert to Poland, Główny urząd statystyczny, *Produkcja globalna i brutto rolnictwa przed wojną i w latach 1946–1958.* The average realized price is also given there.

Row 12. Eggs. The above-quota prices are given in Chlebowczyk,

Beskid, and Felbur, *Materiały do badania relacji cen,* p. 330; the average realized price was estimated as the delivery and free market prices (*ibid.*) weighted by amounts delivered to the state (1.63 million) and sold on free market (.55 million) in 1955. These amounts were estimated from data on total domestic consumption of eggs (*RS 1960,* p. 408), deliveries to the state (*RS 1960,* p. 246), and consumption on farms (Płowiec, "Przyczynek w sprawie badania spożycia ludności chłopskiej," p. 16).

We assumed that the price index calculated in Appendix Table F2 also applies to products omitted from the sample. Using this index as a deflator, we converted the 1956 farm income in kind given officially in above-quota prices into our estimate at average realized farm prices. Farm consumption in kind for the whole period is shown in Appendix Table F3, and detailed notes on the sources follow.

APPENDIX TABLE F3
FARM CONSUMPTION IN KIND
(*Million zlotys*)

	1954	1955	1956
1. Individual farms	21,338	22,668	29,969
2. Producer cooperatives	1,184	1,361	284
3. State farms	452	547	855
Total	22,974	24,576	31,108

NOTES TO APPENDIX TABLE F3

Row 1. 1954–55: *DN 1954–55,* p. 14; 1956: This is the official estimate in above-quota prices (*DN 1956,* p. 25) deflated by the index of 117.6 (see Appendix Table F2, above).

Row 2. 1954–55: This was estimated on the assumption that the value of consumption per member was the same as on individual farms; the latter, as well as the number of members of cooperatives, was estimated from *DN 1954–55,* p. 14; 1956: This is the official estimate in terms of above-quota prices (*DN 1956,* p. 25) deflated by the index of 117.6 (see Appendix Table F2, above).

Row 3. According to Poland, Głowny, urząd statystyczny, *Produkcja globalna i brutto rolnictwa przed wojną i w latach 1946–1958,* p. ix, in some instances official statistics of consumption in kind in state farms include the value of foodstuffs sold by state farms to their employees and to workers' canteens. It appears, however, that these sales also were a part of retail sales to households, and hence we have excluded them here. Consumption in kind on state farms is considered here as originating exclusively in household plots of employees of state farms.

We estimated consumption in kind on state farms at about 70 percent of the net income derived from household plots. This percentage was based on the data shown in Poland, Głowny urząd statystyczny, *Produkcja globalna i brutto rolnictwa przed wojną i w latach 1946–1958,* pp. 3, 19, 23, 25, and 27. The income from plots for 1954–55 in average realized prices was taken from *DN 1954–55,* p. 13. The estimate for 1956 in above-quota prices (*DN 1956,* p. 25) was deflated by the index of 117.6 given in Appendix Table F2.

APPENDIX G: THE STATE BUDGET

This appendix presents estimates of government revenues and expenditures based on official government budgets as well as on the estimated budgets of quasi-governmental organizations. State budget revenues are shown in Appendix Table G1 and explained in notes thereto.

NOTES TO APPENDIX TABLE G1

With certain exceptions, data for 1954 were taken from *RS 1956*, pp. 295–296, and those for 1955–56, from *RS 1957*, pp. 289–290. We note below only those items of Table G1 which require special comment or sourcing.

Row 1A1a. Indirect taxes paid by socialized enterprises

Row 1A1a2. Budget differences in foreign trade. See Appendix Table D1.

Row 1A1a3. Budget differences outside foreign trade were calculated as the total budget differences less those in foreign trade.

Row 1A1a4. It was assumed that the tax on services in 1954 and 1955 represented 1.76 percent of the turnover tax in the socialized sector as it did in 1956. The 1956 figure was derived from data in *RS 1957*, p. 290, and *RS 1959*, p. 360.

Row 1A1a5. "Other" taxes were calculated as the difference between "other" revenue for the socialized sector (shown in *RS 1956*, p. 296, and *RS 1957*, p. 290) and the sum of the following items shown elsewhere in Appendix Table G1: (*a*) land tax (row 1A2a3); (*b*) tax on services (row 1A1a4); (*c*) revenue of budget enterprises (row 2); and (*d*) transfers of surplus depreciation funds (row 6B). Besides tax-like payments, the residual includes revenue of the Ministries of National Defense and Internal Affairs, which in 1957 amounted to about 500 million zlotys.

APPENDIX TABLE G1
STATE BUDGET REVENUES
(*Million zlotys*)

	1954	1955	1956
1. Taxes	95,170	104,001	108,753
A. From enterprises	89,597	97,566	101,497
(1) Indirect taxes	75,258	80,271	80,931
a. Socialized sector	73,789	78,558	79,266
1. Turnover tax	57,257	56,460	48,784
2. Budget differences in foreign trade	12,200	15,400	25,800
3. Budget differences outside foreign trade	2,223	3,859	2,340
4. Tax on services	1,008	994	857
5. Other taxes	1,101	1,845	1,485
b. Private sector	1,469	1,713	1,665
1. Turnover tax	672	815	749
2. Tax on transfer of property rights	23	28	35
3. Residential tax	13	14	14
4. Real estate tax	712	802	844
5. Other taxes	49	54	23
(2) Direct taxes	14,339	17,295	20,566
a. Socialized sector	9,526	12,508	16,348
1. Income tax	1,481	1,649	1,567
2. Transfer of profits	7,981	10,785	14,711
3. Land tax	64	74	70
b. Private sector	4,813	4,787	4,218
1. Income tax	811	765	605
2. Land tax	4,002	4,022	3,613
B. From households	5,573	6,435	7,256
(1) Income tax	4,988	5,747	6,488
(2) Customs duties	363	420	423
(3) Other taxes	222	268	345
2. Revenue of budget enterprises	440	614	791
A. MTS	340	484	641
B. Other enterprises	100	130	150
3. Current transfers	4,171	3,185	2,961
A. From enterprises	3,455	2,437	2,139
B. From households	716	748	822
4. Social security contributions	12,568	13,556	15,511
5. Loans and deposits	969	1,189	1,671
A. From enterprises	447	599	1,140
B. From foreign sector	522	590	531
6. Capital transfers	2,594	1,033	5,601
A. Working capital	2,414	833	4,951
B. Surplus depreciation funds	180	200	650
7. Sales to foreign sector	55	63	63
8. Other revenue	850	641	324
Total revenue	116,817	124,282	135,675

Row 1A1b. Indirect taxes paid by private enterprises

Row 1A1b2. The tax on transfer of property rights (see Reniger, *Dochody państwowe,* p. 171) was assumed to have been paid by private enterprises and households in equal parts, as was the case of this tax in connection with apartment rentals (see Andrzejewski, *Ekonomika gospodarki mieszkaniowej,* p. 205).

Row 1A1b3. The residential tax on tenants was paid almost entirely by private enterprises and households (Reniger, *Dochody państwowe,* p. 176). As a token allowance we put the share paid by enterprises at 10 percent of the total. The tax revenue in 1954 was from *RS 1955,* p. 208.

Row 1A1b4. The real estate tax covers property not subject to the land tax, and is paid by both socialized and private sectors (Reniger, *Dochody państwowe,* p. 173). Official sources show the tax as being paid only by the private sector, and we assumed that any payments by socialized enterprises are included in the category of "other taxes" (see row 1A1a5, above). The tax revenue in 1954 was taken from *RS 1955,* p. 208.

Row 1A1b5. Revenue from other taxes was estimated as follows (in million zlotys):

	1954	1955	1956
1. Wartime enrichment tax	11	12	11
2. City tax	8	11	12
3. Other taxes not otherwise specified	30	31	
Total	49	54	23

The wartime enrichment tax was presumably paid by private enterprise only (see Reniger, *Dochody państwowe,* p. 218), whereas the city tax was paid by households and by private enterprise using housing space (see Andrzejewski, *Ekonomika gospodarki mieszkaniowej,* p. 204), presumably in about the same ratio as the residential tax discussed above (row 1A1b3). All figures for 1955 and 1956 are from *RS 1960,* p. 416, while the 1954 payments were assumed roughly equal to those made in 1955, except for city tax, which was shown in *RS 1955,* p. 208.

Row 1A2a. Direct taxes paid by socialized enterprises

Row 1A2a3. Land tax paid by socialized enterprises was estimated by subtracting payments made by individual farmers (shown in *RS 1956,* p. 296, and *RS 1957,* p. 290) from the total land tax revenues shown in *DN 1954–55,* p. 14 and *DN 1956,* p. 25.

Row 1B. Taxes paid by households

Row 1B3. Other taxes paid by households were the sum of the following four components (in million zlotys):

	1954	1955	1956
Tax on transfer of property rights	23	27	36
Residential tax	114	130	129
City tax	70	95	106
Other taxes	15	16	74
Total	222	268	345

The first three components were calculated by subtraction of shares paid by private enterprise (see rows 1A1b2, 1A1b3, and 1A1b5, above) from total revenues derived from those taxes (see the general sources cited for Appendix Table G1, p. 173, above). The fourth component includes motor vehicle duties, dog taxes, and so forth; it was estimated, for 1954, as a residual in local government revenue (*RS 1955,* p. 208), whereas for 1955 and 1956, the figures were taken from *RS 1960,* p. 416.

Row 2. Revenues of budget enterprises

Row 2A. MTS. See Appendix Table G2, notes to Row 3a.

Row 2B. Other enterprises are enumerated in notes to Appendix Table G2, row 3b. Their revenues were estimated very roughly on the basis of the planned revenues shown in the 1957 central government budget (*DU 1957,* No. 25).

Row 3. Current transfers

Row 3A. Transfers from enterprises were estimated as follows (in million zlotys) and are explained in the notes below:

	1954	1955	1956
1. Payments in connection with land reform ⎱	115	124	118
2. Electricity fees ⎰		18	38
3. Stamp and administration fees	126	127	137
4. Fines, confiscations	135	137	130
5. Court and notary fees	100	103	141
6. Payments into housing fund	118	121	123
7. Other transfers not otherwise specified	2,861	1,807	1,452
Total	3,455	2,437	2,139

1 and 2. 1954: This is the residual in revenue from private enterprises (*RS 1956,* p. 296) after subtraction of wartime enrichment tax and "other" taxes (see notes to row 1A1b5, above). 1955–56: *RS 1960,* p. 416.

3. It was assumed that this was split equally between enterprises and households. See *RS 1956*, p. 296, and *RS 1960*, p. 416.

4 and 5. Households were assumed to pay 10 percent and enterprises 90 percent of these revenues. 1954: These were taken roughly as equal to the 1955 figure. 1955–56: *RS 1960*, p. 417.

6. 1954: *RS 1955*, p. 208. 1955–56: These were estimated on the assumption that the share of these payments in gross cash rent (Appendix Table A4) was the same as in 1954.

7. This item includes, among others, such payments as passport fees, park and patent fees, and interest on loans made by the government. It was estimated as a residual in total budgetary revenue after subtraction of all other items in Appendix Table G1.

Row 3B. Transfers from households were estimated as follows (in million zlotys):

	1954	1955	1956
1. Social, cultural, and health fees	305	331	340
2. Stamp duties, fines, court and notary fees	151	153	168
3. Radio and television fees	260	264	314
Total	716	748	822

1. 1954: *RS 1956*, p. 296. 1955–56: *RS 1960*, p. 417.

2. This is the residual in total revenue from these sources after subtraction of payments by enterprises (see row 3A, above).

3. 1954: It was assumed to be roughly the same as in 1955. 1955–56: *RS 1960*, p. 417.

Row 6. Capital transfers

Row 6B. Surplus depreciation funds were transferred by enterprises into the government budget. Presumably such transfers took place only in light industries (leather, clothing, and textile) and food industries (including meat and milk), as was the case in 1957. These transfers were estimated on the assumption that they accounted for the same share of depreciation allowances in the industries in question as in 1957 (30 percent in light industries and 15 percent in food industries). Depreciation for 1954–55 is given in *DN 1954–55*, p. 8 (state industry only), for 1956 in Poland, Główny urząd statystyczny, *Statystyka Przemysłu 1957*, p. 34, and for 1957 in *DN 1957–58*, p. 25. Planned depreciation transfers for 1957, assumed actually to have taken place, were shown in the 1957 central government budget (*DU 1957*, No. 25, pp. 308, 317).

Row 7. Sales to foreign sector

This estimate is intended to cover the cost of diplomatic representation of foreign countries as well as other expenditures by foreign governments in Poland. It was assumed to be exactly offset by the expenditures of Polish government abroad, shown in Appendix Table G2, row 6b, below.

Row 8. Other revenue.

According to *RS 1956,* this item consists of transfers from past years' appropriations and refunded expenditures.

State budget current and capital expenditures have been broken down into five categories: national economy; health, education, and welfare; national defense; administration, justice, and internal security; and service of the national debt. Detailed estimates are shown in Appendix Table G2 and are explained in the notes that follow.

NOTES TO APPENDIX TABLE G2

Column 1. National economy

Total expenditure on national economy in 1954–56 is given in *RS 1959,* p. 360. We adjusted the 1956 figure downward by (*a*) the current outlays on economic research institutes (588 million zlotys) and on central laboratories (26 million zlotys), as given in *RS 1957,* p. 292; (*b*) the current outlays on atomic energy research (62 million zlotys; estimated in notes to row 2, Appendix Table G3); and (*c*) the investment outlays in the research activities mentioned in (*a*) and (*b*), estimated roughly at 75 million zlotys, that is, one tenth of the total outlays for these activities. The research institutes and laboratories were financed under health, education, and welfare in 1954–55, and we assumed that atomic energy research was treated the same way.

Some insight into the composition of the expenditure on national economy is provided by the official data for 1955–56 (*RS 1960,* p. 417). In both years, however, there remained an unexplained residual amounting to about 10 percent of total outlay on national economy. In order to account for this residual, frequent use was made of central government budgets for 1957–59 (*DU 1957,* Nos. 25, 56; *DU 1959,* No. 16). This enabled us not only to identify various categories of expenditure but also to estimate their magnitude as a basis for the estimates covering 1954–56. Hence, some of our figures for

APPENDIX TABLE G2
STATE BUDGET EXPENDITURES
(Million zlotys)

1954	(1) National Economy	(2) Health, Education and Welfare	(3) National Defense	(4) Administration, Justice, and Internal Security	(5) National Debt	(6) Total
Current expenditures	26,564	23,751	10,410	9,721	40	70,486
1. Wages and salaries, including social security	23,000	6,877	6,592	6,387		19,856
2. Subsidies	11,500	353				23,353
a. Foreign trade	11,500					11,500
b. Other enterprises		353				11,853
3. Budget enterprises	1,499					1,499
a. MTS	949					949
b. Other	550					550
4. Transfer payments	350	10,558			40	10,948
a. To households		10,558				10,558
b. To enterprises	350				40	390
5. Grants to quasi-governmental organizations		200		1,520		1,720
6. Purchases of goods and services	1,715	5,763	3,818	1,814		13,110
a. From enterprises	1,715	5,748	3,818	1,774		13,055
b. From foreign sector		15		40		55
Capital expenditures	42,150	2,204	528	605	512	45,999
7. Government investment	1,602	2,094	528	605		4,829
a. Fixed capital	1,156	1,623	493	565		3,837
b. Capital repairs	446	471	35	40		992
8. Grants to enterprises	40,548	110				40,658
a. Fixed capital	25,144	85				25,229
b. Capital repairs	1,104	13				1,117
c. Working capital	14,300	12				14,312
9. Repayment of debts and new credits					512	512
a. To enterprises					50	50
b. To foreign sector					462	462
Total expenditures	68,714	25,955	10,938	10,326	552	116,485

APPENDIX TABLE G2 (*Continued*)
STATE BUDGET EXPENDITURES
(*Million zlotys*)

1955	(1) National Economy	(2) Health, Education and Welfare	(3) National Defense	(4) Administration, Justice, and Internal Security	(5) National Debt	(6) Total
Current expenditures	31,349	26,349	11,748	10,719	35	80,200
1. Wages and salaries, including social security		7,700	5,829	6,584		20,113
2. Subsidies	27,324	424				27,748
a. Foreign trade	11,400					11,400
b. Other enterprises	15,924	424				16,348
3. Budget enterprises	1,779					1,779
a. MTS	1,154					1,154
b. Other	625					625
4. Transfer payments	400	11,614			35	12,049
a. To households		11,614				11,614
b. To enterprises	400				35	435
5. Grants to quasi-governmental organizations		292		1,624		1,916
6. Purchases of goods and services	1,846	6,319	5,919	2,511		16,595
a. From enterprises	1,846	6,301	5,919	2,466		16,532
b. From foreign sector		18		45		63
Capital expenditures	38,624	2,467	829	572	502	42,994
7. Government investment	1,453	2,339	829	572		5,193
a. Fixed capital	974	1,763	794	532		4,063
b. Capital repairs	479	576	35	40		1,130
8. Grants to enterprises	37,171	128				37,299
a. Fixed capital	26,771	100				26,871
b. Capital repairs	1,454	14				1,468
c. Working capital	8,946	14				8,960
9. Repayment of debts and new credits					502	502
a. To enterprises					77	77
b. To foreign sector					425	425
Total expenditures	69,973	28,816	12,577	11,291	537	123,194

APPENDIX TABLE G2 (Continued)
STATE BUDGET EXPENDITURES
(Million zlotys)

1956	(1) National Economy	(2) Health, Education and Welfare	(3) National Defense	(4) Administration, Justice, and Internal Security	(5) National Debt	(6) Total
Current expenditures	34,491	30,483	11,715	11,183	60	87,932
1. Wages and salaries, including social security		9,152	5,600	7,318		22,070
2. Subsidies	29,527	647				30,174
a. Foreign trade	16,400					16,400
b. Other enterprises	13,127	647				13,774
3. Budget enterprises	2,353					2,353
a. MTS	1,603					1,603
b. Other	750					750
4. Transfer payments	450	13,117			60	13,627
a. To households		13,117				13,117
b. To enterprises	450				60	510
5. Grants to quasi-governmental organizations		372		1,681		2,053
6. Purchases of goods and services	2,161	7,195	6,115	2,184		17,655
a. From enterprises	2,161	7,182	6,115	2,134		17,592
b. From foreign sector		13		50		63
Capital expenditures	40,331	3,092	967	896	659	45,945
7. Government investment	1,992	2,878	967	896		6,733
a. Fixed capital	1,308	2,090	914	847		5,159
b. Capital repairs	684	788	53	49		1,574
8. Grants to enterprises	38,339	214				38,553
a. Fixed capital	29,255	162				29,417
b. Capital repairs	1,844	29				1,873
c. Working capital	7,240	23				7,263
9. Repayment of debts and new credits					659	659
a. To enterprises					63	63
b. To foreign sector					596	596
Total expenditures	74,822	33,575	12,682	12,079	719	133,877

1954–56 must be considered as rough approximations fitting into the general pattern of budget expenditure for the period 1954–59.

In the notes below we show our sources and derivation of figures of Appendix Table G2 by rows.

Row 2a. Subsidies to foreign trade. See negative budget differences in Appendix Table D1.

Row 2b. Subsidies to other enterprises were derived as shown below (in million zlotys):

	1954	1955	1956
1. Financing of planned losses	8,700	13,477	10,091
2. Negative budget differences	2,700	1,818	1,715
3. Other current grants	100	629	1,321
Total	11,500	15,924	13,127

1. 1954: Pirożyński, "Budżet państwowy Polski Ludowej w okresie uprzemysłowienia," p. 13; 1955–56: *RS 1960,* p. 417.

2. These are the total negative budget differences (1954: Pirożyński, "Budżet państwowy Polski Ludowej w okresie uprzemysłowienia," p. 13; 1955–56: *RS 1960,* p. 417) less negative budget differences in foreign trade (row 2a, above).

3. This is the residual in total budgetary expenditures on the assumption that 1954–56 budgets had a structure similar to those in the period 1957–59. The residual would include grants to finance geological work as well as various grants to agriculture (veterinary service, agricultural training, protection of plants, maintenance of drainage systems, and so forth) and banks. Besides subsidies, this residual item may reflect other items as well as errors in estimates in the directly determined expenditures.

Row 3. Budget enterprises. According to Polish budgetary practice, gross receipts and expenditures of agricultural machine and tractor stations (MTS) and some other enterprises are shown in full in the budget under the heading of "national economy."

Row 3a. MTS. Only the activity of state MTS (POM) is financed fully from the budget; the communal MTS (*GOM*), abolished at the end of 1956, were considered as enterprises. For 1955 and 1956 gross revenues and expenditures of the state MTS were obtained from *RS 1957,* p. 302. The 1954 receipts were estimated by subtraction of subsidies (609 million zlotys, see *Życie gospodarcze,* November 17, 1957, p. 7) from total expenditures. Total expenditures were calculated as the product of total area worked by POM (*RS 1956,* p. 165) and average cost per hectare, which was assumed to have been 2 percent below the 1955 figure (shown in Poland, Główny urząd statystyczny, *Państwowe i gminne ośrodki maszynowe w 1956 roku,* p. vi)—the reduction for 1954 was a rough allowance for increases in wages as an element of total costs.

Row 3b. Other. We include here, as financed from the central budget, various agricultural installations (for example, stud farms), a hunting agency, a machinery export enterprise, a marine salvage enterprise, and a harbor administration, and, in the local government budgets, certain communal services. The expenditure on the enterprises listed in the central budget came to about 600 million zlotys in 1957 and to about 700 million zlotys in 1958 (*DU 1957,* No. 25; *DU 1958,* No. 16). In the absence of information for 1954–56, we estimated such expenditures by rough extrapolation, as follows (in million zlotys): *1954,* 350; *1955,* 400; *1956, 500.* Although we treated all of these activities as belonging to the enterprise sector, the classification is a borderline one in some instances. The remaining portion of the entry in Appendix Table G2 represents a similar allowance from local government budgets and must be considered as of a token character.

Row 4b. Transfer payments to enterprises. These include the following categories of budget expenditure on national economy: prizes, cost of foreign economic cooperation, and so-called "other economic activity." We treated the small sums shown here as transfers from government to the enterprise sector, although some of the elements involved might be put into other categories. The only available data refer to the period 1957–59, and the rounded totals were estimated from central government budgets as follows (in million zlotys): *1957,* 470; *1958,* 460; *1959,* 550. A rough extrapolation gives the figures shown in the table.

Row 6a. Purchases of goods and services from enterprises. This item represents outlays on the maintenance of public highways, waterways, streets, squares, and so forth. The figures shown include both personnel costs and other outlays. The latter were derived from the corresponding entry for wages and salaries (row 1) by first dividing it by 1.155 to arrive at wage costs excluding social security contributions and then multiplying the result by 1.5, roughly the ratio of the personal wage bill to material cost in highway and waterway maintenance in 1957 (see below). The results (in million zlotys) were as follows: *1954,* 969; *1955,* 1,043; *1956,* 1,221.

The remaining component (wages and salaries, including social security) covers employment in the maintenance of (*a*) public high-

ways and inland waterways and (*b*) city streets, squares, and so
forth. The totals for *a* and *b* were as follows (in million zlotys):
1954, 746; *1955,* 803; *1956,* 940. They include social security contributions by employers estimated at 15.5 percent of the personal
wage bill. The nonpersonal wage bill was considered nonexistent. In
the case of (*a*), the personal wage bill was given in *RS 1956,* p. 220,
and *RS 1957,* p. 217 (in million zlotys: *1954,* 466; *1955,* 504; *1956,*
598). The residual in the total, comprising the personal wage bill in
(*b*) above, was estimated roughly in an indirect way as the product
of estimated employment (19 thousand) and average annual wages,
assumed to be the same as in highway maintenance (*RS 1956,* p.
220; *RS 1957,* p. 217). Employment was estimated first for 1957
and taken at the same level for 1954–56. For 1957, we began with
total planned outlays for maintenance of city streets, bridges, squares,
and so forth, namely 616 million zlotys (*Finanse,* 1957, No. 4, p.
12), of which, by analogy to highway maintenance, we took 40
percent to represent the personal wage bill (for highways: see the
wage bill, in *RS 1959,* p. 236; social security contributions estimated
at 15.5 percent of the wage bill; material costs in *DN 1957–58,* p.
55). Dividing the personal wage bill by the estimated average annual
wage, which was taken as equal to that in highway maintenance (RS
1959, p. 236), we arrived at a figure approximating employment.

Row 7a. Government investment: Fixed capital. Government expenditure on fixed capital as a part of the outlays on national economy was estimated roughly for the following categories: highways,
bridges, inland waterways, city streets, parks, and city street lighting.
In the case of highways and bridges, we began with figures for 1957
in 1956 prices (*SIB 1958,* p. 21, in million zlotys: highways, 405;
bridges, 161). To these we applied an index of construction of highways in kilometers and bridges in meters (*RPG 1958,* p. 621) to get
figures for 1954–56, also in 1956 prices. Finally, we divided by a
price index (140.7; see *SIB 1958,* p. 188) linking investment expenditures in transportation and communication in 1955 and 1956
to convert the 1954 and 1955 figures in 1956 prices to current prices.
There apparently was no significant change in prices in this sector
from 1954 to 1955 (see *SIB 1958,* p. 189).

Investment expenditures on inland waterways in 1956 amounted
to 171 million zlotys (*RS 1961,* p. 74). We assumed that in real
terms the same expenditure was made in 1954 and 1955, and we
arrived at figures for these years by deflating the 1956 figure by an
index of 140.7, as above.

Investment outlays on city streets, parks, and street lighting were derived from total investment in commercial economy (in million current zlotys, as given by *SIB 1956*, p. 2: *1954*, 1,273; *1955*, 1,137; *1956*, 1,379) by applying thereto the percentage shares given in Ginsbert, *Gospodarka komunalna w Polsce*, p. 214. As with the items above, we assumed no change in price levels in these categories during 1954–55. Our results were as follows (in million zlotys): *1954*, 251; *1955*, 179; *1956*, 323. Official statistics on 1956 investments in communal economy were raised *ex post facto* in *SIB 1958*, p. 3; we chose, however, to use the earlier total and the indicated percentage breakdown to insure parallel treatment with 1954–55. The difference that would follow from using the later source would be relatively insignificant for our purposes.

Row 7b. Government outlays on capital repairs. These were estimated for the same categories as in 7a, above. In the case of streets, parks, and street lights, we estimated capital repairs as the same percentage of total capital repairs in communal economy excluding housing (see notes to 8b, below) as the share of investment in streets, parks, and street lights was in total communal economy investments (see 7a, above). Our results (in million zlotys: *1954*, 97; *1955*, 88; *1956*, 169) must be considered as rough approximations necessary for a breakdown of the state budget for our sectoral accounts. Capital repairs on highways, bridges, and inland waterways were approximated in proportion to fixed capital outlays in these categories (see 7a, above) in the same ratio as capital repairs were to capital investments in city streets, parks, and street lighting (see above).

Row 8a. Grants to enterprises for fixed capital investment. We show here the total grants for investment given in the sources cited below less the amounts shown in 7a and, in 1956, less an additional 75 million zlotys representing estimated investment in research institutions, which was classified under education in column 2 of Appendix Table G2 for all years but included in national economy in the official figures for 1956 (see notes to Appendix Table G3). 1954: *Finanse*, September, 1961, p. 13. 1955 and 1956: *RS 1959*, p. 361.

Row 8b. Grants to enterprises for capital repairs. The figures shown here consist of (*a*) capital repairs in housing, plus (*b*) capital repairs in other sectors of communal economy. *RPG 1958*, p. 753, states that state budget grants for capital repairs were in principle made only to enterprises in housing and communal economy.

a. Capital repairs in housing were taken from *RS 1959*, p. 72, in 1956 prices. We multiplied the 1954 and 1955 figures by 0.91, a factor based on values appearing in *RS 1957*, p. 185, to convert the values to 1954 and 1955 prices. Of the totals thus obtained (in million zlotys: *1954*, 1,064; *1955*, 1,407; *1956*, 1,706), we took roundly one fifth as state budget grants for repairs to private housing. This ratio is based on data in *RPG 1958*, p. 689, and other sources for more recent years. The ratio suggested for these years, around 25 to 30 percent, was lowered to 20 percent for 1954–56 as a rough allowance for lower priority to private housing in the earlier years. Data in *RS 1956*, p. 276, and *RPG 1959*, p. 636, suggest that all of capital repairs in housing (including properties in the ownership of the local governments, other state authorities, and private persons) were fully covered by subsidies.

b. Capital repairs in other sectors of communal economy were shown directly (in million zlotys) in *RPG 1960*, p. 597, as follows: *1955*, 559; *1956*, 723. We estimated 1954 at 492 from the 1955 figure by means of an index given in Ginsbert, *Ekonomika gospodarki komunalnej*, Part III, p. 24. A part of these totals refers to estimated capital repairs of city streets, lights, and parks (see 7b, above), which were financed by the state budget, and the balance (in million zlotys: *1954*, 395; *1955*, 471; *1956*, 554) refers primarily to enterprises. For the latter, we assumed that subsidies from the state budget covered 10 percent of the cost of capital repairs in 1954–55 and 25 percent in 1956. These percentages must be regarded as bordering on guesses in the light of information in *Finanse*, 1959, No. 4, pp. 29, 30, 33. This source indicated that, to the end of 1955, communal enterprises as a whole covered their costs by their charges for services, excepting water supply, street cleaning, and garbage disposal, where deficits were significantly increased. During 1956 a substantial increase in the costs of supplies and labor together with very low depreciation allowances and unrealistically low prices on services led to a sharp increase in deficits of communal enterprises, and there were inadequate funds to cover capital repairs. During 1959 the state budget met 29.2 percent of the cost of capital repairs of communal enterprises.

Row 8c. Grants to enterprises for working capital. 1954: *Finanse*, September, 1961, p. 13, 1955–56: *RS 1959*, p. 361.

Column 2. Health, education and welfare

Budgetary expenditures on health, education, and welfare were divided among five main categories: art and culture, science and research, social welfare, health and physical culture, and education. Detailed estimates are shown in Appendix Table G3 and explained in the notes and tables below (see pp. 186 ff.), with the exception of purchases of goods and services from the foreign sector and from domestic enterprises (rows 6a and 6b), which we explain here. The amounts in question for 1955–56 are orders of magnitude estimated at one half of the budget appropriations for cultural cooperation with foreign countries and study abroad (*RS 1957*, pp. 292–93). The 1954 figure is a guess based on the 1955 figure. Purchases from domestic enterprises (row 6a) is the residual in the total in row 6 as given in Appendix Table G3.

NOTES TO APPENDIX TABLE G 3

Column 1. Total

Row 1. Total expenditures in 1954–55 were estimated as total outlays on "social and cultural services" (*RS 1956*, p. 295), less grants to quasi-governmental organizations, which were transferred from the category "social welfare" to the category "administration." The amount of these grants in 1955 was 229 million zlotys (see the heading *inne świadczenia socjalne* in *RS 1957*, p. 295), and we estimated them roughly at 200 million zlotys in 1954, roughly in the same ratio to the total outlays as in 1955. The 1956 figure represents total outlays on "socialized cultural services" (*RS 1957*, p. 289), plus current and capital outlays on research, central laboratories, and atomic energy (see notes to column *3*, below), less grants to quasi-governmental organizations (1,681 million zlotys; see *RS 1957*, p. 295). Beginning with 1956, outlays on the research noted above formed a part of the expenditure on "national economy" (see *RS 1957*, p. 292), but they were shifted here to insure comparability with 1954 and 1955.

Row 2. Current expenditures were obtained as a residual in total expenditure after subtraction of investment expenditure.

Row 2a. Wages, including social security. See Appendix Table E1, row III A, columns *4* and *7*.

Rows 2b. Transfers, 2c. Subsidies, 2d. Grants to quasi-governmental organizations. These represent the sums of components in columns *2* to *6*.

Row 2e. Purchases of goods and services. This is the residual in total current expenditures.

APPENDIX TABLE G3

BUDGET EXPENDITURES ON HEALTH, EDUCATION, AND WELFARE

(Million zlotys)

	(1) Total	(2) Art and Culture	(3) Science and Research	(4) Social Welfare	(5) Health and Physical Culture	(6) Education
1954						
1. Total	25,955	1,138	970	9,801	5,590	8,456
2. Current expenditures	23,751	890	864	9,789	5,042	7,166
a. Wages, including social security	6,877	255	489		2,244	3,888
b. Transfers	10,558	275		9,633		925
c. Subsidies	353			17	20	41
d. Grants to quasi-governmental organizations	200			100	100	
e. Purchases of goods and services	5,763	360	375	39	2,678	2,311
3. Investment expenditures	2,204	248	106	12	548	1,290
a. Fixed capital	1,623	135	97		370	1,021
b. Capital repairs	471	22	9		171	269
c. Fixed capital grants	85	73		8	4	
d. Working capital grants	12	12				
e. Grants for capital repairs	13	6		4	3	
1955						
1. Total	28,816	1,262	1,108	10,763	6,375	9,308
2. Current expenditures	26,349	992	987	10,751	5,733	7,886
a. Wages, including social security	7,700	288	558		2,587	4,266
b. Transfers	11,614	3		10,511		1,100
c. Subsidies	424	330		17	22	55

APPENDIX TABLE G3 (Continued)

BUDGET EXPENDITURES ON HEALTH, EDUCATION, AND WELFARE

(Million zlotys)

	(1) Total	(2) Art and Culture	(3) Science and Research	(4) Social Welfare	(5) Health and Physical Culture	(6) Education
1954						
d. Grants to quasi-governmental organizations	292			180	112	
e. Purchases of goods and services	6,319	371	429	43	3,012	2,464
3. Investment expenditures	2,467	270	121	12	642	1,422
a. Fixed capital	1,763	133	111		436	1,083
b. Capital repairs	576	28	10		199	339
c. Fixed capital grants	100	88		8	4	
d. Working capital grants	14	14				
e. Grants for capital repairs	14	7		4	3	
1956						
1. Total	33,575	1,600	1,147	12,353	7,785	10,690
2. Current expenditures	30,483	1,314	1,022	12,326	6,913	8,908
a. Wages, including social security	9,152	330	580		3,134	5,109
b. Transfers	13,117	6		12,036		
c. Subsidies	647	536		18	30	1,075
d. Grants to quasi-governmental organizations	372			222	150	63
e. Purchases of goods and services	7,195	442	442	50	3,599	2,662
3. Investment expenditures	3,092	286	125	27	872	1,782
a. Fixed capital	2,090	56	115		583	1,336
b. Capital repairs	788	53	10		279	446
c. Fixed capital grants	162	143		13	6	
d. Working capital grants	23	23				
e. Grants for capital repairs	29	11		14	4	

Row 3. Total investment expenditures were derived in the tabulation below (in million zlotys):

	1954	1955	1956
1. Fixed capital expenditures as shown in the budget	1,708	1,863	2,177
Plus:			
2. Capital repairs as shown in the budget	484	590	810
3. Financing working capital	12	14	23
4. Fixed capital and capital repairs expenditure in industrial research, central laboratories, and atomic energy			82
Equals:			
5. Total	2,204	2,467	3,092

1. 1954: *RS 1956,* p. 296. 1955–56: *RS 1957,* p. 290.

2. 1954: This was estimated on the assumption that capital repairs shown below in columns 2 to 5 for subsectors other than education accounted for roughly 45 percent of all capital repairs, that is, the same as in 1955. 1955–56: RS 1957, p. 290.

3. Estimated below in notes to column 2.

4. Estimated in notes to column 3. This sum was added to insure comparability with 1954–55.

Fixed capital outlays (row 3a) were obtained by subtracting grants for fixed capital (row 3c) from fixed capital expenditures as shown in the budget (see tabulation in the note to row 3, above). In 1956 we added 75 million zlotys, a transfer from the expenditure on "national economy," representing fixed capital investment in industrial research, central laboratories, and atomic energy research (see notes to column 3 below). This reclassification parallels the practice in 1954–55. Outlays on capital repairs (row 3b) were similarly obtained by subtracting grants for capital repairs (row 3d, derived below) from outlays on capital repairs as shown in the budget and adding, in 1956, 7 million zlotys, the estimated capital repairs in the research activities noted above (see notes to column 3). Other items of investment (3c, 3d, 3e) represent row totals of components given in other columns.

Column 2. Art and culture

Budget expenditures under art and culture covered the following activities: (*a*) museums, public libraries, exhibitions, cultural exchange with abroad, Polish Press Agency, and other minor cultural institutions; (*b*) Polish Radio, a state-owned broadcasting corporation; (*c*) theaters, symphony orchestras, and other entertainment services, publishing houses, and the motion picture industry. These enter the state budget only to the extent of their subsidies.

The first two major categories are treated by us as belonging to the government sector proper. The last category is considered as falling in the enterprise sector. Documentation of row entries follow below.

Row 1. Total. 1954: *RS 1956,* p. 296. 1955–56: *RS 1957,* p. 293.

Row 2. Total current expenditures were obtained as a residual in total expenditure after subtraction of investment expenditure.

Row 2a. Wages, including social security. See Appendix Table E1, row III A1, columns *4* to *7*.

Row 2b. Transfers. 1954: It was assumed these were insignificant. 1955–56: These were stipends (see *RS 1957,* p. 295).

Row 2c. Subsidies to enterprises. 1954: These were assumed to represent roughly 30 percent of total current expenditure plus capital repairs and grants for capital repairs. 1955–56: On the basis of central government budgets for 1957–59 (*DU 1957,* No. 25, pp. 283, 289; *DU 1958,* No. 18, p. 215; *DU 1959,* No. 16, pp. 180–81), it was assumed that subsidies accounted for 94 percent of current budgetary grants (including grants for capital repairs, see *RS 1957,* p. 293) to enterprises in 1955–56.

Row 2e. Purchases of goods and services were obtained as the residual item in the total for row 2. As such it may include some, presumably negligible, grants and payments for items other than purchases.

Row 3a. and 3c. Expenditures on fixed capital. The total of these two items was given in *RS 1956,* p. 296, and *RS 1957,* p. 290. Fixed capital grants (row 3c) were estimated on the basis of state budgets for 1957–59 very roughly at 20 percent of total government grants to *khozraschet* enterprises, the other 80 percent being composed of subsidies (row 2c), working capital grants (row 3d), and grants for capital repairs (row 3e), all of which were estimated before determining row 3c. Expenditures on fixed capital (row 3a) were obtained as a residual in the total for rows 3a and 3c.

Rows 3b and 3e. Capital repairs. 1954: The sum of the two items was assumed to represent roughly the same share of the total of current expenditure (capital repairs and grants for working capital) as in 1955 (3 percent).

Column 3. Science and research

Row 1. Total expenditures were the sum of current and investment expenditures (rows 2 and 3).

Row 2. Current expenditures. 1954: In the absence of other information we assumed that total current budget expenditures (including capital repairs) on research, with the exception of atomic energy, represented 40 percent of total current budgetary expenditures on science and higher education as shown in *RS 1956,* p. 296, that is, 821 million zlotys. The corresponding ratios in 1955 and 1956 were 38.5 percent and 36.5 percent respectively (see *RS 1957,* p. 292). The estimated expenditures for 1954 are thus about 10 percent below the expenditures for 1955, as was also the case for general education.

Expenditures on atomic energy were assumed to represent 6 percent of total expenditures on research (including atomic energy), as in 1955–56. Total current budget expenditures on research in 1954 were estimated at 873 million zlotys, of which 9 million zlotys were estimated capital repairs (row 3b) and the balance was entered in row 2.

1955–56: Total current budget expenditures on the research activities enumerated above, but excluding atomic energy, came to 937 million zlotys in 1955 and 970 million in 1956 (*RS 1957,* p. 292). These figures include outlays on capital repairs. Outlays on atomic energy research were estimated on the basis of the 1959 planned budget (*DU 1959,* No. 16, pp. 181 ff) at 6 percent of the total including atomic energy. Proceeding very roughly on the basis of this percentage and the totals excluding atomic energy given above (taken to represent 94 percent of the comprehensive total), we estimated the outlays on atomic energy research (in million zlotys) in 1954, 1955, and 1956, respectively, at 52, 60, and 62. Subtracting the estimated capital repairs (row 3b) from the comprehensive total, we obtained the values shown in row 2.

Row 2a. Wages, including social security. See Appendix Table E1, row III A2, columns *4* and *7.*

Row 2e. Purchases of goods and services were estimated as a residual in total current expenditure after subtraction of wages (row 2a). In addition to purchases of goods and services, the figure contains other payments such as subsidies for publications, some wage-like payments, and grants, which, however, were relatively insignificant and could be ignored.

Row 3a. Fixed capital expenditures. No data on planned investment expenditure in research institutions (excluding atomic energy
research) were available except for 1958, when it amounted to about
8 percent of planned total budgetary expenditure. It was assumed
that investment expenditure during the years 1954–56 was slightly
higher and amounted to 10 percent of total budgetary expenditure
(rows 2, 3a, 3b), including atomic energy. The same percentage was
applied also to research institutes and atomic energy research in
1956, which were transferred from the category "national economy."

Row 3b. Capital repairs. According to central government budgets,
capital repairs in research institutions (excluding atomic energy research) accounted for 1.5 to 2.0 percent of total planned current
budget expenditure (including capital repairs) during 1957–59. We
assumed that capital repairs in all research institutions during 1954–
56 accounted for 1 percent of current budget expenditure, including
capital repairs.

Column 4. Social Welfare
Row 1. Total expenditures were the sum of current and investment
expenditure.

Row 2. Current expenditure was obtained from the state budget
figures (excluding investments but including capital repairs) as shown
in the budget of social welfare, which covered social insurance and
other social services (*RS 1956*, p. 296, *RS 1957*, p. 285), less (*a*)
expenditure on hospitalization (1956 only, 101 million zlotys; see
RS 1957, p. 295) and welfare institutions (1954: assumed equal to
the expenditure in 1955; 1955 and 1956, 138 million zlotys and 251
million zlotys, respectively; see *RS 1957*, p. 295), both of which we
transferred to the category "health and physical culture," less (*b*)
grants to quasi-governmental organizations (*inne świadczenia socjalne*), which we transferred to the category "administration and
justice" (1954: assumed to equal 200 million zlotys, roughly 2 percent of the official social welfare budget, that is, the same ratio as in
1955; 1955–56: *RS 1957*, p. 295), less (*c*) capital repairs (estimated in row 3e below).

Row 2a. We assumed that wages were insignificant in this category
that dealt primarily with grants and transfers.

Row 2b. Transfers represent the sum of pensions and allowances
paid by the social security administration (1954: *RS 1956*, pp. 287–
88; 1955–56: *RS 1957*, p. 295) plus pensions paid by the Ministry

of Railroads. Their total in 1955–56 was included in the total paid by social security administration (*renty* and *zasiłki*), whereas the sum in 1954 was assumed equal to the 1955 figure obtained as the difference between complete and incomplete figures (*RS 1956,* pp. 287–88; *RS 1957,* pp. 285, 295).

Row 2c. Subsidies to enterprises. 1954: This was assumed roughly equal to the 1955 figure, 1955–56: *RS 1957,* p. 295, under the heading *dotacja dla stołówek pracowniczych.*

Row 2d. Grants to quasi-governmental organizations. We identified here, for 1955–56, grants to the Workers Holiday Fund, supervised by the trade unions, and holiday grants (*RS 1957,* p. 295). According to the central government budgets for 1957–59, budgetary expenditure on "social organizations" included grants for fixed capital and capital repairs. The latter (estimated in row 3e, below) were subtracted to obtain current grants in row 2d. The corresponding figure for 1954 was estimated as the residual in total current expenditure after subtraction of transfers (row 2b), subsidies (row 2c), and current purchases (row 2e).

Row 2e. Purchases of goods and services. 1955–56: This was obtained as a residual in current expenditure after subtraction of rows 2b, 2c, and 2d. 1954: This was estimated in proportion to transfers (row 2b) on the basis of the ratio in 1955.

Row 3c. and 3e. Fixed capital grants and grants for capital repairs. According to the 1957–59 central government budgets, grants to the Workers Holiday Fund included grants for fixed capital investment and for capital repairs. On the basis of the 1957 budget (*DU 1957,* No. 25, pp. 243, 361), fixed capital grants were assumed to equal one half of the fixed capital expenditure in each year under "social security and other social services" (*RS 1956,* p. 296, and *RS 1957,* p. 290). Grants for capital repairs were also assumed to equal one half of capital repairs during 1955–56, as shown in the budget (*RS 1957,* p. 290), while the grants for 1954 were assumed to equal the 1955 figure.

Column 5. Health and physical culture

This sector includes expenditures on the following major categories: (*a*) Health service and physical culture (hospitals, sanitariums, clinics, first aid stations, laboratories, drugs and medicines, stadiums, sport events, and so forth), (*b*) *khozrashchet* enterprises controlled by the Ministry of Health, as well as enterprises in charge of sports events, (*c*) quasi-governmental organizations (Polish Red

Cross, sports clubs, tourist clubs). Documentation for the row entries follows.

Row 1. Total expenditures is the sum of current and investment expenditures.

Row 2. Current expenditure was obtained from the current budget expenditure (including capital repairs but excluding investment) as shown in the budget (*RS 1956*, p. 296; *RS 1957*, p. 290), plus expenditure on welfare institutions and hospitalization, transferred from the social welfare budget (see notes to column *4*, above), minus capital repairs (estimated in row 3b and 3e below).

Row 2a. Wages, including social security. See Appendix Table E1, row III A3, columns *4* and *7*.

Row 2b. Transfers. 1954: It was assumed there were none. 1955–56: *RS 1957*, p. 295.

Row 2c. Subsidies to enterprises. 1954: These were assumed to equal roughly the 1955 figure. 1955–56: On the basis of the central government budget for 1957 (*DU 1957*, No. 25), it was assumed that subsidies accounted for 10 percent of expenditure on health and physical culture not listed in detail in *RS 1957*, pp. 293–94.

Row 2d. Grants to quasi-governmental organizations. 1954: These were assumed to represent roundly the same share of total current budget expenditure, including capital repairs, as in 1955. 1955–56: On the basis of the central government budget for 1958 (*DU 1958*, No. 16), we assumed that grants to quasi-governmental organizations accounted for about 50 percent of the expenditure on health and physical culture not listed in detail in *RS 1957*, pp. 293–94.

Row 2e. The amount for purchases of goods and services was obtained as a residual in total current expenditure (row 2) after subtraction of the other components.

Row 3a. Fixed capital was obtained from the sum of investment expenditures as shown in the state budget (*RS 1956*, p. 296; *RS 1957*, p. 290) less fixed capital grants to enterprises (estimated in row 3c, below), plus investment expenditure in welfare institutions transferred to health and physical culture (estimated at 8, 8, and 13 million zlotys for 1954, 1955, and 1956, respectively, namely, one half of the investment under "social security and other social services"; see notes to rows 3c and 3e of column *4*, above, and *RS 1957*, p. 290).

Row 3b. Capital repairs were estimated as equal to capital repairs in health and physical culture (1954: taken at 170 million zlotys, roughly the same share of current expenditure, including capital repairs, as in 1955; 1955–56: *RS 1957*, p. 290), less grants to enterprises for capital repairs (estimated in row 3e, below), plus capital repairs in welfare institutions which we transferred to "health and physical culture" (estimated in notes to rows 3c and 3e of column *4*, above, as one half of the total for "social security and other social services" shown in official sources or estimated).

Row 3c and 3e. Fixed capital grants and grants for capital repairs were assumed to account for 15 percent and 10 percent, respectively, of total budget expenditure on *khozraschet* enterprises in each year. The total itself was estimated from subsidy payments (see row 2c, above), which were taken to represent 75 percent of this total. All of these ratios were based on the planned central government budget for 1957 (*DU 1957*, No. 25) and should be considered as orders of magnitude.

Column 6. Education

Budget expenditures for education in Appendix Table G3 were obtained as residuals in the row totals in column *1*, excepting rows 2a, 2b, and 2c, which we document below.

Row 2a. See Appendix Table E1, row III A4, columns *4* and *7*.

Row 2b. Transfers. 1955–56: These were educational stipends (*RS 1957*, p. 295). 1954: This was estimated from the 1955 total on the assumption that these totals were in the same proportion as stipends to higher education in these years. The latter amounted to 344 million zlotys in 1954 (*Przegląd zagadnień socjalnych*, 1955, No. 1, p. 27) and to 409 million zlotys in 1955 (*RS 1957*, p. 295).

Row 2c. Subsidies. 1955–56: These were grants to *khozraschet* enterprises (*RS 1957*, p. 292). 1954: This was assumed to represent roughly the same share of current budget expenditures on higher education (*RS 1956*, p. 296) as in 1955 (2 percent).

NOTES TO APPENDIX TABLE G2 (continued)

Column 3. National defense

Expenditures from the budget for national defense are thought to cover not only the regular armed forces but also the Internal Security Corps (*KBW*), a kind of riot troops, and border guards (*WOP*), both of which were controlled by the Ministry of Interior (*DU 1954*, No. 54). Such was the situation in 1950 (*DU 1950*, Annex to No. 16, p. 26). The size of budget appropriations for internal security in 1954–56 would also support this assumption.

The breakdown of expenditures on National Defense was estimated as follows (in million zlotys):

	1954	1955	1956
1. Total explicit budget expenditures on defense	10,938	12,577	12,682
2. Military pay and subsistence, including wages of civilian employees	6,592	5,829	5,600
3. Capital repairs	35	35	53
4. Investment expenditures	493	794	914
5. Current purchases	3,818	5,919	6,115

1. *RS 1959*, p. 360. According to *RS 1956*, p. 295, the increase in expenditure between 1954 and 1955 was due to price increases of military supplies.

2. See Appendix Table E1, row III D, columns *4* and *7*.

3. 1954: This was assumed equal to the 1955 figure. 1955: The total value of capital repairs in defense and administration, justice, and internal security (assumed to equal 73 percent of the 1956 figure, which was the ratio in the case of health, education, and welfare) was divided between these categories in proportion to planned budget expenditures on investment in 1955 (see *DU 1955*, No. 15, p. 115). 1956: The residual in capital repairs in the government sector (*DN 1956*, p. 46), after subtracting expenditure on capital repairs in health, education, and welfare institutions (rows 3b and 3c of Appendix Table G3) was allocated among national defense, administration, and internal security, including justice, approximately in the ratio of their respective investment expenditures (see above for national defense and Appendix Table G4 for others).

4. See notes to Appendix Table G4, columns *6* to *8*, below.

5. This was the residual in the total.

Column 4. Administration, justice, and internal security

This item includes the following subsectors: (*a*) central and local government administration (ministries, local councils, government committees, industrial boards); (*b*) administration of justice (courts, office of the prosecutor general); and (*c*) internal security (militia, secret police, fire service, administration of prisons).

In the official budgetary classification, *b* and *c* are shown together under the heading "administration of justice and internal security." An attempt was made to separate these two categories, but the institutional changes that occurred between 1954 and 1956 make the individual totals not strictly comparable. For example, in October,

1956, administration of prisons was transferred from the jurisdiction of the Ministry of Interior to that of the Ministry of Justice (*DU 1956,* No. 41). Judging by the 1957 budget, internal security accounted for a little over 80 percent of the appropriation for internal security and justice.

We show expenditure on maintaining fire brigades as covered by the budget for internal security, since the fire prevention service came under the jurisdiction of the Ministry of the Interior (see *RPG 1958,* p. 140); but the information on this point is not conclusive. The official industrial classification (Annex No. 1 to Order No. 32 of the Chairman of the Central Statistical Office, dated August 14, 1959) lists fire prevention services under "communal economy"; earlier publications on communal services, however, do not mention fire protection (see Ginsbert, *Gospodarka komunalna w Polsce*).

Expenditure on internal security troops and special frontier troops, controlled by the Ministry of Interior, was included with expenditure on national defense (see notes to column *3,* above).

The breakdown expenditure on administration, justice, and internal security is shown in Appendix Table G4 and explained in notes thereto (see pp. 197 ff.).

Column 5. National debt

Budget expenditures on the national debt cover both internal and external debts. *DU 1957,* No. 25, p. 261, indicates two main components of the servicing of internal debt: (*a*) debts incurred during the postwar period through subscription among the population, and (*b*) repayments of deposits plus interest. The former probably refers to various debts owed to the National Bank of Poland, whereas the latter apparently represents the repayment of deposits of various financial institutions that were required to transfer their surpluses to the budget (see Reniger, *Dochody państwowe,* p. 259).

We estimated the debt service as follows (in million zlotys):

	1954	1955	1956
1. Total debt service	552	537	719
Less:			
2. Foreign debt	462	425	596
3. Repayment of internal debt	50	77	63
Equals:			
4. Interest on internal debt including premiums	40	35	60

1. 1954: *RS 1956,* p. 295. 1955–56: *RS 1957,* p. 289.

2. Service of foreign debt was assumed equal to the planned amounts. 1954: *DU 1954,* No. 19, p. 115. 1955: *DU 1955,* No. 15, p. 115. 1956: *DU 1956,* No. 12, p. 65.

3. *RS 1959,* p. 364.

Appendix Table G4 and notes thereto provide the documentation for column *4* of Appendix Table G2.

NOTES TO APPENDIX TABLE G4

Column *1.* Total. This represents the total expenditure on administration, justice, and internal security (*RS 1961,* p. 396) plus grants to quasi-governmental organizations, transferred from the social welfare budget for the sake of comparability (see notes to Appendix Table G3, column *4*). The subtotals for administration, justice, and internal security were obtained as sums of current and investment expenditures.

Column *2.* Current expenditure. Total current expenditure was equal to total expenditure minus investment expenditure (column *6*). The subtotals for (*a*) administration and (*b*) internal security and justice were obtained as follows: Current expenditures, including capital repairs, for the entire sector, were allocated between the two major subsectors in proportion to their planned current budgetary expenditures shown in the state budgets. For 1954 and 1955 we used the corresponding state budgets (*DU 1954,* No. 19, pp. 115–19, and *DU 1955,* No. 15, pp. 115–19). For 1956 we used the 1957 budget (*DU 1957,* No. 25, pp. 242–44), since the proportions given there fit the actualities of 1956 better than the plan for 1956. This was presumably owing to wage increases in the second half of 1956 as well as to political changes which appear to have resulted in lower actual expenditure on internal security than was planned. The figures for administration were increased by the amount of grants to quasi-governmental organizations transferred from the social welfare budget (see notes to Appendix Table G3, column *4*). Capital repairs (estimated in notes to column *8,* below) were subtracted from each subtotal. Current expenditure on justice was estimated on the assumption that the total wage bill, including social security (Appendix Table E1, row III B2), accounted for two thirds of total current budget expenditure, including capital repairs, as was the case in the 1957 state budget (*DU 1957,* No. 25, pp. 328, 346, 348). Here again capital repairs were subtracted from the total and shown separately

APPENDIX TABLE G4

BUDGETARY EXPENDITURE ON ADMINISTRATION, JUSTICE, AND INTERNAL SECURITY

(Million zlotys)

	(1) Total	(2) Current Expenditure	(3) Wages, including Social Security	(4) Grants to Quasi-governmental Organizations	(5) Current Purchases of Goods and Services	(6) Investment Expenditures	(7) Fixed Capital	(8) Capital Repairs
1954								
Total	10,326	9,721	6,387	1,520	1,814	605	565	40
Administration	6,511	6,080	3,799	1,520	761	431	402	29
Justice	311	290	194		96	21	20	1
Internal security	3,504	3,351	2,394		957	153	143	10
1955								
Total	11,291	10,719	6,584	1,624	2,511	572	532	40
Administration	6,856	6,497	4,141	1,624	732	359	330	29
Justice	325	308	206		102	17	16	1
Internal security	4,110	3,914	2,237		1,677	196	186	10
1956								
Total	12,079	11,183	7,318	1,681	2,184	896	847	49
Administration	7,215	6,867	4,742	1,681	444	348	329	19
Justice	428	405	272		133	23	20	3
Internal security	4,436	3,911	2,304		1,607	525	498	27

in Appendix Table G4. Current expenditure on internal security was obtained as a residual in total current expenditure.

Column *3*. Wages, including social security. See Appendix Table E1, rows III B and III C, columns *4* and *7*.

Column *4*. Grants to quasi-governmental organizations were assumed to have been financed from the administration budgets. 1954–55: These were assumed to represent roughly the same share of the administration current expenditure as in 1956 (25 percent; see Appendix Table G4). 1956: This amount was assumed equal to the total shown in the official social welfare budget for 1956 and said to have been financed prior to 1956 out of the administration budget (*RS 1957*, p. 295).

Column *5*. Current purchases of goods and services. This figure was obtained as a residual in current expenditure (column *2*) after subtraction of wages (column *3*) and grants (column *4*). Out of the total residual, we allocated to purchases from abroad (in million zlotys): *1954,* 40; *1955,* 45; *1956,* 50. These estimates were based on the amounts budgeted from 1957 (*DU 1957,* No. 25).

Column *6*. Investment expenditure. This is the sum of expenditures on fixed capital investment and capital repairs.

Column *7*. Fixed capital investment. Total fixed capital investment in administration, justice, internal security and defense was estimated as the residual in total fixed capital investment financed from the budget (*RS 1961,* p. 396) after subtraction of investment grants financed from the category "national economy" (1954: see Appendix Table G2; 1955–56: see *RS 1961,* p. 398) and fixed capital investment financed from the category "health, education and welfare" (1954: see Appendix Table G3, rows 3a and 3c; 1955–56: see *RS 1961,* p. 398). The residual was allocated among central administration, local administration, administration, justice and internal security, and defense according to the planned investment expenditures shown in state budgets for 1954, 1955, and 1957. Within the total for justice and internal security, fixed capital investment in justice was estimated on the assumption that it represented the same share of total expenditure in each year as in the case of administration, and fixed capital investment in internal security was obtained as the residual.

Column *8*. Capital repairs. Capital repairs in administration, justice and internal security, and defense for 1954–55 were assumed to equal 75 million zlotys in each year, roughly in the same ratio to the 1956 figure as in the case of capital repairs plus grants for capi-

tal repairs in health, education, and welfare (see Appendix Table
G3). The value for 1956 (102 million zlotys) was obtained as the
residual in the total cost of capital repairs in the government sector
(*DN 1956,* p. 46) after subtraction of capital repairs in health, education, and welfare (Appendix Table G3). These totals were then
allocated among administration, justice and internal security, and defense, in the same manner as fixed capital investment (see column 7,
above). The figure for capital repairs in justice and internal security
was allocated between the two subsectors in proportion to their
current expenditures.

BUDGETS OF QUASI-GOVERNMENTAL ORGANIZATIONS

The budgets of quasi-governmental organizations are shown in Appendix Table G5 and explained in notes thereto.

APPENDIX TABLE G5
BUDGETS OF QUASI-GOVERNMENTAL ORGANIZATIONS
(*Million zlotys*)

	1954	1955	1956
Expenditures			
1. Wages, including social security	538	541	546
2. Transfers to households	151	155	182
3. Transfers to state budget	16	18	19
4. Purchases of goods and services	1,157	1,384	1,583
Total	1,862	2,098	2,330
Revenues			
5. Membership dues	693	703	727
6. Admission fees	25	39	55
7. Budgetary grants	1,144	1,356	1,548
Total	1,862	2,098	2,330

NOTES TO APPENDIX TABLE G5

Row 1. Wages, including social security. See Appendix Table E1,
row III E, columns 4 and 7.

Row 2. Transfers to households. This item includes statutory benefits paid by trade unions (*RS 1960,* p. 401; 1954 assumed equal to
1955) and benefits paid by loan associations operating under the
aegis of trade unions (*RPG 1958,* p. 363).

Row 3. Transfers to state budgets. This item covers admission
fees to sports events and fees charged by tourist hostels, which, according to Reniger, *Dochody państwowe,* p. 247, are paid into the

state budget as part of the revenue from social and cultural services. The revenue from sports was obtained as the product of the number of spectators attending admission-charging events in each year (*RS 1956*, p. 363; *RS 1957*, p. 373) and the average admission charge in 1956 (*RS 1957*, p. 373), which was assumed valid also for 1954 and 1955. Income of tourist hostels was estimated as the product of the number of nights lodgings provided (*RS 1955*, p. 257; *RS 1957*, p. 370) and the average fee, which was assumed to have been 10 zlotys.

Row 4. Purchases of goods and services. These figures were obtained as a residual in total expenditures, the latter being taken as equal to total revenues.

Row 5. Membership dues. These amounts were roughly estimated as follows (in million zlotys):

	1954	1955	1956
a. Trade unions	400	405	445
b. Communist Party	156	161	160
c. United Peasant Party	28	28	28
d. Youth organization	24	22	11
e. Sports clubs and tourist associations	10	9	8
f. Other organizations	75	78	75
Total	693	703	727

a. 1954: This was assumed roughly equal to the 1955 figure. 1955–56: This was estimated on the basis of data shown in *RPG 1958*, p. 384, showing the percentage composition of income and expenditure, and *RS 1960*, p. 401, Table 12, giving one component in absolute terms. Income was assumed equal to expenditure.

b. This is the rounded product of membership and annual dues. Membership in 1954–55 was taken from *Nowe drogi*, March, 1954, p. 69, and from *ibid.*, June, 1956, p. 102. Membership in 1956 was estimated as equal to that of November, 1957, as given in *RPG 1958*, p. 341. Average monthly dues were estimated at about 10 zlotys, somewhat higher than those paid by trade union members.

c-f. Estimated from membership statistics in *RPG 1958*, p. 351; *RS 1955*, p. 258; *RS 1956*, pp. 359, 393; and *RS 1957*, pp. 371–72.

Row 6. Admission fees. The net revenue was obtained as follows: The 1954 revenue was estimated from the 1955 figure on the basis of the ratio of audiences in both years in trade union movie theaters (*RPG 1958*, p. 369). For 1955–56 it was estimated from data on trade union presentations, the percentage composition of union incomes and expenditures (taken as equal to incomes), and one component of expenditures (see *RPG 1958,* p. 384, and *RS 1960,* p. 401). In order to get gross revenue we added here revenue from sports events and tourist hostels, which eventually was transferred to the budget (see row 3, above).

Row 7. Budgetary grants. This represents the total grants to quasi-governmental organizations (Appendix Table G2, row 5), less grants to religious institutions, which were assumed equal to the wage bill paid in these institutions (Appendix Table E1, row I B).

APPENDIX H: NOTES TO TABLES 6 AND 7

NOTES TO TABLE 6

Columns 1 and 2. Wages and salaries; Social security contributions.
See Appendix Table E1, columns *4* and *7*.

Column 3. Income of self-employed. The total was obtained as the sum of farm income and income of self-employed outside agriculture. Farm income was equal to the sum of farm consumption in kind (Appendix Table F3), income from the sale of farm products before taxes and imputed depreciation (Appendix Table F1, gross revenue less purchases of inputs, including insurance costs), and the value of livestock increments on individual farms and producer cooperatives (1955–56: see *DN 1956*, p. 25; 1954: 811 million zlotys, derived by deflating the 1955 value by an index of 86.2, referred to in the notes to Table 2B, item 12).

The nonfarm income was obtained as the sum of the net income of self-employed outside agriculture (Appendix Table A1) and the income tax paid by the private sector (Appendix Table G1, item 1A2b1). In so far as private industry and transport were concerned, profits, strictly construed, were not distinguished from other income of self-employed. Total nonfarm income was allocated among the subsectors in the following way: net income after taxes was distributed according to the allocation shown in Appendix Table A1, while income tax was distributed on the basis of the percentage distribution of turnover and income tax payments for 1955–56 as shown in *DN 1956*, pp. 20, 28, 38, 42, and *RS 1957*, pp. 300–1, with the 1954 distribution assumed equal to that of 1955. Professional services was the only sector that paid only income tax. Its amount for 1954 was assumed to represent the same percentage share of gross sales as in 1955 (see Appendix A). Private forestry apparently paid no tax.

Column 4. Profit and interest. The total in column *4* equals column *5* less the sum of columns *1, 2,* and *3.* Within the annual totals we estimated very roughly the profits in agriculture, passenger transport, housing, and other services. The balance of the totals was allocated to the indicated sectors in accordance with the percentage distribution of the officially reported profits in industry and handicraft, construction, freight transport and communication, and trade and catering (see *DN 1954–55,* pp. 9, 17, 19, 21; *DN 1956,* pp. 21, 31, 37, 41).

Profits in agriculture were taken equal to the livestock increment on state farms. For 1955–56, see *DN 1956,* p. 25; for 1954 we took the residual in total increments after subtracting increments in the private and cooperative sectors (see above, notes to column *3* and to Table 2B, item 12). Profits in passenger transportation, especially by railroads, were indicated as large prior to 1956, but no figures were given (see Krajewski, "O zmianach cen," No. 1, p. 8). We took as order of magnitude estimates, 1.0 billion zlotys annually in 1954–55 and 0.5 billion zlotys in 1956. We assumed that there were no profits in housing in view of the rather nominal rental rates. In the case of other services, there apparently were profits, perhaps mostly in financial services, and here we took 1.0 billion zlotys each year as an order of magnitude approximation.

Column 5. Value added. Totals are given in Table 5A, item 8. Row entries are sums of columns *1* to *4.*

Column 6. Indirect taxes. Indirect taxes in this context include turnover taxes, positive budget differences other than in foreign trade, and minor indirect taxes. The incidence of indirect taxes by the paying sector are presented in Appendix Table H1 and in the supporting notes.

NOTES TO APPENDIX TABLE H1

Column *1.* Total turnover tax was obtained as the sum of turnover tax and the tax on services as recorded in the budget (Appendix Table G1, items 1A1a1, 1A1a4, and 1A1b1, and turnover tax receipts on exports that were rebated by the government to producers as given in Appendix Table D1). In the notes below we shall derive the composition of the totals in so far as the necessary information permits, but two cautions must be given at the outset. First, row

APPENDIX TABLE H1
INDIRECT TAX RECEIPTS BY SECTOR
(*Million zlotys*)

	(1) Turnover Tax	(2) Positive Budget Differences	(3) Other Indirect Taxes	(4) Total
1954				
1. Industry and handicraft	59,671	1,585	1,064	62,320
2. Forestry				
3. Transport and communications	847			847
4. Trade and catering	4,834	638	86	5,558
5. Housing			748	748
6. Other services	3,585			3,585
Total	68,937	2,223	1,898	73,058
1955				
1. Industry and handicraft	60,453	2,468	1,746	64,667
2. Forestry				
3. Transport and communications	459			459
4. Trade and catering	5,309	1,391	153	6,853
5. Housing			844	844
6. Other services	2,048			2,048
Total	68,269	3,859	2,743	74,871
1956				
1. Industry and handicraft	53,643	1,720	1,452	56,815
2. Forestry	546			546
3. Transport and communications	395			395
4. Trade and catering	2,054	620	56	2,730
5. Housing			893	893
6. Other services	1,852			1,852
Total	58,490	2,340	2,401	63,231

6 (other services) is derived as a residual and accordingly reflects whatever errors the other figures may have. Second, the derivation of the row entries for 1956 proceeded in two steps: (i) a provisional estimate, based on the documentation given below, was made for each entry, and (ii) these provisional estimates were then reduced proportionately in the ratio (0.9032) that their sum was to the total turnover tax as established at the outset (see above). This reduction was necessary because the sum of the provisional estimates was greater than the total receipts that we could identify, and, in the absence of other means of reconciling the conflicting information, a proportional adjustment appeared preferable over some other arbitrary procedure.

Row 1. Industry and handicraft. This is the sum of the tax paid by the socialized sector (*DN 1954–55,* p. 9, *DN 1956,* p. 19, and tax rebates in Appendix Table D1) and the tax paid by the private sector. The latter for 1954 was assumed to equal 80 percent of the 1955 tax, which was roughly the ratio for the private sector as a whole (*RS 1956*, p. 296). For 1955–56 it was obtained as the residual in total receipts of turnover and income tax from the private sector (*RS 1957*, p. 300) after subtraction of income tax estimated in notes to Table 7, column *3*, above.

Row 2. Forestry. For 1956 only, *DN 1956*, p. 28.

Row 3. Transport and communications. 1954: *DN 1954–55*, p. 19 (socialized sector). The tax paid by the private sector was taken as equal to 80 percent of the 1955 tax (as in row 1, above). 1955–56: *DN 1956*, p. 37 (socialized sector). The tax paid by the private sector was taken equal to the residual in total taxes (*DN 1956*, p. 38) after subtraction of the income tax estimated above. In addition, we assumed that one third of the tax on services (Appendix Table G1, item 1A1a4) was paid by passenger transport. This assumption was based on figures shown in the planned and actual central government budgets for 1957 and 1958 (*DU 1957*, No. 25, pp. 276, 33; *DU 1958*, No. 16 p. 205), and on the assumption that the planned budget figures for 1957 were close to the actual tax receipts on that account in 1956.

Row 4. Trade and catering. The tax paid by the socialized sector was taken from *DN 1954–55*, p. 21, and *DN 1956*, p. 41. The tax paid by the private sector in 1954 was taken as equal to 80 percent of the 1955 receipts (as in row 1, above), while payments in 1955–56 were obtained as a residual in the total payment of turnover and income tax (*DN 1956*, p. 42) after subtraction of income tax payments estimated in the notes to column *3* above.

Row 5. Other services. The 1954–55 figures were estimated as residuals in total receipts for each year. 1956 was taken roughly at the 1955 level. A substantial margin of error must be attached to these estimates because of the derivation as residuals or in relation thereto.

Column 2. Positive budget differences. The totals were estimated in Appendix Table G1, item 1A1a3. Budget differences in trade and catering were taken from *DN 1954–55*, p. 21, and *DN 1956*, p. 41, whereas those for industry were obtained as residuals. This procedure was based on *DN 1956*, which showed only these two sectors as being subject to the positive budget differences.

Column 3. Other indirect taxes. As shown in Appendix Table G1, these include the following categories: (*a*) tax on transfer of property rights (1A1b2), (*b*) residential tax (1A1b3), (*c*) real estate tax

(1A1b4), (*d*) other taxes, the nature of which could not be fully established (1A1a5 and 1A1b5). We assumed that *a* to *c* were imposed on housing, while *d* was paid by industry and trade in the same proportion as their payments of turnover tax (see column *1*).

NOTES TO TABLE 6 (continued)

Column 7. Subsidies. The total amount of subsidies shown in Table 3B is broken down by receiving sectors in Appendix Table H2 and explained in the notes below.

APPENDIX TABLE H2
SUBSIDY PAYMENTS BY RECEIVING SECTOR
(*Million zlotys*)

	1954	1955	1956
1. Industry and handicrafts	6,440	10,379	8,383
2. Agriculture	3,114	4,408	4,988
3. Forestry	237	102	24
4. Construction	1,000	1,140	
5. Transport and communications	753	150	200
6. Trade and catering	91		
7. Housing	411	306	217
8. Other services	513	604	877
Total	12,559	17,089	14,689

1. Industry and handicrafts. Obtained as a residual in total subsidy payments (in each year).

2. Agriculture. See Table 2A, items 3A and 3B.

3. Forestry. *DN 1954–55,* p. 15, and *DN 1956,* p. 28.

4. Construction. 1954: This was estimated as a rounded figure on the assumption that net losses (*DN 1954–55,* p. 17) were equal to about one third of gross losses, as this was the ratio existing in 1955. 1955: *DN 1954–55,* p. 17. 1956: According to *DN 1956,* p. 31, there was a substantial net profit in the sector; we assumed, therefore, that net losses were zero.

5. Transport and communications. 1954–55: This is the sum of subsidies in rail and water transport (*DN 1954–55,* p. 19) and in urban transportation. Subsidies in urban transportation were taken arbitrarily at 150 million zlotys in both years, somewhat lower than the estimate for 1956. 1956: As in 1955, no indication was found of any subsidies in the transport sector, other than urban passenger transportation. The planned subsidies for 1958 amounted to 381 million zlotys (*Finanse,* No. 3, 1958, p. 6), while those for 1957 were estimated at 260 million zlotys (*Finanse,* No. 4, 1957, p. 12).

We put their total in 1956 at 200 million zlotys as an order of magnitude.

6. Trade and catering. 1954 only: *DN 1954–55,* p. 21.

7. Housing. Subsidies were estimated as the difference between revenue and expenditure of the state housing administration (see estimates below, in million zlotys). Housing cooperatives received no subsidies while private, non-owner-occupied housing received only government grants for capital repairs. We took half (in proportion to rental payments) the amount of subsidies derived below as applicable to housing construed as services of dwellings; the other half was attributed to industry and handicrafts by way of the residual determination of the latter. Although this is an oversimplification, probably a great part of the space in question went to various handicrafts and industrial workshops.

	1954	1955	1956
1. Rental payments	838	870	900
a. Households	419	435	450
b. Enterprises	419	435	450
2. Total expenditures	2,514	2,610	2,700
3. Grants for capital repairs	854	1,127	1,366
4. Subsidies	822	613	434

1a. See Table A4 (excludes cooperatives).

1b. According to Litterer, "W sprawie czynszów i źródeł finansowania gospodarki zasobem mieszkaniowym," p. 4, total rentals paid by business enterprises equalled that paid by households.

2. Litterer, "W sprawie czynszów i źródeł finansowania gospodarki zasobem mieszkaniowym," indicated that total expenditures were three times the total rental receipts.

3. See notes to Appendix Table G2, row 8b.

4. Row 2 less the sum of rows 1 and 3.

8. Other services. Services that were subject to subsidies were divided into two main categories: (*a*) utilities (gasworks, waterworks, laundries) and (*b*) health, education, and welfare. Total planned subsidies to utilities in 1957–58 amounted to roughly 1 percent of local government budgets. Lacking other information, we assumed that subsidies to municipal utilities during 1954–56 also amounted roughly to 1 percent of the local government budgets (*RS 1956,* p. 295; *RS 1957,* p. 289). The final estimates were rounded to the nearest ten million zlotys. Subsidies to health, education, and welfare are shown in Appendix Table G3, item 2c.

Column 9. Depreciation allowances
  See Appendix Table H3 and notes thereto below.

Appendix Table H3
DEPRECIATION ALLOWANCES BY SECTOR
(Million zlotys)

	1954	1955	1956
1. Industry and handicrafts	4,728	5,597	11,630
2. Agriculture	4,249	4,784	4,901
a. State farms	298	342	448
b. Private and collective farms	3,951	4,442	4,453
3. Forestry	30	36	61
4. Construction	463	523	651
5. Transport and communications	1,843	2,080	3,439
a. "Material"		1,196	1,920
b. "Nonmaterial"		748	1,311
c. Urban transport		136	208
6. Trade and catering	252	278	276
7. Housing	2,930	3,298	3,736
a. Socialized farm housing		200	200
b. Other		3,098	3,536
8. Other services	302	344	391
9. Total (excluding row 2b)	10,846	12,498	20,632
10. Total (including all rows)	14,797	16,940	25,085

  1954: Total allowances (Table 2A, item 6, plus imputed capital consumption on private and collective farms estimated in Appendix Table F1), less depreciation in socialized industry (*DN 1954–55,* p. 8) and in private industry (taken at 100 million zlotys, roughly the same as in 1955; see *DN 1956,* p. 20), were allocated among the remaining sectors on the basis of the 1955 percentage distribution. The figure thus derived for agriculture was split between private and collective farms (see Appendix Table F1) and state farms (the residual).
  1955–56: For industry and handicrafts, forestry, construction, "material" transport and communications, and trade and catering, see *DN 1956,* pp. 19, 28, 31, 37 and 41.
  2. Agriculture. 1955: This represented the total allowances in the "material" sector of the economy (*DN 1956,* p. 13), less depreciation in the sectors listed above, less depreciation in "other material production," which was estimated as equal to the same percentage of "material" depreciation as in 1956 (see *DN 1956,* p. 46), and less depreciation in socialized farm housing, which was assumed to equal the estimated value for 1956 (see below). 1956: This was the depreciation in agriculture, including socialized farm housing (*DN*

1956, p. 46), less depreciation in the latter category, estimated at 200 million zlotys (see notes to Appendix Table I5, below).

5b. "Nonmaterial" transport and communications. 1955: Depreciation in 1956 was 17.1 percent above the depreciation in 1955 in 1956 prices (*DN 1956*, p. 46). The value in 1956 prices was deflated to 1955 prices with the aid of the index implicitly given in the corresponding values for the "material" transport and communications sector in 1955 (*DN 1956*, pp. 37, 46). 1956: *DN 1956*, p. 46.

5c. Urban transport. This was estimated as 4 percent of the replacement value of fixed assets in both years. The latter was estimated in Appendix I, pp. 222–23.

7a. Socialized farm housing. See item 2, above.

7b and 8. Other housing and other services. 1955: The residual in total depreciation allowances was allocated among the two sectors according to the 1956 percentage distribution. 1956: For housing, see *DN 1956*, p. 46; other services were taken as equal to the sum of depreciation in "other material production," communal services and "other nonmaterial production" (see *DN 1956*, p. 46) less depreciation in urban transportation (estimated as item 5c, above).

NOTES TO TABLE 6 (continued)

Column 10. Gross national product. This is the sum of columns *8* and *9*.

NOTES TO TABLE 7

Item 1. Personal consumption. See Table 5B, item 3.

Item 1a. Civilian. This is the residual in personal consumption.

Item 1b. Military. See Table 1B, item 2B2a.

Item 2. Government consumption. This is the value of government services (Table 3A, item 1) less current expenditure on national defense (Appendix Table G2, column *3*). For detailed composition, items 2a to 2d, see Appendix Table G3. In all instances government consumption is the sum of wage costs and current purchases.

Item 2e. Internal security. See Appendix Table G4.

Item 2f. Administration and justice. This is the sum of current expenditures, excluding transfers, in administration and justice (Appendix Table G4) plus item 6a, column *1,* of Appendix Table G2.

Item 2g. Quasi-governmental organizations. See Appendix Table G5.

Item 3. National defense. See Appendix Table G2, column *3,* current expenditures.

Item 4a. Fixed capital. This is the sum of fixed capital investment in the enterprise sector (Table 2C, items 6A and 6B) and in the government sector (Table 3C, item 4).

Item 4b. Increase in inventories. See Table 2C, item 6C.

Item 4c and *5. Net foreign investment* and *Other.*

The sum of items 4c and 5 was obtained from Table 4A, item 2, as the formal surplus of nation on current account as determined by domestic prices. Within this surplus we identify as net foreign investment the equivalent in domestic zlotys of (*a*) the commodity balance in foreign trade zlotys and (*b*) the net earnings from services; the residual in the surplus is entered as item 5. Component (*a*) in million zlotys was as follows: *1954,* 300 (import surplus); *1955,* 500 (import surplus); *1956,* 2,400 (export surplus); see, for 1954, *DN 1954–55,* p. 3, for 1955–56, *DN 1956,* p. 14). Component (*b*) is equal to the sum of items 3B and 3C in Table 4A.

APPENDIX I: NOTES TO TABLES 8 AND 9

The percentage distribution of GNP by sectors of origin at factor cost given in Table 8 is based on Appendix Table I1, for which we show below our sources and methods.

NOTES TO APPENDIX TABLE I1

Returns to labor

See Table 6, sum of columns *1, 2,* and *3.* We assumed that the income of self-employed persons represented only returns to labor. For the nonagricultural sectors, the magnitudes involved under this assumption are so small that some allowance for a return to nonlabor factors of production would have negligible effect on the structure of GNP at factor cost. In the case of agriculture, our decision to treat all income at market prices as returns to labor was based on a comparison of this income per employed person with average wages in other sectors of the economy.

The results of our comparisons will depend on our definition of the labor force in agriculture and on the valuation of consumption in kind. If we take as the labor force the number of persons actively engaged in agriculture (interpolated figures based on the 1950 and 1960 censuses for private agriculture and the employment on collective farms plus the 1954–56 figures for employment on state farms; see *RS 1962,* pp. 28, 46, 213) and if we adjust farm income as shown in Table 6 (wages and salaries plus income of self-employed) to exclude nonfarm producers of agricultural products (we deducted 10 percent on the basis of comparable Czechoslovak and Hungarian data, for example, see Hungary Central Statistical Office, *Statisztikai időszaki közlemények* [Series of Statistical Periodicals], Vol. VIII [Budapest, 1961], p. 18), then average income per capita in all agriculture represented the following percentages of average wages in other employments (1954, 1955, and 1956, respectively): in socialized industry, 53, 55, 61; in socialized agriculture, including allowances for clothing, fuel, and purchases at reduced prices of certain farm products (*deputaty*), 78, 79, 89 (see *RS 1962,* p. 392). These figures are based on the valuation of all farm production, including that consumed in kind, at average realized prices.

If we convert the family help included in the agricultural labor force into man-equivalents and value consumption in kind at retail prices less trade margins, then the percentages given above will rise. For our rough comparison we multiplied the numbers of family help by 0.75 to convert them into man-equivalents. This ratio was suggested by 1955 average wages paid to hired farm help (man, woman, and youth in various types of work; see *RS 1962,* p. 204). An upward adjustment to consumption in kind was approximated on the basis of Polish official figures (*DN 1954–55,* p. 3), reduced by 10 percent for the nonfarm producers of agricultural products. Then the ratios of farm income per man-equivalent to average wages in socialized industry were as follows: *1954,* 77 percent; *1955,* 79 percent. We do not have at hand the corresponding data to estimate the ratio for 1956; however, a rough extrapolation based on data in average realized prices shows about 87 percent. In comparison with average wages paid in socialized agriculture, the average farm income per man-equivalent in 1955 was about 12 percent higher, but this advantage would be reduced somewhat by allowance for auxiliary income from garden plots of the socialized farm employees.

These ratios probably exaggerate the relative level of farm income because the official valuation of income in kind in 1955 given in *DN 1954–55,* p. 3, is a great deal higher than the figure given implicitly by *DN 1956,* p. 25, by comparison with the former source. The latter source values consumption in kind at above-quota delivery prices and refers (p. 23) to "great practical difficulties" in applying retail prices less trade margins.

The ratios of average farm income to average wages in socialized agriculture and socialized industry that we cited above suggest that our assumption that all farm income represents only a return to labor is reasonable. One would expect average income in agriculture to be lower than average industrial wages.

Adjusted depreciation
See Appendix Table I5.

Appendix Table 11

GROSS NATIONAL PRODUCT BY SECTOR OF ORIGIN AT FACTOR COST

(Billion current zlotys)

	Returns to Labor			Adjusted Depreciation			Nonlabor Returns			GNP		
	1954	1955	1956	1954	1955	1956	1954	1955	1956	1954	1955	1956
Industry and handicraft	46.9	51.4	59.8	7.4	7.9	10.9	10.3	11.7	14.7	64.6	71.0	85.4
Agriculture	54.9	60.0	74.1	4.1	4.1	4.4	11.4	12.6	12.6	70.4	76.7	91.1
Forestry	1.5	1.6	2.1	.1	.1	.2	.4	.4	.5	2.0	2.1	2.8
Construction	13.7	13.9	15.4	.4	.4	.6	1.7	2.0	2.8	15.8	16.3	18.8
Transportation and communication	10.0	10.5	12.5	2.2	2.3	3.4	3.4	3.8	5.2	15.6	16.6	21.1
Trade and catering	10.2	10.8	12.9	.6	.6	.8	4.0	5.0	4.9	14.8	16.4	18.6
Housing	.3	.4	.4	8.9	9.0	9.8	21.1	22.8	22.8	30.3	32.2	33.0
Other services	4.4	4.7	5.3	1.0	1.0	1.4	1.9	2.2	2.8	7.3	7.9	9.5
Education	3.9	4.3	5.1							3.9	4.3	5.1
Art and culture	.2	.3	.3							.2	.3	.3
Science and research	.5	.6	.6							.5	.6	.6
Public health	2.3	2.5	3.1							2.3	2.5	3.1
Internal security	2.4	2.3	2.3							2.4	2.3	2.3
Administration and justice	4.0	4.4	5.0							4.0	4.4	5.0
Quasi-governmental organizations	.6	.6	.6							.6	.6	.6
Defense	6.6	5.9	5.6							6.6	5.9	5.6
Domestic and religious services	.8	.8	.8							.8	.8	.8
Total	163.0	175.0	205.9	24.7	25.4	31.5	54.1	60.5	66.4	241.8	260.9	303.8

NOTE: Totals may differ slightly from the sums of indicated items because of rounding.

Nonlabor returns

The annual totals were taken equal to the GNP at market prices (see Table 6) less the adjusted value of the category "other" (representing the domestic zloty value of that part of foreign trade that is exactly balanced in foreign-exchange zlotys and thus has no counterpart in obligations due from the rest of the world; see Appendix Table I6, row 5, column 6) and less the sum of the labor returns and depreciation shown in the present table. These totals were allocated among the sectors of origin in proportion to their current (depreciated) values of fixed capital and working capital (see Appendix Table I2).

GNP.

This is the sum of components noted above.

NOTES TO APPENDIX TABLE I2

Fixed capital

See Appendix Table I3.

Working capital

Industry and trade: 1954–55, see Ficowski, "Struktura zapasów w gospodarce narodowej w latach 1950–1955," pp. 23–24; 1956, Wojciechowska, "Ogólne tendencje kształtowania się zapasów w gospodarce uspołecznionej," p. 14. Agriculture and forestry: Working capital in socialized agriculture and forestry in 1954–55 (Ficowski, p. 24) amounted to about one half the value of gross output as shown in *DN 1954–55,* pp. 12, 15. In *DN 1956,* p. 25, the valuation of 1955 gross output (and 1956 as well) was shown on a different higher basis because of changes in methodology. A comparison of the original and the revised figures implies that working capital would represent about one third of gross output as shown in the more recent figures. For lack of a better basis, we took as order-of-magnitude estimates of working capital in 1954 and 1955 one half the gross output of both socialized and private agriculture in 1955 as shown in *DN 1954–55,* p. 12, and one third the corresponding 1956 figure as given in *DN 1956,* p. 25. In forestry, because the valuation of gross output did not change significantly for 1955 as given in *DN 1954–55,* p. 15, and *DN 1956,* p. 28, we took one half the gross output in each year as a guess for the value of working capital. Construction: For our very rough approximation we estimated working

APPENDIX TABLE 12

CURRENT VALUES OF FIXED AND WORKING CAPITAL

(Billion zlotys)

	1954				1955				1956			
	Fixed Capital	Working Capital	Total	Percent	Fixed Capital	Working Capital	Total	Percent	Fixed Capital	Working Capital	Total	Percent
Industry	83.5	30.2	113.7	19.0	89.7	30.7	120.4	19.3	123.5	42.3	165.8	22.2
Agriculture	81.0	44.3	125.3	21.0	82.0	47.9	129.9	20.8	86.6	55.3	141.9	19.0
Forestry	3.2	.9	4.1	.7	3.3	1.0	4.3	.7	4.0	1.9	5.9	.8
Construction	3.4	15.3	18.7	3.1	3.8	17.1	20.9	3.3	5.7	25.6	31.3	4.2
Transportation and communication	33.5	3.3	36.8	6.2	35.5	3.6	39.1	6.3	52.6	5.3	57.9	7.8
Trade and catering	9.8	34.7	44.5	7.4	10.4	41.5	51.9	8.3	13.2	42.0	55.2	7.4
Housing	232.8	0	232.8	39.0	235.6	0	235.6	37.7	256.5	0	256.6	34.4
Other services	21.5	0	21.5	3.6	22.7	0	22.7	3.6	31.6	0	31.6	4.2
Total	468.7	128.7	597.4	100.0	483.0	141.8	624.8	100.0	573.8	172.4	746.2	100.0

capital at 4.5 times the value of fixed capital, a ratio suggested by our estimates for Czechoslovakia and Hungary (Alton and associates, *Czechoslovak National Income and Product, 1947–48 and 1955–1956,* p. 225, and their *Hungarian National Income and Product in 1955,* p. 226). Transportation and communication: As an order-of-magnitude estimate we took working capital equal to 10 percent of fixed capital. Housing and other services: We assumed that working capital was relatively negligible for the purpose of our factor cost adjustment.

NOTES TO APPENDIX TABLE I3

Replacement values in 1956 prices
    See Appendix Table I4. These values are the estimated costs in 1956 prices of replacing the installed capacity by new fixed capital of equivalent capacity.

Replacement values in current prices
    These values were obtained by deflating the replacement values in 1956 prices by indexes of investment costs linking 1954, 1955, and 1956, derived, except for housing and agriculture, from data given in *SIB 1958,* p. 188. These indexes are strictly applicable only to the socialized sector, but in view of the relatively insignificant amounts of private capital in the private sector, no attempt was made to derive separate deflators for the latter. Components of fixed capital in "other services" (see Appendix Table I4) were separately deflated, and the results were combined in the figures given in the present table.
    Fixed capital in housing in 1956 prices was deflated separately for the socialized and private sectors (see Appendix Table I4), using indexes of investment costs given in *SIB 1958,* p. 188, and *RS 1957,* p. 180. Similarly fixed capital in agriculture was deflated by sectors, using deflators implicitly given in *SIB 1956,* p. 2, linking investment outlays in 1954 and 1955, both in 1955 prices, to their corresponding values in 1956 prices. We assumed that there was no significant change in prices of fixed capital from 1954 to 1955. Our assumption is supported by data on "limited" investments in agriculture given in *RS 1955,* p. 140.

Current values of fixed capital
    These values are defined as the replacement values in current prices minus the capital consumed through use of the assets. We con-

APPENDIX TABLE 13
FIXED CAPITAL IN THE POLISH ECONOMY
(Billion zlotys, values in 1956 prices and in current prices)

	Replacement Value (in 1956 prices)			Replacement Value (in current prices)			Current Value (in current prices)		
	1954	1955	1956	1954	1955	1956	1954	1955	1956
Industry and handicraft	178.5	191.7	205.4	138.9	149.2	205.4	83.5	89.7	123.5
Agriculture	135.8	138.2	140.2	131.0	132.7	140.2	81.0	82.0	86.6
Forestry	6.0	6.2	6.4	5.1	5.3	6.4	3.2	3.3	4.0
Construction	7.7	8.6	9.6	5.7	6.4	9.6	3.4	3.8	5.7
Transportation and communication	77.2	81.7	86.0	54.9	58.1	86.0	33.5	35.5	52.6
Trade	19.4	20.5	21.4	15.9	16.8	21.4	9.8	10.4	13.2
Housing	396.1	402.2	409.3	371.3	375.8	409.3	232.8	235.6	256.6
Other services	45.2	47.8	50.5	34.4	36.4	50.5	21.5	22.7	31.6

verted values at replacement costs into current (after depreciation) values on the basis of Polish census data, showing by six major types of fixed capital (buildings, means of transportation, machinery groups, and so forth) the capital used up as a percentage of the replacement cost of the assets (see Róg, "Charakterystyka środków trwałych na podstawie wyników powszechnej inwentaryzacji," p. 3). We combined these ratios into a single ratio for each industrial sector, using as weights the amounts of the six major types of fixed capital in that sector of the socialized economy as of January 1, 1961 (see Poland, Główny urząd statystyczny, "Ogólne wyniki powszechnej inwentaryzacji środków trwałych wedlug stanu w dniu 1 1 1961 r.," p. 4). By subtracting the resulting average percentage of capital used up from 100 we finally arrived at coefficients relating replacement values to current (depreciated) values.

Notes to Appendix Table I4

The figures shown in Appendix Table I4 were derived in working tables and supplementary calculations that are omitted here to save space. In the notes below we shall describe the methodology and specify the sources leading to our results.

Separate calculations were made for the socialized and private sectors with certain exceptions, namely, transportation and communication and "other services," where figures for the entire economy were estimated directly.

Fixed capital in the socialized sector

Our estimates are based on a census of fixed capital in socialized business enterprises accounting for depreciation carried out in 1960 and showing the value of assets at the end of 1959 in 1956 prices (see Róg, "Charakterystyka środków trwałych na podstawie wyników powszechnej inwentaryzacji") and on a revaluation of fixed assets as of January 1, 1961, in prices of July, 1960, carried out subsequently (see *MRS 1963,* pp. 50–54; Poland, Główny urząd statystyczny, "Ogólne wyniki powszechnej inwentaryzacji środków trwałych według stanu w dniu 1 1 1961 r.," pp. 2–5; and *RS 1963,* pp. 89–92).

The January 1, 1961, revaluations gave the results in million zlotys, 1960 prices, (*a*) for the economy as a whole, indicating the percentage shares owned by the socialized and private sectors in each of the industrial sectors (industry, agriculture, construction, and so forth) and covering not only business enterprises (the *khozraschet*

APPENDIX TABLE 14

FIXED CAPITAL STOCK IN THE POLISH ECONOMY, BY SECTOR OF OWNERSHIP

(Billion zlotys, replacement cost at 1956 prices, end of year figures)

	1954			1955			1956		
	Socialized	Private	Total	Socialized	Private	Total	Socialized	Private	Total
Industry	175.7	2.8	178.5	188.9	2.8	191.7	202.5	2.9	205.4
Agriculture	20.8	115.0	135.8	25.2	113.0	138.2	29.9	110.3	140.2
Forestry	6.0	.0	6.0	6.2	.0	6.2	6.4	.0	6.4
Construction	7.5	.2	7.7	8.4	.2	8.6	9.4	.2	9.6
Transportation and communication			77.2			81.7			86.0
Trade	19.0	.4	19.4	20.1	.4	20.5	21.0	.4	21.4
Housing	91.6	304.5	396.1	97.5	304.7	402.2	103.4	305.9	409.3
Other services			45.2			47.8			50.5
Communal services			35.5			37.6			39.8
Enterprises in health, education, finance, etc.			9.7			10.2			10.7

organizations included in the census) but also other organizations (for example, budget-financed establishments not covered by the census) for which estimates were provided and (b) for a more narrowly defined socialized sector consisting of business enterprises keeping accounts of depreciation. The coverage under (b) for most sectors corresponded to that reported by Róg for the census as of December 31, 1959.

Since we wanted to take into account the more detailed and more comprehensive figures available in the results for January 1, 1961, we needed to establish indexes for deflating from 1960 to 1956 prices. We derived these in two steps, as follows.

1. We estimated the January 1, 1960, values of fixed capital at replacement cost in 1960 prices for the more restricted definition of the socialized sector (see (b), above) proceeding from the results for January 1, 1961, by subtracting net investment in 1960 prices in each industrial sector in the year 1960 (see *DN 1955–1960*, pp. 82–83). Since net investment as defined in Polish statistics consists of new investment plus capital repairs less depreciation, our results will be more or less correct if the new capacity installed during the year less the capacity retired in that year is approximated by net investment. If we take into account the fact that a part of capital repairs is designated simply to restore existing capacity and another part to expand the existing capacity and that depreciation as it is calculated in Poland is intended to cover for each fixed capital asset both the capital repairs to keep its capacity intact and the eventual replacement of that capacity, then our results may be reasonably good approximations. Because of lack of information, we also could not take into account such refinements as the changing proportions of unfinished investment, the rate of growth of the stock of various types of fixed assets, and their length of life, which have relevance to the approximation of net change in capacity (new capacity minus retirements) by net investment.

2. We compared our results for the value of fixed assets in the various industrial sectors in 1960 prices for January 1, 1960, as derived above with the corresponding figures given by Róg for the same date (December 31, 1959) in 1956 prices, thereby deriving the price indexes defined by the two sets of values.

With the aid of these price indexes we converted the values in 1960 prices for the socialized fixed assets in the various industrial sectors as of January 1, 1961, in the more comprehensive definition (*MRS 1963*, pp. 51–52) into 1956 prices. Then, by subtracting net investment in 1956 prices (see *DN 1955–1960*, p. 79) for intervening years in the period 1955–1960, we arrived at the estimated replacement values in 1956 prices for the years 1954, 1955, and 1956.

Fixed capital in the private sector

Our calculations for the private sector followed the same procedures as for the socialized sector. The January 1, 1961, values for the replacement cost of private fixed capital by industrial branches was given in *MRS 1963*, pp. 51–52; data on net investment year by year for the period of 1955–60 in 1956 prices were given by *DN 1955–1960*, p. 79. We did not have a basis for deriving separate price indexes for the private industrial sectors, and therefore we used the deflators linking 1960 and 1956 prices derived above for the socialized sector.

We had some reservation about applying to private agriculture the price index derived for socialized agriculture, since it was very low in comparison with the indexes derived for other industrial sectors. This means that in 1960 prices the value of fixed assets in agriculture is considerably greater in relation to the values of fixed assets in industry and other branches of production than it is in 1956 prices. The consequence for our factor cost adjustment is that the returns to capital in agriculture may be underestimated in relation to returns to capital in other branches of production.

Fixed capital in transportation and communication and other services

The Polish census enumeration of fixed capital in the socialized sector did not cover the state railways, since they were not required to keep accounts for depreciation, and the more comprehensive estimates for the entire economy do not indicate what part of the total capital in transportation and communication may be properly attributed to the enterprise sector and what part to public highways and other facilities not ordinarily regarded as business capital. Lacking a better basis, we estimated the fixed capital in transportation and communication in 1956 by dividing the depreciation allowances officially estimated for the sector (see *DN 1956*, p. 46) by 4 percent, an assumed rate based on Czechoslovak schedules (see Alton and associates, *Czechoslovak National Income and Product, 1947–1948 and 1955–1956*, p. 228). Figures for 1954 and 1955 were derived from our result by subtracting net investment in 1956 prices (see *DN 1955–1960*, p. 79) as an approximation to changes in installed capacity. Finally, our results were adjusted upward to account for fixed capital in urban passenger transportation not covered in our estimates above. These adjustments were estimated on the assumption that the amount of fixed capital per employee was the same in urban as in nonurban transportation and communication. Employment in the latter was taken from *RS 1960,* p. 49. Employment in urban transportation was obtained as follows: 1954, estimated on the assumption that employment in 1955 was 10 percent above that in 1954, which was the case for communal services as a whole; 1955, see *BS,* 1957, No. 4, p. 23; 1956, 1958, No. 5, p. 29. Our adjustment amounted (in billion zlotys, 1956 prices) to the following sums: *1954,* 4.3; *1955,* 4.8; *1956,* 5.2.

A similar lack of clear definition of the fixed capital and net investment in communal and other services led us to an improvised estimate in this sector. We assumed that the ratio of fixed capital in socialized communal services to that in socialized housing in 1954– 56 in 1956 prices was the same as that on January 1, 1961, in 1960 prices. The latter was derived from *MRS 1963,* p. 53. We assumed that private capital in communal services was sufficiently small to be neglected and that our rough estimate for the socialized sector covered the entire economy. Finally, the figures we obtained were adjusted downward to account for the transfer of urban passenger transportation from the sector of communal services to transportation and communication (see immediately above).

Our rough estimates for fixed capital in enterprises in health, education, finance, and so forth are rule-of-thumb figures based on the assumption that they were one half the values shown in each year for trade. This ratio was suggested by figures for December 1959 given by Róg, "Charakterystyka środków trwałych na podstawie wyników powszechnej inwentaryzacji," p. 4.

Coverage of Polish data on net investment and fixed capital

Our estimates for fixed capital by industrial sector in 1954–56 was derived from Polish official data on fixed capital on January 1, 1961, extrapolated to 1954–56 on the assumption that net investment figures could be used to approximate changes in capacity at replacement cost. We have indicated above (p. 221) our impression that the rough estimates obtained in this way may be reasonably good approximations.

But we have also made another simplifying assumption, namely, that the coverage of the official data on fixed capital as regards definitions of industrial sectors is the same as that for the official data on investments. Such is not quite the case, however, for fixed capital data were determined on the basis of the principal activity of the enterprise, whereas, in the first instance, investment data are based on the main activity of the investor on a plant basis (thus a multi-plant enterprise engaged in more than one line of activity would have each plant separately classified) and, in the second instance, investment outlays on housing, trade facilities, and health, educational, and cultural facilities are classified by their designations regardless of the basic activity of the investor. We were unable to make adjustments to insure fuller comparability of the fixed capital and investment data, and it may be worth noting that the same simplifying assumptions were followed in Polish discussions (see Artur Markowski and Mieczysław Rakowski, "O efektywności inwestowania w latach 1956–1960" (Concerning the Efficiency of Investment in the Years 1956–1960), *Inwestycje i budownictwo*, 1962, No. 4, p. 6).

One of the consequences of the enterprise basis of classification of fixed capital data is that a substantial part of the fixed capital in dwellings is classified in nonhousing sectors. *MRS 1963*, p. 51 (footnote), shows 745 billion zlotys (1960 prices) of fixed capital at replacement cost in dwellings, but the same source (pp. 52–53) identifies only 627 billion zlotys of fixed capital in the housing sector. We made no attempt to identify and adjust for the difference by industrial sectors for lack of information. No doubt there are similar problems connected with fixed capital in health, educational, cultural, and trade facilities arising from enterprise basis of classification.

NOTES TO APPENDIX TABLE I5

Fixed capital at replacement costs

See Appendix Table I3.

Depreciation rate

These rates were estimated as weighted averages of Czechoslovak official rates for buildings (2.4 percent), machinery (9.1 percent), and means of transportation (11.7 percent) (see *Statistický obzor* [Prague], 1956, No. 1, p. 437). The weights were January 1, 1961, values of fixed capital at replacement cost in 1960 prices in each of the Polish industrial sectors (see *MRS 1963*, pp. 51–53). In deriving the weights, we put constructions (*budowle*) in the same group as buildings, and we put technical equipment in the group with machin-

APPENDIX TABLE 15

ADJUSTED DEPRECIATION ALLOWANCES

	Fixed Capital at Replacement Cost (billion current zlotys)			Depreciation Rate (percent)	Depreciation Allowances (billion current zlotys)		
	1954	1955	1956		1954	1955	1956
Industry	138.9	149.2	205.4	5.3	7.4	7.9	10.9
Agriculture	116.6	118.1	124.8	3.5	4.1	4.1	4.4
Forestry	5.1	5.3	6.4	2.7	.1	.1	.2
Construction	5.7	6.4	9.6	6.5	.4	.4	.6
Transportation and communication	54.9	58.1	86.0	4.0	2.2	2.3	3.4
Trade and catering	15.9	16.8	21.4	3.8	.6	.6	.8
Housing	371.3	375.8	409.3	2.4	8.9	9.0	9.8
Other services	34.4	36.4	50.5	2.8	1.0	1.0	1.4
Total	742.8	766.1	913.4		24.7	25.4	31.5

ery. For housing and communal and other services we used as weights the capital distribution in the socialized sector only; for other branches of production we used the all-economy figures as weights. In agriculture, livestock and orchards were left out of the weights (only 89 percent of the total was used, and the same percentage was applied to the 1954–56 replacement values when computing the adjusted depreciation allowances). For transportation and communication we used 4.0 percent, an approximation based on a slightly higher figure used for Czechoslovakia (see Alton and associates, *Czechoslovak National Income and Product, 1947–1948 and 1955–1956*, p. 228).

Depreciation allowances

These were derived as the products of fixed capital and the depreciation rate.

NOTES TO TABLE 9

Table 9, showing the GNP by end uses at market prices at factor cost, is based on Appendix Tables 16 and 17, which are documented below.

NOTES TO APPENDIX TABLE 16

Column 1. Total personal consumption is given in Table 1B, items 3A and 3B; the components (rows 1b to 1g) are also in Table 1B under items 3A and 3B; retail sales (row 1a) is the residual in the total.

Total government consumption was taken from Table 6; wages and salaries (inclusive of social security contributions and wages in kind) were given in Appendix Table E1. Commodities are the residual in the total.

National defense sources and procedures are the same as for governmental consumption; see above.

Gross investment figures were taken from Table 7 with some adjustment to show separately the increment to livestock in agriculture based on Appendix B, note to Table 2B, item 12. The increase in basic herds was subtracted from the figures for fixed capital, and the increase in the turnover, or fattening, herds was deducted from the figure on inventories. The sum of the two deductions appears in row 4c.

The remaining item, "other," is given in Table 6.

Column 2. The totals of indirect taxes were taken from Appendix Table H1. In order to distribute the totals among end uses, the latter were divided into three groups: (i) those that were tax exempt, (ii) those for which the tax element could be estimated directly, and (iii) the remaining end uses, to which an average rate of tax was applied.

(i) Tax-exempt end uses included the following: farm market sales at full market prices, farm income consumed in kind valued at average realized prices, domestic and religious services, all wages and salaries in government and defense as representing services of personnel, military procurements, a part of fixed capital investment, a part of the increase in inventories, and farm investment in kind. In some of these uses it is evident that no formal transactions took place and that no tax was levied (farm consumption and invesment in kind); in others, no evidence could be found that taxes applied (farm market sales, domestic and religious services, military procurements, a part of fixed capital investment in the state-owned sector, and a part of the increase in inventories, that is, outside of trade). Services of government employees and defense personnel as measured in their remuneration obviously were not taxed, although pay in kind taken as an element of personal consumption was subject to indirect taxes. Our exclusion of the foregoing end uses is clearly an oversimplification when account is taken of indirect effects; for example, a commodity subject to the turnover tax sometimes enters the cost of intermediate products that support the excluded end uses. At this

APPENDIX TABLE 16
GNP BY END USE
(Billion zlotys)

1954	(1) Value in Market Prices	(2) Indirect Taxes	(3) Accounting Profits	(4) Subsidies	(5) Adjusted Base	(6) Factor Cost
1. Personal consumption	148.1	59.8	12.8	6.1	81.6	134.3
a. Retail sales	111.5	56.8	12.5	5.5	47.7	62.9
b. Farm market sales	5.8				5.8	5.8
c. Gross rent	2.5	.7		.4	2.2	31.7
d. Farm consumption in kind	23.0	1.8	.2		23.0	30.4
e. Military subsistence	3.5	.5	.1	.2	1.7	2.2
f. Wages in kind	1.0				.4	.5
g. Domestic and religious services	.8				.8	.8
2. Government consumption	24.2	5.3	1.1	.5	18.3	19.8
a. Commodities	10.4	5.3	1.1	.5	4.5	6.0
b. Wages and salaries	13.8				13.8	13.8
3. National defense	10.4				10.6	11.9
a. Procurements	3.8			.2	4.0	5.3
b. Military pay and subsistence	6.6			.2	6.6	6.6
4. Gross investment	58.6	4.4	1.7	5.1	57.6	75.7
a. Fixed capital	42.6	2.7	1.0	3.7	42.6	56.3
(i) Taxed	5.2	2.7				
(ii) Tax-free	37.4					
b. Increase in inventories	14.3	1.5	.7	1.4	13.5	17.9
(i) Taxed	2.9	1.5				
(ii) Tax-free	11.4					
c. Farm investment in kind	1.0				1.0	1.0
d. Net foreign investment	.6	.2			.4	.5
5. Other	9.1	3.6	.5	.6	5.6	(8.6)[a]
Total	250.4	73.1	16.1	12.5	173.7	241.8[a]

APPENDIX TABLE I6 (*Continued*)
GNP BY END USE
(*Billion zlotys*)

1955	(1) Value in Market Prices	(2) Indirect Taxes	(3) Accounting Profits	(4) Subsidies	(5) Adjusted Base	(6) Factor Cost
1. Personal consumption	158.6	60.3	16.7	8.7	90.3	146.0
a. Retail sales	120.2	57.5	16.4	8.2	54.5	70.6
b. Farm market sales	6.4				6.4	6.4
c. Gross rent	2.5	.8		.3	2.0	33.6
d. Farm consumption in kind	24.6				24.6	32.0
e. Military subsistence	3.1	1.5	.2	.2	1.6	2.1
f. Wages in kind	1.0	.5	.1		.4	.5
g. Domestic and religious services	.8				.8	.8
2. Government consumption	26.8	5.8	1.6	.5	19.9	21.4
a. Commodities	12.0	5.8	1.6	.5	5.1	6.6
b. Wages and salaries	14.8				14.8	14.8
3. National defense	11.7			.5	12.2	14.1
a. Procurements	5.9			.5	6.4	8.3
b. Military pay and subsistence	5.8				5.8	5.8
4. Gross investment	63.4	6.4	2.6	6.9	61.3	79.3
a. Fixed capital	45.6	2.7	1.4	5.1	46.6	60.6
(i) Taxed	5.6	2.7				
(ii) Tax-free	40.0					
b. Increase in inventories	16.0	3.3	1.1	1.8	13.4	17.4
(i) Taxed	6.8	3.3				
(ii) Tax-free	9.2					
c. Farm investment in kind	.8		.1		.8	.8
d. Net foreign investment	.9	.4			.4	.5
5. Other	6.1	2.4	.4	.5	3.8	(5.7) a
Total	266.6	74.9	21.3	17.1	187.5	260.9 a

APPENDIX TABLE 16 (Continued)
GNP BY END USE
(Billion zlotys)

1956	(1) Value in Market Prices	(2) Indirect Taxes	(3) Accounting Profits	(4) Subsidies	(5) Adjusted Base	(6) Factor Cost
1. Personal consumption	180.9	54.6	19.0	9.0	116.3	171.7
a. Retail sales	135.5	52.2	18.6	8.6	73.3	89.0
b. Farm market sales	7.1				7.1	7.1
c. Gross rent	2.5	.9		.2	1.8	34.4
d. Farm consumption in kind	31.1				31.1	37.8
e. Military subsistence	2.8	1.1	.3	.2	1.6	1.9
f. Wages in kind	1.1	.4	.1		.6	.7
g. Domestic and religious services	.8				.8	.8
2. Government consumption	30.1	5.0	1.7	.5	23.9	25.4
a. Commodities	13.1	5.0	1.7	.5	6.9	8.4
b. Wages and salaries	17.0				17.0	17.0
3. National defense	11.7			.3	12.0	13.4
a. Procurements	6.1			.3	6.4	7.8
b. Military pay and subsistence	5.6				5.6	5.6
4. Gross investment	81.4	4.7	4.9	5.0	76.8	93.2
a. Fixed capital	61.8	2.9	3.3	3.3	58.9	71.7
(i) Taxed	7.5	2.9				
(ii) Tax-free	54.3					
b. Increase in inventories	13.4	.4	1.2	1.3	13.1	15.9
(i) Taxed	1.0	.4				
(ii) Tax-free	12.4					
c. Farm investment in kind	1.3				1.3	1.3
d. Net foreign investment	4.9	1.4	.4	.4	3.5	4.3
5. Other	-3.8	-1.1	-.4	-.2	-2.5	(-3.5) [a]
Total	300.3	63.2	25.2	14.6	226.5	303.8 [a]

[a] Item 5 is excluded from the total in column 6.

stage we do not have sufficient information to quantify such effects, but they probably are relatively unimportant. Indirect taxes in Poland were designed to burden primarily personal consumption. In principle, transactions between producing socialized enterprises were exempt from tax, although enterprises in the private sector and in parts of the cooperative sector were often treated on the same basis as the population. We shall show under (iii) the devision of those end uses that were taxed only in part.

(ii) In the case of gross rent (item 1c), net foreign investment (4d), and other (5), the incidence of indirect taxes could be approximated directly. For item 1c, see Appendix Table H1. For items 4d and 5, we applied the average rate indicated for exports (see Appendix Table D1).

(iii) The end uses shown in Appendix Table I6 that were not already enumerated under (i) and (ii) above were assumed to be taxed at the same average rate. Before explaining the derivation of this rate, we shall show the separation of items 4a and 4b (fixed capital and increase in inventories) into taxed and tax-free components.

We took as subject to tax only that part of the change in inventories that belonged to domestic trade. On the basis of information given in Ficowski, "Struktura zapasów w gospodarce naradowej w latach 1950–1955," p. 23, we took the figures for trade at 2.9 billion zlotys in 1954 and 6.8 billion zlotys in 1955. *DN 1956*, p. 46, gives 1.0 billion zlotys for 1956.

Within fixed capital investment we assumed that only investment by private and cooperative enterprises was subject to indirect taxes. On the basis of data pertaining to new investment (*SIB 1956*, p. 5) in 1955 and 1956, we estimated that private and cooperative investment accounted for about 12.2 percent of the total gross fixed capital investment in the years 1954–56. Accordingly, the following amounts were considered taxed (in billion zlotys): *1954*, 5.2; *1955*, 5.6; and *1956*, 7.5. These figures probably will lead to an overestimate when we apply an average rate of tax to them because some cooperative investment particularly may have been tax-free or taxed at a preferential rate. We may consider any overestimate to offset an underestimate of indirect tax on the balance of fixed capital. Although we assumed this balance pertaining to the state sector was tax-free, no doubt some small part of it was bought at retail contrary to the intentions of the planning authorities, and to some small degree there were indirect effects arising from taxed products being used as inputs into the production of investment goods.

We estimated the indirect tax on the items in (iii), above, at an average rate determined by dividing the total tax less the tax directly allocated under (ii), above, by the sum of the items in column *1* subject to the average rate (1a, 1e, 1f, 2a, 4a(i), 4b(i)).

Column *3*. Total accounting profits (Table 6) were distributed among end uses roughly on the basis of the sector of origin of the profits and judgments as to the end uses served by sectors. Thus, profits in transportation and communication, trade, and other services were allocated to retail sales (item 1a) and government current purchases (item 2a) in proportion to their values in column *1*. The very small profits in agriculture were allocated to retail sales, those in construction to fixed capital investment, and those in industry, to the following end uses in proportion to their values in column *1*: retail sales, military subsistence (under personal consumption), wages in kind, government current purchases, increase in inventories, net foreign investment, and other (item 5).

Column *4*. Subsidies were first identified by sectors of origin (see Table 6) and then roughly allocated to end uses on the basis of judgments as to which uses benefited by products coming from the various branches of production. In some instances (for example, construction, agriculture, domestic trade, and housing), the subsidies by sectors of origin could be directly associated with major end uses with a fair degree of reliability; in others, we tried to take account of the diffusion and indirect effects to some extent by allocating subsidies among selected components of all the major end uses (for example, subsidies in industry, forestry, and transportation and communication). There was scant basis for any refinement; on the other hand, the amounts involved are relatively small, and, within a considerable range of alternative allocations, the resulting structure of GNP by major end uses would be only slightly affected.

Subsidies in industry and forestry were distributed among retail sales, military subsistence, wages in kind, government current purchases, military procurements, fixed capital investment, increase in inventories, net foreign investment, and other (item 5) in proportion to their market values less indirect taxes and accounting profits (columns *1, 2, 3*). In the same manner we allocated subsidies in agriculture to retail sales, military subsistence, increase in inventories, net foreign investment, and other (item 5); in transportation and communication to retail sales, government current purchases, fixed capital investment, and increase in inventories; and in trade and other services to retail sales and government current purchases. Subsidies in construction were allocated to fixed capital investment, and those in housing to gross rent.

Column 5. This is the sum of columns *1* and *4* less the sum of columns *2* and *3*.

Column 6. In passing from the entries in column *5* to those in column *6*, we observe first that the values in column *5* represent primarily labor costs plus depreciation. To approximate factor cost in column *6* we must allocate to selected end uses the remaining non-labor returns represented by the totals of columns *2* and *3* less the total of column *4*. We excluded certain items as ineligible for such augmentation because (*a*) either they consisted entirely of labor services or (*b*) they were assumed to be already at high enough values to approximate factor cost. Under *a* we included private professional services (as a component of retail sales, in billion zlotys, 0.7, 0.8, and 0.9 in 1954, 1955, and 1956, respectively; see Appendix Table A3), domestic and religious services, and wages and salaries in government and defense. Under *b* we included farm market sales and farm investment in kind, both of which were considered already to include full returns to all factors of production in their values as shown in column *5*.

The allocation of nonlabor returns among the remaining end uses was carried out in three steps. First, we determined an average rate of increase for the eligible items by dividing the total to be allocated (columns *2* plus *3* less *4*) by the sum of the eligible items in column *5*. This rate, however, was applied only to item 5, "other," to arrive at its value in column *6*. We then used this value in our factor cost adjustment by sectors of origin (Appendix Table I1). Second, we estimated the value of gross rent (item 1c) at factor cost by taking the gross value added by housing at factor cost as shown in Appendix Table I1 and increasing it by the value of current inputs from other sectors into housing services. This increase at factor cost was very roughly approximated for all years at 1.4 billion zlotys on the basis of the 1956 value of gross rent (Appendix Table I6, item 1c, column *1*) plus subsidies to housing less labor costs and indirect taxes (Table 6). Current purchases at market prices included turnover tax and profits, and we assumed these elements roughly covered nonlabor factor charges in these purchases. Depreciation in housing as shown in Polish official sources for the most part appears to be an imputation for national accounting purposes, and hence we did not consider it a charge against gross rent at market prices. Third, we diminished the total to be allocated (columns 2 plus 3 less 4) by the amounts already allocated to item 5, "other," and to gross rent (item 1c), and we distributed the balance to the remaining eligible end uses proportionately to their values in column 5. In this connection we recall that item 1a, retail sales, was first diminished by the value of private professional services to arrive at the value used in the pro rata allocation. The value of the excluded services was, of course, added back to the factor cost value of the remainder of retail sales to arrive at the value in column 6.

In Appendix Table I7 we present a breakdown of government consumption (item 2 in Appendix Table I6).

APPENDIX TABLE I7

GOVERNMENT SECTOR SERVICES AT FACTOR COST

(Billion zlotys)

	1954		1955		1956	
	Market Prices	Factor Cost	Market Prices	Factor Cost	Market Prices	Factor Cost
Education	6.2	5.2	6.7	5.6	7.8	6.8
Labor services	3.9	3.9	4.3	4.3	5.1	5.1
Current purchases	2.3	1.3	2.4	1.3	2.7	1.7
Art and culture	.6	.5	.7	.5	.8	.6
Labor services	.2	.2	.3	.3	.3	.3
Current purchases	.4	.2	.4	.2	.5	.3
Science and research	.9	.7	1.0	.8	1.0	.9
Labor services	.5	.5	.6	.6	.6	.6
Current purchases	.4	.2	.4	.2	.4	.3
Health	4.9	3.8	5.6	4.2	6.7	5.4
Labor services	2.3	2.3	2.5	2.5	3.1	3.1
Current purchases	2.6	1.5	3.1	1.7	3.6	2.3
Internal security	3.4	3.0	3.9	3.2	3.9	3.3
Labor services	2.4	2.4	2.3	2.3	2.3	2.3
Current purchases	1.0	.6	1.6	.9	1.6	1.0
Administration and justice	6.6	5.5	7.0	5.9	7.8	6.8
Labor services	4.0	4.0	4.4	4.4	5.0	5.0
Current purchases	2.6	1.5	2.6	1.5	2.8	1.8
Quasi-government services	1.7	1.2	1.9	1.3	2.1	1.6
Labor services	.6	.6	.6	.6	.6	.6
Current purchases	1.1	.6	1.3	.7	1.5	1.0
Total government	24.2	19.8	26.8	21.4	30.1	25.4

NOTES TO APPENDIX TABLE 17

Total government consumption and its components by branch of services at market prices were taken from Table 7. Labor services were taken from Table 6, the sum of columns *1* and *2;* current purchases are the residual in each branch total after subtraction of labor charges. The labor component at factor cost is the same as at market prices. The factor cost total, including current purchases, is taken from Appendix Table 16. The factor cost total for current purchases shown in Appendix Table 16, item 2a, was distributed among branches in Appendix Table 17 in proportion to their values at market prices.

SOURCES CITED

Alton, Thad Paul. Polish Postwar Economy. New York, Columbia University Press, 1955.

Alton, Thad Paul, and associates. Czechoslovak National Income and Product, 1947–1948 and 1955–1956. New York, Columbia University Press, 1962.

———— Hungarian National Income and Product in 1955. New York, Columbia University Press, 1963.

Andrzejewski, Adam. Ekonomika gospodarki mieszkaniowej (The Economics of Housing). Warsaw, Państwowe Wydawnictwo Naukowe, 1955.

———— Polityka mieszkaniowa, zagadnienia ekonomiczne i socjalne (Housing Policy: Economic and Social Problems). Warsaw, Wydawnictwo Arkady, 1959.

Baran, S., and W. Witakowski. Finansowanie inwestycji (Investment Financing). Warsaw, Polskie Wydawnictwo Gospodarcze, 1957.

Bergson, Abram. Soviet National Income and Product in 1937. New York, Columbia University Press, 1953.

———— The Real National Income of Soviet Russia since 1928. Cambridge, Harvard University Press, 1961.

Bergson, Abram, and Hans Heymann, Jr. Soviet National Income and Product, 1940–48. New York, Columbia University Press, 1954.

Biuletyn budownictwa mieszkaniowego (Bulletin of Housing Construction), 1958. Warsaw. A supplement to the monthly Miasto (City).

Bogusławski, J. "Kilka słów o równowadze rynkowej" (A Few Words about Market Equilibrium), Trybuna ludu (Tribune of the People), March 31, 1957.

Cegielski, A., and C. Kucharski. "O niektórych zagadnieniach rozwoju prywatnej gospodarki miejskiej w Polsce Ludowej" (About Some Problems of the Development of Private Urban Economy in People's Poland), Finanse (Finances), X, No. 1 (January, 1959).

Chlebowczyk, Alojzy, Lidia Beskid, and Stefan Felbur. Materiały do badania relacji cen (Contributions to Research on the Relation of Prices). Warsaw, Państwowe Wydawnictwo Naukowe, 1958.

Clark, Colin. "Russian Income and Production Statistics," *Review of Economic Statistics,* November, 1947.

"Dochody realne ludności chłopskiej z produkcji rolniczej w latach 1956–58" (The Real Income of Farm Population from Agricultural Production during the Years 1956–58), Poland, Główny urząd statystyczny (Central Statistical Office), *Biuletyn Statystyczny* (Statistical Bulletin), Supplement, February, 1959.

Finanse (Finances). 1956. Warsaw.

Ficowski, S. "Struktura zapasów w gospodarce narodowej w latach 1950–1955" (The Structure of Reserves in National Economy during the Years 1950–1955), *Wiadomości narodowego banku polskiego* (News of the Polish National Bank) (Warsaw), No. 1 (1957).

Fiszel, Henryk. Prawo wartości a problematyka cen w przemyśle socjalistycznym (The Law of Value and the Problem of Prices in Socialist Industry). Warsaw, Państwowe Wydawnictwo Naukowe, 1956.

Fiutowski, S., and C. Kozłowski. "Szacunek wyposażenia gospodarstw indywidualnych w maszyny rolnicze" (Estimate of Furnishing Private Farms with Agricultural Machinery), *Zagadnienia ekonomiki rolnej* (Problems of Agricultural Economy) (Warsaw), No. 3, 1957.

Food and Agriculture Organization of the United Nations. Agricultural Sector Accounts and Tables: A Handbook of Definitions and Methods. Geneva, 1956.

Frankel, S. "Lekceważone źródło dewiz" (The Neglected Source of Foreign Exchange), *Życie gospodarcze* (Economic Life), April 5, 1959.

Ginsbert, Adam. Ekonomika gospodarki komunalnej (The Economics of Communal Services). Part III. Warsaw, Państwowe Wydawnictwo Naukowe, 1955.

―――― Gospodarka komunalna w Polsce (Communal Economy in Poland). Warsaw, Wydawnictwo Arkady, 1959.

Gorzelak, E., and Z. Kozłowski. "Zagadnienie cen porównywalnych produktów rolnych w planie 5-letnim" (Problem of the Comparable Prices of Agricultural Products in the Five-Year Plan), *Ekonomista* (Economist) (Warsaw), No. 4 (1956).

Gospodarka planowa (Planned Economy). 1959. Warsaw.

Grabowski, C. "Uwagi o strukturze pieniężnych dochodów i wydatków ludności Polski w r. 1953" (Remarks about the Structure of Money Incomes and Expenditures of the Polish Population in 1953), *Ekonomista* (Economist) (Warsaw), No. 2 (1955).

Handel zagraniczny (Foreign Trade). 1957. Warsaw.

Holzman, Franklyn D. Soviet Taxation. Cambridge, Harvard University Press, 1955.

Hungary. Central Statistical Office. Adatok és adalékok a népgazdaság fejlődésének tanulmányozásához 1949–1955 (Data and Additional Facts for the Study of the Development of National Economy, 1949–1955). Budapest, 1957.

———— Statisztikai évkönyv (Statistical Yearbook) 1949/1955. Budapest, 1957.

Inwestycje i budownictwo (Investment and Construction). 1961. Warsaw.

Jędrychowski, S. Polityka partii i rządu w dziedzinie podziału dochodu narodowego (Party Policy in the Distribution of National Income). Warsaw, Książka i Wiedza, 1958.

Kantor, Jan, and Ignacy Osipow. Statystyka przemysłu (Statistics of Industry). Warsaw, Polskie Wydawnictwa Gospodarcze, 1954.

Karpiński, A. Zagadnienia socjalistycznej industrializacji Polski (Problems of Socialist Industrialization of Poland). Warsaw, Polskie Wydawnictwa Gospodarcze, 1958.

Kołodziej, E. "Zaopatrzenie rolnictwa w środki dla produkcji rolnej" (Supplying Agriculture with the Means for Agricultural Production), *Handel Wewnętrzny* (Internal Trade) (Warsaw), July–August, 1957.

Krajewski, J. "O zmianach cen" (About Price Changes), *Przegląd kolejowy* (Railroad Review) (Warsaw), No. 1 (1956).

Krasicki, W., and W. Misiuna. "Perspectywiczny plan rozwoju produkcji zwierzęcej" (Perspective Plan of Development of Livestock Production), *Gospodarka planowa* (Planned Economy), March, 1959.

Krynicki, Józef. Problemy handlu zagranicznego Polski 1918–1939 i 1945–1955 (Problems of Polish Foreign Trade, 1918–1939 and 1945–1955). Warsaw, Państwowe Wydawnictwo Naukowe, 1958.

Krzeczkowska, E., B. Szybisz, and L. Zienkowski. Tablice przepływów międzydziałowych i międzygałeziowych w gospodarce narodowej Polski w 1956 r. (Tables of Intersectoral and Interbranch Flows in the National Economy of Poland in 1956), *Ekonomista* (Economist) (Warsaw), No. 1 (1958).

Lipiński, Edward. Rewizje (Revisions). Warsaw, Państwowe Wydawnictwo Naukowe, 1958.

Litterer, W. "Szacunek zasobów mieszkaniowych użytkowanych przez ludność pozarolniczą" (An Estimate of Housing Stock Used by the Nonagricultural Population), *Biuletyn budownictwa mieszkaniowego* (Bulletin of Housing Construction), VIII, No. 4-M (April, 1957).

———— "W sprawie czynszów i źródeł finansowania gospodarki zasobem mieszkaniowym" (About Rents and Sources of Financing Housing), *Biuletyn budownictwa mieszkaniowego* (Bulletin of Housing Construction), VIII, No. 5-M (May, 1957).

Montias, John M. Central Planning in Poland. New Haven, Yale University Press, 1962.

Niewadzi, Czesław. Małe przedsiębiorstwa przemysłowe w gospodarce narodowej (Small Industrial Enterprises in National Economy). Warsaw, Polskie Wydawnictwa Gospodarcze, 1958.

Nowe drogi (New Ways). 1956. Warsaw.

Nowe rolnictwo (New Agriculture). 1957. Warsaw.

Pirożynski, Z. "Budżet państwowy Polski Ludowej w okresie uprzemysłowienia" (The State Budget of People's Poland during the Industrialization Period), *Finanse* (Finances), September, 1961.

Płowiec, U. "Koncepcja dochodów realnych ludności wiejskiej" (The Concept of Real Incomes of Rural Population), *Przegląd statystyczny* (Statistical Review) (Warsaw), No. 1 (1958).

———— "Przyczynek w sprawie badania spożycia ludności chłopskiej" (Contribution to the Research on Consumption of the Peasant Population), *Wiadomości statystyczne* (Statistical News), March–April, 1958.

Polaczek, S. "Próba obliczenia siły nabywczej złotego w stosunku do walut zagranicznych" (An Attempt to Estimate the Purchasing Power of Zloty in Relation to Foreign Currencies), in Poland, Komisja planowania przy radzie ministrów (Planning Commission of Council of Ministers), Prace i materiały zakładu badań ekonomicznych (Contributions and Materials of the Institute of Economic Research), Warsaw, March–April, 1957.

Poland. Główny urząd statystyczny (Central Statistical Office). *Biuletyn statystyczny* (Statistical Bulletin). Warsaw, 1957.

———— Dochód narodowy Polski (National Income of Poland) 1954–1962. Warsaw, 1957–62.

———— Elektryfikacja wsi 1950–1959 (Electrification of the Village, 1950–1959). Statystyka Polski (Statistics of Poland), Vol. 48. Warsaw, 1961.

———— "Klasyfikacja gospodarki narodowej" (Classification of National Economy), *Biuletyn statystyczny* (Statistical Bulletin), No. 8 (1959), insert.

———— Mały rocznik statystyczny (Concise Statistical Yearbook) 1957–1963. Warsaw, 1957–63.

———— "Ogólne wyniki powszechnej inwentaryzacji środków trwałych według stanu w dniu 1 1 1961 r." (Over-all Results of the General Census of Fixed Capital as of January 1, 1961), *Biuletyn statystyczny* (Statistical Bulletin), No. 1 (1963), insert.

———— Państwowe gospodarstwa rolne w 1956 roku (State Farms in 1956). Statystyka Polski (Statistics of Poland), Series F, Vol. 1. Warsaw, 1958.

———— Państwowe i gminne ośrodki maszynowe w 1956 roku (State and Cooperative Agricultural Machine Centers in 1956). Statystyka Polski (Statistics of Poland), Series F, Vol. 2. Warsaw, 1958.

———— Produkcja globalna i brutto rolnictwa przed wojną i w latach 1946–1958 (Gross Production and Output of Agriculture before the War and in the Years 1946–1958). Warsaw, 1960.

———— Rocznik statystyczny (Statistical Yearbook) 1955–1963. Warsaw, 1955–63.

———— Statystyka cen (Statistics of Prices) 1957. Statystyka Polski (Statistics of Poland), Series F, Vol. 8. Warsaw, 1959.

———— Statystyka handlu zagranicznego (Statistics of Foreign Trade), 1961. Statystyka Polski (Statistics of Poland), Vol. 62. Warsaw, 1962.

———— Statystyka inwestycji i budownictwa (Statistics of Investment and Construction) 1956, 1958. Statystyka Polski (Statistics of Poland), Series E, Vols. 3, 40. Warsaw, 1958–60.

———— Statystyka kultury (Statistics of Culture) 1958. Statystyka Polski (Statistics of Poland), Vol. 39. Warsaw, 1960.

———— Statystyka przemysłu (Statistics of Industry) 1957. Statystyka Polski (Statistics of Poland), Vol. 22. Warsaw, 1959.

———— Statystyka przemysłu: statystyka produkcji, zatrudnienia i płac (Statistics of Industry: Statistics of Production, Employment, and Wages). Statystyka Polski (Statistics of Poland), Series E, Vol. 8. Warsaw, 1958.

———— Statystyka rolnictwa 1946–1957 (Agricultural Statistics, 1946–1957). Warsaw, 1961.

Poland. Rada ekonomiczna przy radzie ministrów (Economic Council of the Council of Ministers). Główne problemy sytuacji gospodarczej kraju (Main Problems of Economic Situation of the Country). Warsaw, Polskie Wydawnictwa Gospodarcze, 1958.

────── Sytuacja gospodarcza kraju w roku 1958 (Economic Conditions of the Country in 1958). Warsaw, Polskie Wydawnictwa Gospodarcze, 1959.

Poland. Rada ministrów (Council of Ministers). Dziennik ustaw (Journal of Laws). 1947–1948, 1951–1952, 1954, 1956–1959. Warsaw, 1947–59.

Polskie towarzystwo ekonomiczne, oddział w Poznaniu (Polish Economic Society, Poznan Chapter). Problemy gospodarcze drobnej wytwórczości (Economic Problems of Small-Scale Production). Roczniki i sprawozdania (Yearbooks and Reports) Part III. Poznań, Państwowe Wydawnictwo Naukowe, 1958.

Poniatowski, J. "Rolnictwo" (Agriculture), *Kultura* (Culture) (Paris), No. 4, Home Issue (1953).

Przegląd statystyczny (Statistical Review). 1958. Warsaw.

Przegląd zagadnień socjalnych (Review of Social Problems). 1957. Warsaw.

Przełaskowski, W. "Rozwój indywidualnego oszczędzania w krajach socjalistycznych" (Development of Personal Savings in Socialist Countries), *Z prac zakładu nauk ekonomicznych* (Works of Institute of Economics). No. 1 (February, 1961).

Reniger, Henryk. Dochody państwowe (Incomes of the State). Warsaw, Państwowe Wydawnictwo Naukowe, 1955.

Rocznik polityczny i gospodarczy (Political and Economic Yearbook) 1958. Warsaw, Polskie Wydawnictwo Gospodarcze, 1958.

Róg, S. "Charakterystyka środków trwałych na podstawie wyników powszechnej inwentwaryzacji" (Characteristics of Fixed Capital on the Basis of Results of Census), *Inwestycje i budownictwo* (Investment and Construction), No. 4 (April, 1961).

Skałuba, Z. "Sytuacja mieszkaniowa na wsi w końcu 1955" (The Housing Situation in the Countryside at the End of 1955), *Przegląd zagadnień socjalnych* (Review of Social Problems), No. 5 (1957).

Słowo powszechne (The Universal Word). 1958. Warsaw.

Soviet Studies. 1955. Glasgow.

Spulber, Nicolas. The Economics of Communist Eastern Europe. New York, Wiley, 1957.

Stone, Richard. "Functions and Criteria of a System of Social Accounting," in International Association for Research in Income and Wealth, *Income and Wealth,* Series I, ed. Eric Lundberg. Cambridge, Bowes and Bowes, 1951.

Szularzewicz, J. "Perspektywy rozwojowe produkcji drobiarskiej" (Prospects for the Development of Poultry Output), *Nowe rolnictwo* (New Agriculture), November, 1957.

Taylor, J. The Economic Development of Poland, 1919–1950. Ithaca, N.Y., Cornell University Press, 1952.

Thor, A. "Stan electryfikacji wsi w Polsce oraz wydatki ludności wiejskiej związane z elektryfikacją" (The Level of Electrification in Poland and the Expenditures of the Rural Population Connected with Electrification), *Zagadnienia ekonomiki rolnej* (Problems of Agricultural Economy), No. 4 (34) (1959).

Tokarski, Z. "Metoda szacunku zasobów gotówkowych ludności pochodzących z plac i dochodów pokrewnych" (Method of Estimation of Cash Resources of the Population Derived from Wages and Related Incomes), *Wiadomości narodowego banku polskiego* (News of Polish National Bank) (Warsaw), No. 6 (1958).

Trybuna ludu (Tribune of the People). 1956. Warsaw.

United Nations. Economic Bulletin for Europe. Geneva.

———— A System of National Accounts. Studies in Methods, No. 2. New York, United Nations, 1953.

United States. Bureau of the Census. Statistical Abstract of the United States: 1956. Washington, D.C., 1956.

United States. Department of Commerce. U.S. Income and Output: A Supplement to the *Survey of Current Business*. Washington, D.C., 1958.

Wanatowski, A. "Próba oceny rozmiarów rocznego zużycia budynków wiejskich i przeciętnego stopnia ich zużycia w 1957 r." (An Attempt of Estimation of Annual Depreciation of Farm Residential Housing and the Average Rate of Its Depreciation in 1957), *Wiadomości statystyczne* (Statistical News), March, 1958.

Weralski, M. Finanse i kredyt Polskiej Rzeczypolpolitej Ludowej (Finances and Credit of Polish People's Republic), Part I. Warsaw, Polskie Wydawnictwo Gospodarcze, 1957.

Wesołowski, J. "Usługi morskie w bilansie rozrachunkowym i płatniczym" (Maritime Services in the Balance of Payments), *Handel zagraniczny* (Foreign Trade), No. 6 (1957).

Wiadomości statystyczne (Statistical News). 1958. Warsaw.

Wiles, Peter. "Are Adjusted Rubles Rational?" *Soviet Studies,* October, 1955.

Wojciechowska, U. "Ogólne tendencje kształtowania się zapasów w gospodarce uspołecznionej" (General Tendencies in the Development of Inventories in the Socialized Economy), *Finanse* (Finances), No. 3 (1958).

Wyler, J. "The National Income of Soviet Russia," *Social Research,* December, 1946.

Wyźnikiewicz, J. "O dalszy rozwój eksportu niewidocznego" (About Further Development of Invisible Exports), *Finanse* (Finances), XI, No. 5 (May, 1960).

Zagadnienia ekonomiki rolnej. 1959. Warsaw.

Zienkowski, Leszek. Jak oblicza się dochód narodowy (How National Income Is Calculated). 1st ed. Warsaw, Polskie Wydawnictwa Gospodarcze, 1957; 2d ed., 1959.

Zwass, A. "Rola bodźców ekonomicznych w prawidłowym kształtowaniu zapasów" (The Role of Economic Incentives in the Correct Formation of Reserves), *Wiadomości narodowego banku polskiego* (News of Polish National Bank) (Warsaw), No. 3 (1958).

Życie gospodarcze (Economic Life). 1959. Warsaw.

KEY TO TABLE ITEMS

Item	Page		Item	Page
Table 1A	13		Table 1C	15
1	138, 140, 142		1	31, 117
2	101		2	31, 117
			3	31, 117–18
			4	31–32, 118
Table 1B	14–15			
1	21, 101		Table 2A	15–16
2A(1)a	21–22, 101		1A	32, 119
b	22, 101–103		B	32, 119
c	22–23, 103		C	32, 119
(2)a	23, 103		D	32, 119
b	23–24, 103		E	32, 119
(3)	24, 104		2	32, 119
(4)	24, 104		3	32, 119
B(1)	24–25, 104		A	119–20
a	25		B	120
b	25		C	120
c	25–26		4	33, 120
d	26		5A	33–34, 120
e	26		B	34, 120
(2)	104		6	34, 120–21
a	26		7A	35
b	26		(1)	121
(3)a	26, 104		(2)	121
b	26–27, 104		(3)	121
3A	27, 104		B	35, 121
B(1)	27–28, 104		C	35, 122
(2)	28, 106–107			
(3)	28–29, 107–109		Table 2B	16
(4)	29–30, 112–13		1	35, 122
(5)	30, 113		2	35, 122
(6)	30, 113		3	35, 122
(7)	30, 113		4	35, 122
(8)	30, 113		5	35, 122
C(1)	30–31, 117		6	35–36, 122
(2)	31, 117		7	36, 122
(3)	31, 117		8	36, 122
(4)	31, 117		9	36, 122
4	31, 117		10	36, 122

Item	*Page*
11	36, 122
12	36, 122–23
Table 2C	17
1	37, 123
2	37, 123
3	37, 123
4	37, 123
5	37, 123
6	37–38
A	123
B	123–24
C	124
7	38, 124
8	38, 124
Table 3A	17
1	38–39, 125
2	39, 125
3	39, 125
4	39–40, 125
5	40, 125
Table 3B	18
1A	40–41, 125–26
B	41, 126
C	41, 126
D	41, 126
E	126
(1)	41–42, 126
(2)	42, 126

Item	*Page*
2	42
3A	42, 126
B	42, 126
4	42–44, 126
5	44, 126
Table 3C	18
1	44, 127
2	44, 127
3	44, 127
4	44–46, 127
5A	46, 127
B	46, 127
6	46, 127
Table 4A	19
1	47–49, 128–34
2	134
3A	47–49, 134
B	49, 134
C	49–50, 134–35
Table 4B	19
1	135
2	135
Table 4C	19
1	51, 135
2	51, 135
3	51, 135
4	51–52, 136

INDEX

Accounting profits, 74–75, 227–29 (*table*); *see also* Turnover tax

Accounts, framework of, 2–5; *see also* Appropriation accounts; Capital accounts; Production accounts

Administration and justice, 14 (*table*), 24, 25; expenditures, 177–79 (*table*), 195–96, 198 (*table*); in GNP (*tables*), 56–58, 62, 77, 82, 87, 214; wage bill, 139–43 (*table*), 152; at market prices and at factor cost, 233 (*table*)

Agriculture, 6, 7; income from, 14 (*table*), 16 (*table*), 22–23, 36, 103, 162 (*table*), 163–64; consumption in kind, 14 (*table*), 16 (*table*), 23–24, 32, 35, 36, 165–70, 169 (*table*), 227–29 (*table*); market purchases from, 14 (*table*), 28, 106–7, 227–29 (*table*); investment in kind, 35, 227–29 (*table*); and land tax, 36, 162 (*table*); in GNP (*tables*), 56–58, 77, 81, 82, 87, 89 (*table*), 214 (*table*); market prices, 76; in factor cost, 77–78, 79; share in national income (*tables*), 95, 98; retail purchases for consumption, 105; capital consumption, 121; wage bill (*tables*), 138, 140, 142; wage-like payments in, 159 (*table*); selected estimates in, 161–70; current expenditure, 162 (*table*), 162–63; depreciation (*tables*), 162, 164–65, 209, 225; insurance, 162 (*table*), 165; taxes, 162 (*table*), 165; index of prices, 167 (*table*); subsidy payments to, 207 (*table*); current values of fixed and working capital, 216 (*table*); fixed capital, 218 (*table*); fixed capital stock, 220 (*table*)

Appropriation accounts: defined, 4; household sector, 14–15 (*table*), 21–31; enterprise sector, 16 (*table*), 35–37; government sector, 18 (*table*), 40–44; *foreign sector,* 19 (*table*), 50–51; consolidated, 20 (*table*)

Armed forces, *see* Military

Art and culture (*tables*), 56–58, 62, 77, 82, 87, 214; wage bill, 139 (*table*), 141 (*table*), 143 (*table*), 150–51; budget expenditures on, 186–87 (*table*), 188–89; at market prices and at factor cost, 233 (*table*)

Association of Polish Youth, 30

Budget differences: enterprise sector, 16 (*table*), 33, 42–44, 120, 171, 172 (*table*); foreign sector, 47–48, 126, 130–34, 135, 172 (*table*); by sectors, 205 (*table*), 206

Budget enterprises, 172 (*table*), 174, 177–79 (*table*), 180

Budgets, state, *see* State budgets

Capital account(s): defined, 4; household sector, 15 (*table*), 31–32; enterprise sector, 17 (*table*), 37–38; government sector, 18 (*table*), 44–46; foreign sector, 19 (*table*), 51–52; consolidated, 21 (*table*)

Capital consumption allowances: in enterprise production account, 16 (*table*), 34, 120–21; in enterprise capital account, 17 (*table*); in consolidated accounts (*tables*), 20, 21; in factor-cost, 69, 79; as form of return to capital, 75–76; as a source of finance, 93 (*table*)

Capital repairs, 17 (table), 32, 37, 120–21, 123–24
Catering, see Trade and catering
City tax, 174 (table)
Coal deliveries to USSR, 65
Collective farms, 23, 36
Commercial Services, 102 (table), 103
Communication services, see Transportation and communication
Communist Party, 26, 201 (table); see also Quasi-governmental organizations
Compensation of employees, see Wages and salaries
Consolidated accounts, 52–54; production, 20 (table); appropriation, 20 (table); capital, 21 (table)
Construction: in GNP (tables), 56–58, 77, 81, 87, 89, 214; share in national income (tables), 95, 98; income of self-employed in, 102 (table); wage bill, 138 (table), 140 (table), 142 (table), 146; wage-like payments in, 159 (table); subsidy payments to, 207 (table); depreciation allowances (tables), 209, 225; current values of fixed and working capital, 216 (table); fixed capital, 218 (table); fixed capital stock, 220 (table); see also Housing
Cooperatives: nonagricultural, 14 (table), 16 (table), 22, 24, 36, 104; agricultural, 22, 161, 169; labor, 24, 35, 36; income tax paid by, 35; housing, 146, 147
Culture, see Art and culture
Czechoslovakia (tables), 89, 92
Customs duties, 172 (table)

Debt, national, 177–79 (table), 196–97
Defense: military investments, 44–46; in GNP (tables), 56–58, 62, 77, 82, 87, 214, 227–29; in resource allocation, 92 (table); wage bill, 139 (table), 141 (table), 143 (table), 154–56; expenditures, 177–79 (table), 194–95
Depreciation allowances, 56–58 (table), 61, 76, 209 (table), 209–10, 225 (table); funds, surplus, 172 (table), 175; adjusted, 214 (table); rate, 224–25; see also Capital consumption allowances

Director's fund, 22, 158, 159 (table)
Direct taxes, see under Taxes
Domestic and religious services, 13 (table), 20 (table), 21; contribution to GNP (tables), 56–58, 77, 81, 87, 214 (table), 227–29 (table); wage bill, 138 (table), 140 (table), 142 (table), 144

Economic enterprise, see Enterprise sector
Economic policy, 5–9
Education: stipends, 26; contribution to GNP (tables), 56–58, 62, 77, 82, 87, 214 (table); wage bill, 139 (table), 141 (table), 143 (table), 151–52; expenditures on, 186–87 (table), 194; at market prices and at factor cost, 233 (table); see also Health, education, and welfare
Employment income, see Income; Wages and Salaries
Enterprise sector: identified, 3; household sector purchase from, 14 (table), 15 (table), 20 (table), 27–30, 32; household sector income from, 14 (table), 21–24; sales to foreign sector, 15 (table), 16 (table), 32, 33; household sector lending to, 15 (table), 17 (table), 31; transfers from household sector, 15 (table), 17 (table), 31–32; sales to enterprise sector, 15 (table), 20 (table), 32; sales to government sector, 15 (table), 17 (table), 20 (table), 32, 39–40, 105 (table), 125, 177–79 (table), 181–82; production account, 15–16 (table), 32–35; compensation of employees, 16 (table); transfers to government sector, 16 (table), 17 (table), 18 (table), 36, 38, 124, 172 (table), 177–79 (table), 181; transfers from government sector, 16 (table), 17 (table), 18 (table), 37, 42, 46; interest payments to household sector, 16 (table), 35; appropriation account, 16 (table), 35–37; loans to government sector, 17 (table), 18 (table), 38, 172 (table); gross investment, 17 (table), 21 (table), 37–38; capital account, 17 (table), 37–38; direct taxes from, 18 (table), 41; subsidies from government sector to

state farms, 15 (table), 33; subsidies from government sector to
MTS, 15 (table), 33; subsidies from
government sector, 18 (table), 42–
44, 126; saving, 20 (table); value
added to national income, 20 (table); as source of finance, 93 (table); wage bill, 138–43 (table),
145–149; wage-like payments in,
159 (table); indirect taxes from,
172 (table), 173; government repayment of debts and new credits,
177–79 (table); grants to, 177–79
(table)
Entertainment, 28, 107–111, 109 (table), 147, 148, 149
Exports, 19 (table), 33–34, 47–48,
63–64; see also Foreign sector; Imports

Factor cost: standard of, 68–76; relationship to market price, 69–76,
86–89; GNP at (tables), 77, 81, 82,
87, 89; see also Gross national
product
Farming and farms, see Agriculture;
State farms
Finance, sources of, 92–94, 93 (table)
Finance and insurance, 147, 148, 149
Five-Year Plan, 8
Fixed capital, 17 (table), 32, 37, 123;
in GNP, 62 (table), 63, 82 (table),
227–29 (table); in factor-cost
standard, 69; current values, 216
(table); in Polish economy, 217–
24, 218 (table)
Fixed capital stock, 220 (table)
Foreign exchange, 46–50, 51, 64
Foreign sector: identified, 3; transfers
to household sector, 15 (table), 19
(table), 21 (table), 51–52, 136;
enterprise sales to 15 (table), 32;
enterprise purchases from, 16 (table), 33; government purchases
from, 17 (table), 40, 125, 177–79
(table); transfers from government
sector, 18 (table), 19 (table), 21
(table), 51, 135; government sector
lending to, 18 (table), 19 (table),
51, 135; production account, 19
(table), 46–50; appropriation account, 19 (table), 50–51; capital
account, 19 (table), 51–52; balance
on production account, 20 (table);

net lending to, 21 (table); in GNP,
62 (table), 63, 82 (table); trade estimates, 134 (table); loans to government, 172 (table); government
sales to, 172 (table), 176; government sector repayment of debts and
new credits to, 177–79 (table); subsidies to, 177–179, (table); investment, 211, 227–29 (table); see also
Exports; Imports
Forestry: in GNP (tables), 56–58, 77,
81, 87, 89, 214; share in national
income, (tables), 95, 98; income of
self-employed in, 102 (table), 103;
wage bill (tables), 138, 140, 142;
wage-like payments in, 159 (table);
indirect taxes from, 205 (table);
subsidy payments to, 207 (table);
depreciation allowances (tables),
209, 220; current values of fixed
and working capital, 216 (table);
fixed capital, 218 (table); fixed
capital stock, 220 (table)

General Savings Bank, 24
Gomułka, Wladyslaw, 6, 7, 65
Government sector: identified, 3;
transfers to household sector, 14
(table), 18 (table), 26–27, 42, 104,
177–79 (table); household sector
income from, 14 (table), 24–27;
enterprise sector sales to, 15 (table), 17 (table), 20 (table), 32,
39–40, 125; household sector payments to, 15 (table), 30–31, 93
(table); interest payments to enterprise sector, 16 (table), 35; prizes
to enterprise sector, 16 (table), 35;
transfers to enterprise sector, 17 (table), 18 (table), 37, 42, 46, 177–79
(table), 181; transfers from enterprise sector, 17 (table), 18 (table),
38, 124; enterprise sector lending to,
17 (table), 18 (table), 38, 172 (ta-
ble); services, 17 (table), 20 (ta-
ble), 38–39, 233 (table); production account, 17 (table), 38–40;
purchases from foreign sector, 17
(table), 40, 125; transfers to foreign sector, 18 (table), 19 (table),
21 (table), 51, 135; lending to foreign sector, 18 (table), 19 (table),
46, 51, 135; investment, 18 (table),

Government sector (*Continued*)
21 (*table*), 44–46; indirect tax receipts, 18 (*table*), 40–41; appropriation account, 18 (*table*), 40–44; direct tax receipts, 18 (*table*), 41; transfers from households, 18 (*table*), 41–42; subsidies to enterprise sector, 18 (*table*), 42–44, 126; capital account, 18 (*table*), 44–46; value added to national income, 20 (*table*); wages and salaries, 20 (*table*); saving, 20 (*table*), 126–27; in GNP (*tables*), 62, 81, 82; in resource allocation, 92 (*table*); enterprise sector payments, 93 (*table*); consumption, 105 (*table*), 210, 226, 227–29 (*table*); indirect tax receipts, 125–26; wage bill, 139 (*table*), 141 (*table*), 143 (*table*), 149–158; foreign sector lending to, 172 (*table*); sales to foreign sector, 172 (*table*), 176; grants to enterprise sector, 177–79 (*table*), 183–84; see also Administration and justice; Art and culture; Education; Internal Security; Public health; Quasi-governmental organizations; Science and research; State budgets

Gross investments, 4, 62 (*table*), 63, 82 (*table*), 92 (*table*), 226, 227–29 (*table*), 230

Gross national product (GNP): 1–2, 4, 8; consolidated production account, 20 (*table*); at market prices, by sector of origin, 55–61, 56–58 (*table*), 87 (*table*), by end use, 61–66, 62 (*table*), 82 (*table*), 225–33, 227–29 (*table*); at factor cost, 67–85, at factor cost, by sector (*tables*), 77, 81, 87, 89, 214; by sector of origin, 86–89; resource allocation, 92 (*table*); returns to labor in, 212–13, 214 (*table*); nonlabor returns, 214 (*table*), 215

Handicrafts: household sector purchases, 14 (*table*), 29–30, 32, 112–13; in GNP (*tables*), 56–58, 77, 81, 87, 214; share in national income, 95 (*table*), 98 (*table*); income of self-employed in, 102 (*table*); wage bill, 138 (*table*), 140 (*table*), 142 (*table*), 145–46; wage-like pay-

ments in, 159 (*table*); indirect taxes from, 205 (*table*), 205–6

Health and Physical culture, 186–87 (*table*), 192–94

Health, education, and welfare, 14 (*table*), 25; wage bill, 139 (*table*), 141 (*table*), 143 (*table*), 149–50; expenditures, 177–79 (*table*), 184–85, 186–87 (*table*); at market prices and at factor cost, 233 (*table*)

Household sector: identified, 3; production account, 13 (*table*), 21; purchases from enterprise sector, 14 (*table*), 15 (*table*), 20 (*table*), 27–30, 32, 107–12; income from enterprise sector, 14 (*table*), 21–24; income from government sector, 14 (table), 24–27, 104; appropriation account, 14–15 (*table*), 21–31; lending to enterprise sector, 15 (*table*), 17 (*table*), 31; transfers to enterprise sector, 15 (*table*), 17 (*table*), 31–32; transfers from foreign sector, 15 (*table*), 19 (*table*), 21 (*table*), 31, 51–52, 136; saving, 15 (*table*), 20 (*table*), 31, 93 (*table*); payments to government sector, 15 (*table*), 30–31, 93 (*table*), 172 (*table*), 175; capital account, 15 (*table*), 31–32; enterprise sector interest payments to, 16 (*table*), 35; taxes from, 18 (*table*), 41, 172 (*table*), 174; transfers to government sector, 18 (*table*), 41–42; transfers from government sector, 18 (*table*), 42, 200 (*table*); consumption, 62 (*table*), 82 (*table*), 92 (*table*), 225–26, 227–29 (*table*); selected services purchased by, 107–12; handicraft purchases, 112–13; wage bill, 138 (*table*), 140 (*table*), 142 (*table*), 144; transfer payments to, 177–79 (*table*); see also Domestic and religious services

Housing: cash and imputed gross rent, 14 (*table*), 30, 113–17, 114 (*table*); in GNP (*tables*), 56–58, 77, 81, 82, 87, 89 (*table*), 214; at factor cost, 80; in market prices and at factor cost compared, 88–89; wage bill, 139 (*table*), 141 (*table*), 143 (*table*), 146–47; wage-like payments in, 159 (*table*); indirect taxes from, 205 (*table*); subsidy payments to, 207 (*table*), 208; depreciation allowances, 209 (*table*), 210, 225 (*table*); current values of fixed and working capital, 216 (*table*); fixed capital, 218 (*table*); fixed capital stock, 220 (*table*); gross rent, 227–29 (*table*); *see also* Construction

Imports, 19 (*table*), 47–48, 63–64, 93 (*table*), 128–34; *see also* Exports; Foreign sector

Income: self-employed, 14 (*table*), 16 (*table*), 22, 35, 36, 56–58 (*table*), 59–60, 77–78, 101–3, 102 (*table*), 203; agricultural, 16 (*table*), 36, 77–78, 79, 103, 162 (*table*); *see also* Wages and salaries

Income, national, *see* National income

Income tax, 35–36, 41, 172 (*table*)

Indirect taxes, *see* Taxes, indirect

Industry: in GNP (*tables*), 56–58, 77, 81, 87, 89, 214; share in national income, 95 (*table*), 98 (*table*); income of self-employed in, 102 (*table*); wage bill, 138 (*table*), 140 (*table*), 142 (*table*), 145–46; wage-like payments in, 159 (*table*); indirect taxes from, 205 (*table*), 205–6; subsidy payments to, 207 (*table*); depreciation allowances (*tables*), 209, 225; current values of fixed and working capital, 216 (*table*); fixed capital, 218 (*table*); fixed capital stock, 220 (*table*)

Interest paid: enterprise to household sector, 14 (*table*), 16 (*table*), 35; government to enterprise sector, 16 (*table*), 35; in GNP, 56–58 (*table*), 60, 204

Internal security, 14 (*table*), 24, 25; in GNP (*tables*), 56–58, 62, 77, 82, 87; wage bill, 139 (*table*), 141 (*table*), 143 (*table*), 152–54; expenditures, 177–79 (*table*), 194, 195–96, 198 (*table*); at market prices and at factor cost, 233 (*table*)

Inventory: increase in, 17 (*table*), 38, 62 (*table*), 63, 124, 227–29; changes, enterprise sector, 15 (*table*), 20 (*table*), 32; in GNP, 82 (*table*)

Investment: gross, 4, 62 (*table*), 63, 82 (*table*), 92 (*table*), 226; enterprise sector, 17 (*table*), 37–38; government sector, 18 (*table*), 44–46, 177–79 (*table*), 182–83; gross domestic, 21 (*table*); retail purchases for, 105 (*table*)

Jędrychowski, S., cited, 44–45

Justice, *see* Administration and justice

Land: tax, 36, 41; in factor-cost standard, 69; rent, 76; improvement, 80

Loans: household to enterprise sector, 15 (*table*), 17 (*table*), 31; enterprise to government sector, 17 (*table*), 18 (*table*), 38, 172 (*table*); government to foreign sector, 18 (*table*), 19 (*table*), 21 (*table*), 51, 135; foreign to government sector, 172

Machine-tractor stations, *see* MTS

Maritime services, 19 (*table*), 49–50, 134–35

Market prices: valuations, 1–2, 69–76, 227–29 (*table*); GNP structure at, 53, 55–61, 56–58 (*table*), 61–66, 62 (*table*), 82 (*table*), 87 (*table*); in factor-cost standard, 69; relationship to factor cost, 86–89

Merchant marine, *see* Maritime services

Military: household sector income from, 14 (*table*), 24, 25, 26; subsistence, 14 (*table*), 26, 32, 227–29 (*table*); investments, 44–46; consumption, 62 (*table*); *see also* Defense

MTS ("machine-tractor stations"), 15 (*table*), 22, 33, 120, 172 (*table*), 177–79 (*table*), 180–81

National defense, *see* Defense; Military

National economy, state budget, expenditures on, 176–80, 177–79 (*table*)

National income, 8, 20 (*tables*); official statistics, 94–100, 95 (*table*); at *1956* conventional prices, 98 (*table*); *see also* GNP

National Reconstruction Loan, *1946*, 38

National wage bill, 137–60

Net national product, 20 (*table*), 56–58 (*table*), 61

Oddziały Zaopatrzenia Robotniczego, 27
Output, *see* Gross national product

Personal consumption, *see* Household, consumption
PKO, 51–52, 136
Police, *see* Internal security
Polish-Soviet Friendship Society, 30
Population, 5
Prices, *see* Market prices
Private enterprise, 6, 7, 22, 35, 36; *see also* Enterprise sector
Product, national, *see* Gross national product; Net national product
Production account: defined, 4; household sector, 13 (*table*), 21; enterprise sector, 15–16 (*table*), 32–35; government sector, 17 (*table*), 38–40; foreign sector, 19 (*table*), 46–50; consolidated, 20 (*table*)
Professional services, 22, 28, 36, 102 (*table*), 103, 109
Profits: distributed to members of non-agricultural cooperatives, 14 (*table*), 24, 104; transfer of, 41, 72–73, 172 (*table*); in GNP, 56–58 (*table*), 60, 204
Property rights, tax on transfer of, 172 (*table*), 173, 174 (*table*)
Public administration, *see* Administration and justice
Public health, in GNP (*tables*), 56–58, 62, 77, 82, 87, 214; *see also* Health, education, and welfare

Quasi-governmental organizations: household sector income from, 14 (*table*), 24, 26; transfer payments to household sector, 14 (*table*), 26–27; dues paid to, 15 (*table*), 18 (*table*), 30–31, 41; contribution to GNP (*tables*), 56–58, 62, 77, 82, 87, 214; wage bill, 139 (*table*), 141 (*table*), 143 (*table*), 156–57; grants to, 177–79 (*table*); grants for health, education, and welfare, 186–87 (*table*); budgetary expenditures on administration and justice and internal security, 198 (*table*), 199; budgets of, 200 (*table*); services at market prices and at factor cost, 233 (*table*); *see also* Government sector

Recreation and holidays, 107–11, 109 (*table*)
Religious services, *see* Domestic and religious services
Rent, *see* Housing; Land
Research, *see* Science and research
Resource allocation, 89–92, 92 (*table*); *see also* Gross national product; National income
Retail trade, 14 (*table*), 27, 32, 102 (*table*), 103, 104–6, 105 (*table*), 227–29 (*table*)
Retained earnings, 16 (*table*), 36, 122–23

Salaries, *see* Wages and salaries
Savings: household sector, 15 (*table*), 31, 35, 93 (*table*); government sector, 18 (*table*), 44, 126–27; consolidated accounts (*tables*), 20, 21
Science and research, in GNP (*tables*), 56–58, 62, 77, 82, 214; wage bill, 139 (*table*), 141 (*table*), 143 (*table*), 151; budget expenditures on, 186–87 (*table*), 190–91; at market prices and at factor cost, 233 (*table*)
Self-employed: income of, 14 (*table*), 16 (*table*), 22, 35, 36, 77–78, 101–103, 102 (*table*); in GNP, 56–58 (*table*), 59–60, 203
Services: household sector purchases, 14 (*table*), 28–29, 32, 107–12; wage bill, 139 (*table*), 141 (*table*), 143 (*table*), 147–148; *see also* Domestic and religious services; Government services
Shipping, *see* Maritime services
Six-Year Plan, 7, 8, 70
Social security contributions: household sector, 13 (*table*), 15 (*table*), 21, 31; enterprise sector, 16 (*table*), 35, 93 (*table*); government sector, 17 (*table*), 18 (*table*), 39, 41, 93 (*table*); administration, 26; in GNP, 56–58 (*table*), 59; in total wage bill, 138–43 (*table*), 157–58; in state budget revenues, 172 (*table*)
Social welfare (*tables*), 186–87, 191–92; *see also* Health, education, and welfare

State budgets, 94, 171–202; revenues, 172 (*table*); expenditures, 177–79 (*table*)

State farms, 15 (*table*), 22, 119–20, 169, 209 (*table*)

Statistics: sources and reliability of, 9–12; official, *1956*, 94–100

Subsidies: receipts in enterprise sector, 15 (*table*), 32–33; government to enterprise sector, 18 (*table*), 42–44, 126; in GNP, 56–58 (*table*), 61, 207–8, 227–29 (*table*), 231–32; in factor cost, 74–75; in foreign trade, 177–79 (*table*); health, education, and welfare, 186–87 (*table*); payments by receiving sector, 207 (*table*)

Taxes: direct, from household sector, 15 (*table*), 18 (*table*), 31, 41, 93 (*table*), from enterprise sector, 16 (*table*), 18 (*table*), 35–36, 41, 93 (*table*), 172 (*table*), 173–74; indirect, enterprise sector, 16 (*table*), 33–34, 93 (*table*), 120, 171, 172 (*table*), 173, government sector receipts, 18 (*table*), 40–41, 125–126, in consolidated accounts, 20 (*tables*), in GNP, 56–58 (*table*), 60–61, 204, 226, 227–29 (*table*), receipts by sector, 205 (*table*), 206–7; land, 36, 162 (*table*), 172 (*table*), 173; residential, 40, 172 (*table*), 173, 174 (*table*); services, 72, 171, 172 (*table*); in factor-cost standard, 72–74; real estate, 172 (*table*), 173; *see also* Turnover taxes

Three-Year Plan, 5–6

Trade, foreign, *see* Foreign sector

Trade, retail, 14 (*table*), 27, 32, 102 (*table*), 103, 104–6, 105 (*table*), 227–29 (*table*)

Trade and catering, in GNP (*tables*), 56–58, 77, 81, 87, 89, 214; share in national income (*tables*), 95, 98; income of self-employed in, 102 (*table*), 103; wage bill, 139 (*table*), 141 (*table*), 143 (*table*), 146; wage-like payments in, 159 (*table*); indirect taxes from, 205 (*table*); subsidy payments to, 207 (*table*); depreciation allowances (*tables*), 209, 225; current values of fixed

and working capital, 216 (*table*); fixed capital, 218 (*table*); fixed capital stock, 220 (*table*)

Transfer payments: government to household sector, 14 (*table*), 18 (*table*), 26–27, 42, 104, 177–79 (*table*); household to government sector, 15 (*table*), 18 (*table*), 31, 41–42, 172 (*table*), 175; household to enterprise sector, 15 (*table*), 17 (*table*), 31–32; foreign to household sector, 15 (*table*), 19 (*table*), 21 (*table*), 31, 51, 136; government to enterprise sector, 17 (*table*), 18 (*table*), 37, 42, 46, 177–79 (*table*), 181; enterprise to government sector, 17 (*table*), 18 (*table*), 38, 42, 93 (*table*), 124, 172 (*table*), 174–75; government to foreign sector, 18 (*table*), 19 (*table*), 21 (*table*), 51; budget expenditures on health, education, and welfare, 186–87 (*table*)

Transit services, 19 (*table*), 49, 134

Transportation and communication: and foreign trade, 48; in GNP (*tables*), 56–58, 77, 81, 87, 89, 214; share in national income (*tables*), 95, 98; income of self-employed in, 102 (*table*); purchases by household sector, 107–10, 109 (*table*); wage bill, 138 (*table*), 140 (*table*), 142 (*table*), 146; wage-like payments in, 159 (*table*); indirect taxes from, 205 (*table*), 206; subsidy payments to, 207 (*table*); depreciation allowances (*tables*), 209, 225; current values of fixed and working capital, 216 (*table*); fixed capital, 218 (*table*), 222–23; fixed capital stock, 220 (*table*)

Turnover taxes: 16 (*table*), 72–74, 76; in foreign trade, 33–34, 48, 126, 130–34, 135; in state budget revenues, 171, 172 (*table*); receipts by sector, 205 (*table*)

Travel allowances, 105 (*table*), 106

Union of Soviet Socialist Republics, 65, 92 (*table*)

United Nations Relief and Rehabilitation Administration, 5

United Peasant Party, 201 (*table*)

Utilities, 107, 108, 109 (*table*), 111–12

Wage bill, national, 137–60
Wages and salaries: enterprise to household sector, 13 (*table*), 14 (*table*), 21–22; household to enterprise sector, 14 (*table*), 23; government to household sector 14 (*table*), 24–27; enterprise sector, 16 (*table*), 35; government sector, 17 (*table*), 20 (*table*), 39; household sector, 20 (*table*); in GNP, 56–58 (*table*), 59; in factor-cost, 69, 70, 77; national wage bill, 137–60; total wage bill, 138–43 (*table*); state

budget expenditures, 177–79 (*table*); budget expenditures on health, education, and welfare, 186–87 (*table*); budgetary expenditures on administration, justice, and internal security, 198 (*table*); in budgets of quasi-governmental organizations, 200 (*table*)

Welfare, *see* Health, education, and welfare

Working capital: enterprise sector, 17 (*table*), 37; in factor-cost standard, 69; in state budget revenues, 172 (*table*); in GNP, 215–17; current values, 216 (*table*)